One Bite Won't Kill You

Other Cookbooks by Ann Hodgman

Beat This! Cookbook
Absolutely Unbeatable, Knock-'em Dead Recipes
for the Very Best Dishes

Beat That! Cookbook
More Outrageously Delicious Recipes
from the author of *Beat This!*

One Bite Won't Kill You

More than 200 Recipes to Tempt Even the Pickiest Kids on Earth*

*And the Rest of the Family Too

Ann Hodgman   Illustrations by Roz Chast

Houghton Mifflin Company · Boston New York · 1999

For information about permission to reproduce selections
from this book, write to Permissions, Houghton Mifflin Company,
215 Park Avenue South, New York, New York 10003.

Library of Congress Cataloging-in-Publication Data
Hodgman, Ann.
One bite won't kill you : more than 200 recipes to tempt even the pickiest kids on Earth, and the rest of the family too / Ann Hodgman ;
illustrations by Roz Chast.
p. cm
ISBN 0-395-90146-4
1. Cookery, American. I. Title.
TX715.H72333 1999
641.5973—dc21
99-32151
 CIP

Book design by Lisa Diercks
Typeset in Meridien and Doghouse

Printed in the United States of America
QUM 10 9 8 7 6 5 4 3 2

For my parents and my children, and for Patty Marx

Lord, I did not freely choose you till by grace you set me free;
for my heart would still refuse you had your love not chosen me.
—Josiah Conder

The enemy crieth so, and the ungodly cometh on so fast: for
they are minded to do me some mischief, so maliciously are
they set against me.

My heart is disquieted within me: and the fear of death is
fallen upon me.

Fearfulness and trembling are come upon me: and an horrible
dread hath overwhelmed me.

And I said, O that I had wings like a dove: for then I would
flee away, and be at rest.

Lo, then would I get me away far off: and remain in the
wilderness.
—Psalm 55

I know the rent is in arrears,
The dog has not been fed in years,
It's even worse than it appears, but it's all right. . . .
—Jerry Garcia

Contents

Introduction

my kids were going to be good eaters. That was the plan.

After all, I'm a great eater myself. Too great an eater, to judge by my girth. The only foods I don't like are eggplant and boiled eggs. Oh, and also celery and olive oil and margarine and skim milk, but who needs those? Every other kind of food, I love.

I also love to cook. My children, I figured, would be exposed to fine cooking at such an early age that they wouldn't be able to *help* becoming little gourmets.

I'd gradually make their food spicier and spicier; by three, they'd be eating raw habaneros for breakfast. As soon as they could wield a fork, I'd introduce them to chopsticks; as soon as they could heft their own bottles, I'd start teaching them about wine. Garlic and onions? No problem! Mushrooms? They'd *beg* for them! They would leap onto each new food trend as avidly as I do myself. And they'd love all kinds of exotic takeout as well, so that on nights I didn't feel like cooking, I could still be proud of what a great job I was doing.

There wouldn't be any fights about food in my house, either. None of these just-one-bite debates and no-dessert-until-your-plate-is-empty remonstrances. Nothing like what I remember from my own childhood, when my brother wept about eating even one pea and my sister threw up whenever she looked at a tomato and I learned how to hide unwanted food in my cheek pouches for hours at a time. In *my* house, mealtimes would be simultaneously peaceful and adventurous. I would never need to coax *my* kids to eat. Or to bribe them. After all, they'd love main courses and vegetables as much as desserts—maybe even more!

But why am I even bothering to set this up? You already know the punch line. For a long, long time my children were the worst eaters I've ever seen (always with the exception of my vomit-at-will sister, now an adult who still won't eat tomatoes). They didn't like *anything*—or at least not anything interesting or healthful. Candy, ice cream, and fast food, they could handle. True, there were a dreadful couple of years when my son didn't like french fries and my daughter didn't like hamburgers, so even McDonald's became a minefield. True, there were years when the only soup the kids would eat was canned Campbell's Chicken Alphabet, poured into a strainer and rinsed repeatedly until all that poisonous broth was gone. True, they used to eat only the frosting on their cake and leave what they call "the breading" on the plate. But we're over that now.

We're not over the food fights, though. Every night I

flinch when one of the kids walks into the kitchen and asks what's for dinner. (My friend Nora, who has five children, has solved this problem by always replying, "We're having Yuck, I Hate It.") Sometimes they don't even bother asking what I'm making; they just say, "What stinks?" I know that at least one of the items on the menu, and probably more than one, will be greeted with howls of disgust. I know that if I pick a food one of the kids likes, the other will hate it, that most vegetables will have to be either disguised or force-fed, and that the no-dessert threat is the only way to get through the main course.

The kids will undoubtedly leap to correct me as soon as they read this. My daughter, Laura, now fifteen, is finally developing a palate; my son, John, now eleven, hasn't quite reached the point of eating anything with green flecks in it, but at least he doesn't retch quite as loudly when I make him try something new. So I'm here to tell you there's hope.

On the other hand, there are also new complications. The kids go to a school where lunch is served to them—no bringing things from home—and I've never dared ask, "So what did you have for lunch?" since the day one of them answered, "A roll and some water. I hated everything else they were serving." Laura now eats no red meat, which pretty much limits "acceptable" animal protein to poultry;

she doesn't really like legumes, salad, or fish (and it goes without saying that John hates all these things), and she would prefer that all our food contain less than one gram of fat. She loves most vegetables, a taste John still hasn't caught up to, but it's not as easy as it used to be to force her to drink a daily quart of milk—and as every single god-damn newspaper points out every single goddamn day, the teen years are the time girls are supposed to be laying in the best supply of calcium to prevent osteoporosis later . . .

Fortunately, though, I'm not alone. Practically every-one else I know also has kids who are the worst eaters in the world.

My friends Graydon and Cynthia have one hundred children—oh, no, wait, just four. Years ago their second son, Max, brought home his preschool's snail for the weekend. Almost immediately the snail disap-peared. Graydon and Cynthia hunted all over their apart-ment with no success. Then one of them noticed black flecks on the face of their third son, eighteen-month-old Spike, who had eaten the snail, shell and all. As Graydon said, "What can the snail have thought?"

When you consider all the things little kids *do* eat, it's amazing what they won't touch. A one-year-old baby can wolf down the most grown-up, complicated foods in the world—salad, Chinese takeout, live snails—for week after week and then suddenly, one day, decide abruptly and permanently that she will never again look at anything but Cheerios and chicken fingers. I can remember the exact day this happened with my daughter, who as a toddler loved barbecue sauce so much that she ate it plain, with a spoon. One night she took a lick of barbecue sauce, burst into tears, and didn't touch it again for years. Almost immediately thereafter, the phrase "too 'picy" entered her vocabulary.

But how could something she'd been eating on Thursday suddenly seem too spicy on Friday? And what about all the babies in other cultures—the cultures that have *really* spicy foods? Does this happen to them, too? What do their mothers do when it does?

This isn't Anthropology 101, so I don't have to answer those last two questions. I'm just wondering about them. In any case, turning against certain foods is certainly not something to blame a baby for. I don't know why toddlers suddenly become picky, but I do know that they're not refusing food solely to rattle our chains. It's much more likely that once babies reach the symbolically charged age of one, we start loading our own chains onto their tiny forms.

Consider the timing. As soon as a baby starts eating

"real" food, her parents—bored with "demand" feeding—tend to decide that she's ready to participate in organized family meals. No more horrible orange gunk from a miniature spoon at odd intervals! Let's pull the high chair right up to the table and introduce Baby to three square meals a day!

From Baby's point of view, though, the fact that she can now pick up a cube of cheese doesn't mean she's ready to sit at the table for half an hour watching older people talk to each other. It's not surprising that as soon as she realizes that three squares are now a fact of life—and, furthermore, that while she's parked at the table her parents are going to *stare* at her all the time, calibrating what goes into her mouth—she starts resisting.

Our family pediatrician, Evan Hack (who is married to our other family pediatrician, Diane D'Isidori), says that toddlers "are like cows—they do better grazing than eating three meals a day." Small amounts, fed frequently, are easier to get into a baby. *One tablespoon* of food is considered a "serving" for anyone under two.

Dr. Hack points out that different textures can also bother very small children more than we realize. Some babies clench their little jaws tight shut when offered food with even the tiniest chunks in it. Others hate anything smooth. "When my second son was four months old," Dr.

Hack says, "I made him a three-month supply of homemade baby food and froze it." (My heart sank when I heard this; making my own baby food was something I was never able to bring myself to do.) "He never ate it. He just never liked smooth foods. Even now, the only smooth foods he likes are ice cream and butternut squash." (My heart sank again on hearing that there's a child out there who likes squash.)

Age one is also about the time most babies are introduced to fast food. If Baby is the first child, this is the time her weary parents finally give in "just this once." One night they're too tired to prepare the pristine, organic, hand-chopped supper they've served her up until then; they pop her into the car seat and take her to McDonald's. If she's the second or third in the family, she's generally familiar with fast-food restaurants and has been longing for the day she was old enough for her own Happy Meal. ("Small Coke?" a nephew of mine once piped up hopefully from the back seat as his mother pulled up to the drive-in window at a bank.) In any case, the minute she tries her first industrial french fry, she's going to decide it's *way* better than any food *you've* ever made her. As C. S. Lewis said in *The Lion, the Witch and the Wardrobe,* "There's nothing that spoils the taste of good ordinary food half so much as the memory of bad magic food." A one-year-old girl I know was served her first french fries minced up in some rice by her careful parents.

She managed to find, pick out, and eat every piece of fry before she touched any of the rice.

I don't think this is all that bad, by the way, and I'm not railing against it particularly. It's just a fact of modern life. It's certainly not going to go away. Like their older siblings, many babies and toddlers know there are alternatives to wholesome home-cooked meals. I believe they store this information somewhere—perhaps down in back of the sofa cushions, where they stuffed that leaking ballpoint pen—and start to use it against you somewhere in their second year of life.

However it happened, you've got this little being who hates everything you serve her, even things she liked yesterday. You don't necessarily have time to serve her eight tiny meals a day, especially if there are older kids in the family. (If there were disposable high-chair trays, letting a toddler graze would be a lot easier.) You don't necessarily have time to screen out all the junk that can lure her away from real food. You don't want to *care* about this stuff like those intense, horrible parents you've seen around and vowed never to become. At the same time, you don't really want your child raised on a diet of chopped Snickers bars and Surge. And this is going to continue for years and years . . .

So that's what this book is for. The following recipes

won't impress anyone much over the age of sixteen, and I can't promise you they'll impress everyone under the age of sixteen. But not one of them is too 'picy. They've all been tested by parents who are at least as desperate as you, and they've all worked for at least one other real, actual child out there. Which doesn't mean *your* children will like every recipe in the book. But if you can expand your repertoire of things-they-don't-hate by even one recipe, aren't you way better off?

I promise, too, that if a friend you wanted to impress suddenly dropped in and saw what you were feeding your kids, none of these recipes would embarrass you. At least not too much. (Unless the friend is really an unbearable snob. In which case, dump her!) It would be easy to get your kids to eat, say, cans of frosting for dinner—but you wouldn't want anyone to catch you doing it. The foods herein are not something you'd necessarily serve to company, but many of them fall under the rubric of I Grew Up on This Kind of Thing. And some of them would be just *fine* for company. Some of them, you'll be out-and-out *proud* to serve.

There's something else I have to tell you. At least five nights out of seven, we either read or watch *The Simpsons* while we eat.

There. Now you know you're a better parent than I am. So cheer up and start cooking.

A Note about These Recipes

Several notes, actually. First, they vary tremendously. Some are easy to make; some have millions of steps. Some serve a party's worth of people; some serve half a toddler. Some are relatively sophisticated; some are cretinously simple.

That's because I don't know you, and I don't know your kids. I assume that you're reading this book because you want to serve foods your children will like. But I don't know how much you like to cook or how much time you have for cooking. I don't know whether your House Rules require that your children finish everything on their plates —in which case, you're going to want to make foods they *can* finish—or whether you're a Just One Biter, in which case you may try foods that are more challenging.

The recipes vary, too, in their healthfulness. Some of them are pretty lean; some are—let's find a tactful way to say this—old-fashioned. Some of them use convenience foods or highly processed ingredients: for better or for worse, many children like those. My mother once overheard my younger sister saying wistfully, "Remember the time she bought us Wonder Bread?" I've given you what I think works best, but I won't get mad if you substitute lower-fat or more "moral" ingredients.

Once I was sorting through some posters while sitting

on the floor in the Sunday school room at my church. I kept putting my hand on a crusty part of the carpet, until it finally occurred to me to look down. Lying there was a flat, flat, leathery dead frog. I reacted the way some children react to onions in their meat loaf. Throughout this book, you'll see that any "dead frogs"—onions, garlic, hot spices, green flecks—have been marked with ***. Only you know how your kids will react to those ingredients. Perhaps you're used to chopping up an onion so fine that your children won't see it and hence won't notice it; perhaps you can only trick them with onion powder; perhaps even a *picture* of an onion makes them retch. My kids used to accept garlic but not flecks of onion, so I often substituted garlic for onions. When you see the ***, go ahead and adapt the ingredients to suit your family. Or leave them out. Once in a while, I consider onions or garlic or mustard or Tabasco to be so crucial to a recipe that I haven't starred them. But you may think the recipe would be just fine without them—or, indeed, without any detectable flavor at all. . . . Just do what you have to do to get the food into your children with the minimum of fuss.

I've tried to be casual about the size of the dishes and pans you cook stuff in. I don't know what you own, and usually it doesn't make a massive difference whether you use a 2-quart soufflé dish or the foil pan you keep under the sink to catch drips from the pipe. When it does make a difference, I've been specific. And when I tell you to use a "nonreactive" pan, it means one that won't turn gray or give the food an off-taste if you cook acid-based ingredients—orange juice, vinegar, canned tomatoes—in it. Aluminum is the chief culprit here, but once in a while cast-iron skillets act up if you cook large amounts of acidic liquids in them.

I'm very bossy about butter. I hate salted butter, which is why I always specify unsalted. I'm trying to convert everyone to my point of view. But I can't see you in the kitchen, remember. If you want to use something else, just don't tell me about it. Do bear in mind, though, that margarine is no better for anyone than butter, and it's much less stable when heated. You can't fry things in it, and its texture sometimes breaks down when you bake with it.

For maximum success, the eggs you use in these recipes should always be large—not extra-large or jumbo. When I say to sift flour, it means it really makes a difference; otherwise, don't worry. Almost anything is easier to bake on baking parchment than on a greased baking sheet. You can find baking parchment in the "paper" aisle of many supermarkets, near the lunch bags.

There aren't too many "foreign" ingredients here, but I do call for sesame oil quite often. Just in case you don't already know, "sesame oil" means the deeply flavored, golden brown kind you can find in gourmet shops and the Asian section of the grocery store—not the bland, pale yellow kind you can find in the salad oil section.

Many people with young children perform a kind of culinary triage to get a meal onto the table. If a recipe calls for cinnamon and they happen to have some cinnamon in the house that doesn't have moths in it—and they can reach it quickly, before the baby drops his macaroni and cheese off the high-chair tray onto the cat—then they'll put in the cinnamon. Knowing how chaotic things can get, I've tried not to be too bossy about the quality of the ingredients you use. But I can't help mentioning that **Penzeys** sells wonderfully good herbs and spices by mail, much better than what you can buy in a regular store; they're less expensive too. I strongly recommend getting onto their mailing list—call them at (414) 679-7207 to order a catalog, which will also be great bedside reading. So is the **King Arthur Flour Baker's Catalog** (800-827-6836), which anyone who bakes more than once a year should definitely have on hand. Where else are you going to get car-shaped sprinkles to put on your three-year-old's cupcakes?

The "Most Important" Meal of the Day

"I had a very healthy breakfast this morning," said my son, John, recently. "Lemonade and Nutter Butters." From which it will be seen that I was still sleeping while John broke his fast. Unfortunately, I'm *always* sleeping while my children stock up on the nutrition they need for the busy day ahead. My husband wakes up with them on school mornings; on weekends, they forage for themselves on yew berries and pine sap from the yard. Or Nutter Butters, as the case may be. Breakfast just isn't that big a deal in our house. Naturally this makes me feel guilty and ashamed, though not as guilty as another mother I know should feel: her son, at a friend's house for the night, ate Lucky Charms *with Pepsi on them* for breakfast.

Still, breakfast isn't really a problem meal—at least as far as getting kids to eat it. When I was a horrible, eating-disordered teen, my breakfast was a cup of water that I drank with a spoon. But my mother left me alone, thank God. You may have a struggle on your hands if you insist on serving eggs to your children (or to me), especially soft-boiled ones. And working in enough milk might cause a little trouble. But most breakfast foods are easy to like. Cereal, toast, pancakes, muffins, bacon, sausage—what's the problem?

Speaking of bacon: my friends Andy and Barbara were once eating breakfast with their son, Will, when he was

The Recipes

about two and a half. Scrambled eggs and bacon were on the menu. After he had cleaned his plate, Will asked for some more eggs, and Barbara obliged. "No," said Will. "I want more of *those* eggs"—he pointed at the bacon. "That's bacon," said Andy. Will said firmly, "Daddy, *we need more bacon.*"

Anyway, I doubt you need much breakfast advice from me, even if I were qualified to give it. Keep the meal simple during the week. Train your children to get as much of their breakfast ready for themselves as possible—and certainly to pour their own cereal and toast and butter their own bagels. Remember that if they want to eat foods that aren't traditionally "breakfasty," that's fine. Is there any reason that leftover lasagna, one of my favorite breakfasts, is unsuitable? Don't make a big deal about table manners this early in the morning; it's important not to start the day fighting. Dreamily reading the back of the cereal box with their elbows on the table is as much as most children can manage. Remember, they don't have the benefits of caffeine to get them going. "Why can't humans hibernate?" growled a six-year-old I know one morning when his father was trying to drag him out of bed.

And for the times when you actually want to cook a nice breakfast, here are a few recipes that are worth the effort.

Amish Friendship Bread

This recipe, from my friend Lisa Lasagna in Victoria, B.C., is one of those pass-it-along affairs. You give some of the batter to friends so they can start their own friendship bread, which they pass on to friends, and soon everyone in the world is Amish. As the batter bubbles, rises, bakes, gets eaten, and gets turned into more batter that goes into more bags, so do the friendships. The bread itself is more like a loaf cake than bread—you can serve it for dessert if you want.

I'm not sure I want someone handing me a bag of batter without warning. It would be like one of those health-class assignments where you have to take care of a pretend baby for a few weeks. Or like a living chain letter—one I'd feel even guiltier about breaking than I do regular chain letters (which I always break and always have, so don't anyone ever send me one). But the bread is good for breakfast, dessert, or snacks, and it's *way* fun to make from scratch. And, as Lisa says, you've got to love a recipe whose main direction is "Mush the bag." There was never a better cooking instruction for children.

"When gas builds up in the bag, let it out" is a good one, too.

 Never use a metal bowl or spoon for mixing the batter. Never refrigerate the batter.

I'm assuming you're starting this recipe from the beginning. In other words, no one has given you any batter—which means you have to make your own sourdough starter before you do aaaaaaanything else. The Internet has hundreds of versions of Amish Starter, including several recipes you have to pay for. Huh! Really *friendly.* Some of the versions take 17 to 22 days because you rely entirely on the batter's fermenting by itself; some take only 10, because you cheat and use a little yeast at the beginning. Guess which version I picked?

 It Happens To Everyone

My daughter Boco thinks that butter is a food. Of course, it *is* a food, and a central ingredient in the foods that all honest people would admit to liking, but she thinks it is a dish to be savored on its own. Because I feel I should be embarrassed at the sight of her eating plain butter (it proves, once and for all, that I am indeed a derelict parent), I have been known to slide some bread under her butter. Particularly in coffee shops and restaurants, where I could get a bad rep.

—Lisa Birnbach

Day 1: In a nonmetallic bowl, mix together 1 cup flour, ½ cup sugar, and 1 envelope (2½ teaspoons) active dry yeast. Stir in 1 cup lukewarm water. Blend the ingredients well. Pour/scrape the batter into a 1-gallon zipper-lock bag, which you should then put into another bag, because if the first bag broke, you'd go insane. Put the double bag into a bowl, for the same reason, and let it sit, sealed, for 24 hours. It will begin to fizz and bubble and look ugly. Don't worry.

Day 2: Mush the bag. Let out any gas that's built up.

Day 3: Mush the bag. Let out the gas.

Day 4: Mush the bag. Let out the gas.

Day 5: Mush the bag. Let out the gas.

Day 6: Heads up! Add 1 cup *each* flour, sugar, and milk to the bag. Mush the bag.

Day 7: Mush the bag. Let out the gas.

Day 8: Mush the bag. Let out the gas.

Day 9: Mush the bag. Let out the gas.

Day 10: Pour the batter into a large nonmetallic bowl and add 1 cup *each*—yes—flour, sugar, and milk. Mix well. Pour 1 cup of the batter into each of four 1-gallon zipper-lock bags. (Don't cheat and use a lesser plastic bag, the kind you use a twist-tie on.) One's for you; the others are for three friends, or enemies, *along with a set of instructions.* Write the date on each bag. This is important, because *the date for your friends is the new Day 1.*

Now preheat the oven to 325 degrees. Lavishly grease two 9-x-5-inch loaf pans or one large Bundt pan. Coat the inside of the pan(s) with 3 tablespoons sugar mixed with 1 teaspoon cinnamon. (It won't all stick. Save the remainder for the top.)

To your 1 cup of batter, in a large bowl, add:

>   2 cups flour, sifted with:
>>   2 teaspoons cinnamon
>>   1½ teaspoons baking powder
>>   ½ teaspoon baking soda
>>   ½ teaspoon salt
>   1 cup sugar
>   1 3-to-4-ounce box instant vanilla pudding
>   3 large eggs
>   1 cup vegetable oil
>   ½ cup milk
>   1 teaspoon vanilla

Beat well. Stir in:

>   1 cup chocolate chips, raisins, or chopped nuts.

Scrape the batter into the prepared pan(s) and sprinkle the top with the remaining cinnamon sugar.

Bake for 1 hour; or, if you use the Bundt pan, about ¼ hours. In either case, a toothpick inserted into the middle of the bread should come out clean.

Let the bread stand for 20 to 30 minutes before you take it out of the pan(s) and cool it on a rack. It would be a shame if it broke in half at *this* point.

Makes 2 loaves or 1 Bundt pan.

Breakfast 'Za

When my husband and I were young and waggish, we always called pizza "'za" and mushrooms "shrooms." The 'za has kind of evaporated from our language, but I still write "shrooms" on my shopping lists. However, this recipe is not a real 'za—more like a delicious cheesy, sausage-y, hash-brown cake. And no shrooms in it, thank God.

1 8-ounce tube refrigerated crescent roll dough

1 pound breakfast sausage, cooked, drained, and crumbled or chopped

1 cup frozen hash brown potatoes, thawed and shredded

6 ounces cheddar, grated (about 1½ cups)

3 large eggs

¼ cup milk

Salt and pepper to taste

¼ cup grated Parmesan (about 1 ounce), for topping

Preheat the oven to 375 degrees. Grease a 12-inch deep-dish pizza pan.

Pop out the crescent dough and pat it into the pan like a pizza crust, pressing the perforations together. Cover it with the sausage, potatoes, and cheese.

Beat together the eggs, milk, and salt and pepper in a small bowl. Carefully pour over the pizza. Sprinkle with the Parmesan.

Bake the pizza for 20 to 25 minutes, or until it's set. Serve warm or at room temperature.

Serves 4.

Blueberry-Raspberry Muffins

Not only are these the best muffins on earth, but they're also much sturdier than regular muffins. They can be made well ahead of time and frozen. Leftovers can even be refrozen. Moreover, a basket of these muffins can sit out on the counter all day and not get dried out around the edges. This works well when you have a houseful of guests who all wake up at different times.

  2 cups flour

  2 teaspoons baking powder

  1 teaspoon baking soda

  1 teaspoon salt

  4 large eggs

  1 16-ounce container sour cream

  10 tablespoons (1¼ sticks) unsalted butter

  2 cups light brown sugar, packed

  2 cups old-fashioned rolled oats

  1 cup fresh or frozen (not thawed) blueberries

  1 cup fresh or frozen (not thawed) raspberries

  About 2 tablespoons sugar, for topping

Preheat the oven to 375 degrees. Line two 12-cup muffin tins with muffin-cup liners. *This recipe won't work without them.*

Combine the flour, baking powder, baking soda, and salt in a small bowl. Set aside.

Beat the eggs with the sour cream in a large bowl until thoroughly combined. In a medium saucepan, over medium heat, melt together the butter and brown sugar, stirring to dissolve the sugar. Cool slightly, then beat this mixture into the egg mixture. Stir in the oats.

Fold in the flour mixture and then—very gently—fold in

the berries. Fill the muffin cups two-thirds full. Drop a generous pinch of sugar onto the top of each muffin.

Bake the muffins for 25 to 28 minutes, or until the edges are medium-brown and the tops are firm. Cool the pans on a rack for 5 minutes; then remove the muffins (in their papers) and finish cooling them.

Makes 2 dozen muffins.

Bacon-Cheese Muffins

These make wonderful go-alongs with soup and salad, as well as a good breakfast. They look especially good if you use orange cheddar instead of white. My original recipe suggested that they be served at "coffee breaks." But when does anyone ever cook for a coffee break?

4 bacon strips

2 cups flour

2 tablespoons sugar

1 tablespoon baking powder

1/2 teaspoon salt

1/4 teaspoon paprika

1 large egg, well beaten

1 1/2 cups milk

4 ounces extra-sharp cheddar, grated (about 1 cup)

1/4 cup grated Parmesan (about 1 ounce), for topping
  (optional)

Preheat the oven to 400 degrees. Fill 18 muffin cups with muffin liners, or grease them well. (The liners would be my preference.)

Cook the bacon until crisp; drain on paper towels, crumble, and set aside. Reserve 3 tablespoons of the bacon fat.

Sift together the dry ingredients into a medium bowl. Melt the bacon fat if it isn't still liquid. Make a well in the center of the dry ingredients and pour the melted bacon fat, beaten egg, and milk into it. Stir lightly just to blend (it's okay if the batter has a few lumps). Working swiftly but gently, fold in the crumbled bacon and the cheddar.

Fill the muffin cups two-thirds full. If you like, sprinkle a generous pinch of grated Parmesan onto each muffin. Bake the muffins for 20 minutes, or until the tops are brown and a toothpick that you poke in reveals that it's fully baked. (You're not using the toothpick like a cake tester; you're using it to peek inside the cupcake.)

Serve the muffins hot or at room temperature. They don't keep more than a day, and they don't freeze too well, so go nuts!

Makes 14 to 18 muffins.

 ### It Happens
To Everyone

When my daughter was three, we fed her an oat bran cereal with a brand name that had the word "healthy" in it (we were living in California). She took one spoonful and offered this evaluation: "It has no taste." We soon moved to New York and started giving her cereals shaped like cartoon characters, with colors that usually appear on sports cars. I was surprised, then, when at the age of nine she developed a sudden, avid taste for "breakfast bars"—made by a company with the word "healthy" in it. When I asked her what she liked about them, she said, without any reservations: "They taste like candy."

—Andy Borowitz

Baked French Toast

I don't like French toast as a rule, and I almost never make it. To me, it's not worth standing up at a stove for. Which is why this recipe, which my daughter, Laura, found somewhere, makes so much sense. If you use a nice dense French or Italian bread, and slice it nice and thick, you'll end up with a chewy, moist "toast" that has a molten, caramelized topping—almost like a crème brûlée crust. I said I didn't think the honey would taste right, but Laura disagreed. When she copied the recipe for me, she wrote HONEY-Baked French Toast at the top, with lots of underlining. When I tested the recipe, I saw that she was right.

4 tablespoons (½ stick) unsalted butter

3 tablespoons honey (or maple syrup)

⅔ cup fresh orange juice (or apple cider)

4 large eggs

¼ teaspoon cinnamon

A pinch of nutmeg

¼ teaspoon salt

6 thick slices bread

Preheat the oven to 375 degrees.

Put the butter and honey or syrup into a 9-x-13-inch nonreactive baking dish. Heat them in the oven until the butter is melted and the honey is bubbling. Take them out of the oven and stir well.

Whisk together the juice or cider, eggs, spices, and salt in another baking dish. Dip each slice of bread in the juice mixture, turning it once to coat well, and then carefully set the pieces of bread in the honey-buttered pan.

Bake for 15 to 20 minutes, or until well browned. "Do *not* flip bread over or anything," wrote Laura. But that's during baking; you'll want to flip it over so the honey-butter side is up when you serve it, since that's the "sauce" for the French toast.

Serves 4.

I Can't Believe
I'm Doing This

Very young children who have crushes on cartoon characters can sometimes be tricked into eating something named after the character. I'm too mortified to suggest any names, however.

Apricot-Orange Kugel

I've never "gotten" sweet noodle kugels as a dinnertime side dish. They work better, to me, when served at breakfast, being a sort of cross between pudding and strata. The cottage cheese and eggs give this kugel a lot of protein; the apricots and orange juice make it more interesting than the bland kugels you sometimes find in delis.

1 pound medium egg noodles

1/2 cup dried apricots, cut into fine slivers

1 cup chopped almonds, toasted at 300 degrees for 10 minutes (optional)

3/4 cup sugar

8 tablespoons (1 stick) unsalted butter, melted

1 16-ounce container sour cream

1 cup small-curd cottage cheese

1 tablespoon grated orange rind

1 cup fresh orange juice

2 teaspoons vanilla

6 large eggs, separated

1/4 teaspoon salt

1/2 cup plus 1 tablespoon apricot preserves

1/2 cup plus 1 tablespoon orange marmalade

Preheat the oven to 350 degrees. Grease a 9-x-13-inch baking dish.

Cook the noodles in a large pot of water as directed on the package, but don't salt the cooking water. Drain the noodles and immediately rinse them with cold water; then drain very well and put the noodles into a big bowl. Toss them together with the dried apricots and almonds (if using).

Beat the sugar, melted butter, sour cream, cottage cheese, orange rind, orange juice, and vanilla in another big bowl until smooth. Beat in the egg yolks thoroughly. Fold this mixture gently but thoroughly into the noodles.

In a separate bowl (sorry about all these bowls), whip the egg whites with the salt until stiff. Carefully fold them into the noodle mixture.

Transfer the kugel to the baking dish. Bake for 45 minutes. Stir together the apricot preserves and marmalade and spread on top of the kugel. Return to the oven for 15 minutes. You're supposed to serve this hot, but I actually like it better cold   for what that's worth.

Serves 10 to 12.

Caramel-Apple Bread Pudding

Now *this* is what I call French toast. Thanks to Kris Creighton for saving the day. Start this the night before.

2 large tart apples, peeled, cored, and thinly sliced

1/4 cup water

3/4 teaspoon cinnamon

1/2 cup light brown sugar, packed

2 tablespoons light corn syrup

2 tablespoons (1/4 stick) unsalted butter

1/4 cup chopped pecans ***

3 large eggs, lightly beaten

1 1/4 cups milk or half-and-half

1 teaspoon vanilla

1/4 teaspoon nutmeg

A pinch of salt

8–10 slices French or Italian bread

The night before you want to serve this for breakfast, put the apples and water into a small pan. Bring them to a boil, reduce to a simmer, and cover the pan. Cook the apples over medium-low heat for 5 to 7 minutes, or until they're tender, stirring them a couple of times.

Drain the apples in a colander and transfer them to a small bowl. Gently stir in the cinnamon. Set aside.

Combine the sugar, corn syrup, and butter in the same saucepan. Cook over medium heat until the mixture comes to a boil. Meanwhile, grease an 8-inch square baking dish.

Pour the sugar mixture into the baking dish. Sprinkle on the optional pecan pieces.

Beat the eggs, milk or half-and-half, vanilla, nutmeg, and

ALWAYS subscribe to *The Practical Palate,* Kristina Creighton's wonderfully cheering newsletter, which is full of comforting chat and homey recipes for families. If it were up to me, every other recipe in this book would be one of hers. As it is, I've had to narrow it down to five. (*The Practical Palate,* P.O. Box 169, Granville, VT 05747 or PracPalate@aol.com).

salt in a medium bowl. Arrange half the slices of bread in the baking dish. (You may have to trim them to fit.) Spoon the apples on top; arrange the rest of the bread on top of the apples. Carefully pour the egg mixture onto the bread and press it down slightly. Cover the dish tightly with plastic wrap and chill it overnight.

The next morning, take the baking dish out of the fridge and preheat the oven to 325 degrees.

Remove the plastic wrap and bake the pudding for 45 minutes, or until well browned. Take it out of the oven and immediately run a knife around the edge to loosen it. Let the pudding stand for 15 minutes.

Carefully invert the pudding onto a serving dish, cut it into triangles, and serve. The leftovers are delicious cold.

Serves 10 to 12.

Cinnamon Toasties

These aren't a breakfast cereal, as the name would suggest. They're a spiral of bread and sweetened cream-cheese filling—sort of like a simplified cheese Danish. *Very, very* yummy.

The original recipe said you could serve sour cream with them. But even I think that's a bit much. You have to start the recipe at least 4 hours ahead.

1 2-pound loaf sliced white bread

2 8-ounce packages cream cheese, at room temperature

2 large egg yolks

1/2 cup sugar

1/2 teaspoon vanilla

A pinch of salt

1 1/2 cups light brown sugar, packed

1 teaspoon cinnamon

1 1/2 cups (3 sticks) unsalted butter, melted

At least 4 hours ahead, or the night before, cut the crusts off each slice of bread and use a rolling pin to roll the slices as thin as possible. Beat the cream cheese, egg yolks, sugar, vanilla, and salt in a large bowl until light and fluffy. Spread this mixture on one-third of each slice of bread. (Obviously you may end up with more bread than cream cheese, or vice versa. Don't have a cow about it.) Roll up the slices as tightly as you can, pressing down on the edges to seal them.

Grease a cookie sheet or line it with parchment paper.

Combine the brown sugar and cinnamon in a shallow baking dish. Dip each rolled-up piece of bread into the melted butter, coating it on all sides, then immediately coat it with the brown-sugar mixture. Put the rolls on the cookie sheet seam side down and freeze them for at least 4 hours, or until you are ready to use them. (The rolls can be wrapped and frozen for up to 2 months.)

When you're ready to go, preheat the oven to 375 degrees.

Use a sharp knife to slice each frozen roll into 3 or 4 sections. Return the slices to the greased or parchment-covered cookie sheet, sliced side down. Bake them for 5 minutes, turn them over, and bake them for 5 more minutes, or until browned. Serve immediately.

Makes 32 rolls, each producing 3 or 4 slices; in other words, a lot.

Cranberry-Swirl Coffee Cake

I 've never seen this recipe anywhere but in my kitchen and in my aunt Elsie's. She lived in Assonet, Massachusetts, down the street from my other aunt, Gail. We'd spend the night at Gail's and have breakfast at Elsie's.

8 tablespoons (1 stick) unsalted butter, at room temperature

1 cup sugar

2 large eggs

2 cups flour

1 teaspoon baking powder

1 teaspoon baking soda

1/2 teaspoon salt

1 8-ounce container sour cream

1 teaspoon almond extract

1/2 teaspoon vanilla

8 ounces whole cranberry sauce

Preheat the oven to 350 degrees. Lavishly grease and flour a 10-inch tube pan, tapping out the excess flour.

Beat the butter and sugar together in a large bowl with an electric mixer until fluffy. Add the eggs and beat until light. Stir together the dry ingredients in one small bowl; stir together the sour cream and extracts in another. Add the dry ingredients and sour cream alternately to the egg mixture, beginning and ending with the sour cream.

Put one-third of the batter into the tube pan and swirl half the cranberry sauce into it. Repeat the process, and cover the second "layer" with the last third of the batter.

Bake the coffee cake for 55 minutes to 1 hour, or until a cake tester inserted into the middle comes out clean. Cool on a rack for *at least* 1 hour before you turn it out onto the rack or a plate.

Serves 8 to 10.

Moom's Quick Coffee Cake

W e usually had this on Sundays. You can whip it up in about a second, which is key if you have to get four kids to church by 9:00 A.M., as my mother did.

This makes a thin coffee cake, which is why it bakes so quickly. If you prefer, you can use an 8-inch square pan and bake the cake for 20 minutes.

Coffee Cake

1 cup flour

1/2 cup sugar

1 tablespoon baking powder

1 teaspoon cinnamon

1/4 teaspoon salt

1/2 cup milk

1 large egg, well beaten

4 tablespoons (1/2 stick) unsalted butter, melted

Topping

2 tablespoons sugar

1 teaspoon cinnamon

2 tablespoons flour

1 tablespoon unsalted butter, melted

1/4 cup chopped walnuts or pecans (optional, but even when we were kids we liked them—why, when we didn't like nuts in anything else?)***

Preheat the oven to 450 degrees. Grease a 9-x-13-inch pan.

For the coffee cake: Sift the dry ingredients together twice into a medium bowl. (*Do* it.) Beat in the milk and egg, and then the melted butter. Put the batter into the pan.

ALWAYS *lightly* spoon flour into your measuring cup and *lightly* smooth off the top with a knife edge; never dip the cup into your canister and scoop it out and pack down the top. Cup for cup, "scooped" flour may weigh up to 2 ounces more than "spooned" flour. And too much flour will definitely make your baked goods taste worse. I'm telling you all this because I bet you don't sift flour when cookbooks say you should. Not that you have to feel too guilty about that. As Marion Cunningham points out in *The Fannie Farmer Cookbook,* today's flour is sifted plenty of times before it gets to the store: "We find that many cakes are just as good when made with unsifted flour, and this certainly makes them easier to prepare. At least one major flour company, after extensive research, has arrived at similar conclusions."

For the topping: Combine all the ingredients and sprinkle them evenly over the batter.

Bake the coffee cake for 10 minutes and serve it immediately. Find your white gloves, and get to church!

Serves 6.

Puffy Pancake

This recipe is from my grandmother. I can't count the number of times we've had it for breakfast and supper. My children don't like it with the lemon juice, but they're very, very wrong—so I'm giving you the recipe the way I got it. If your children (falsely) believe it to be "too sour," you can just squeeze lemon juice onto your own piece. That's what I have to do, all because of my wrong, wrong children.

You'll need a 14-inch skillet with a heatproof handle for this recipe—either that, or you'll need to make it in two batches in two 10-inch skillets.

4 large eggs

1/8 teaspoon nutmeg

1 cup flour

1 cup milk

A pinch of salt

8 tablespoons (1 stick) unsalted butter

1/4 cup confectioners' sugar, plus more for sprinkling

3 tablespoons fresh lemon juice, for sprinkling

Preheat the oven to 425 degrees.

Beat together the eggs and nutmeg in a small bowl. Lightly beat together the flour, milk, salt, and egg mixture in a medium bowl; it's fine to leave the batter a bit lumpy.

Melt the butter in a 14-inch skillet with a heatproof handle. (I use a cast-iron one.) When the butter is melted and sizzling and just about to turn brown, turn off the heat and pour the batter into the skillet.

Bake the pancake for 15 to 20 minutes, or until puffy and golden brown. Sprinkle it with the 1/4 cup sugar and return to

ALWAYS remember that if you're making pancakes for your family, things will go a lot smoother if you just stay standing at the stove, fryin' and flippin' and servin' away. In other words, don't try to make the pancakes ahead of time and sit down with your family. If you do, you'll just be jumping up and down all the time anyway, to check the skillet as you cook the second helpings. This is one instance in which it's actually more relaxing to sacrifice yourself and just wait on the others.

the oven for a minute or two. ("Use a potholder here," wrote my mother in the margin. "I grabbed the handle, like a *fool*.") Then sprinkle it with the lemon juice and serve immediately, passing around more confectioners' sugar at the table.

Serves 4.

Variation: Sauté 2 peeled, cored, and chopped apples in the butter until they're tender. Add 1/4 teaspoon of cinnamon to the eggs. Pour the batter on top of the apples and proceed on schedule.

Also, ALWAYS pour your kids' pancake syrup yourself, until they're so old that they won't let you. (Until they go to college, maybe.) Let them demonstrate their independence in other ways, and try never to let them realize this task *can* be done by people other than a parent. And ALWAYS melt some butter in the same pan you use to heat the syrup if you want to prevent one more mess-making step.

Orange-Blossom Waffles

I was astonished when I visited my husband's family for the first time—before we got married—and David and his sister made a batch of late-night waffles. Waffles for a *treat*? Lugging out the waffle iron and later having to wash it, all for waffles? But my kids inherited the same inexplicable fondness. So I'm sticking this recipe in here to show that I support them no matter what they do.

1/2 cup pecans, toasted at 300 degrees for 10 minutes

1 1/3 cups flour

2 tablespoons sugar

4 teaspoons baking powder

1/2 teaspoon salt

1/4 teaspoon nutmeg or mace

2 1/2 teaspoons grated orange rind, divided

2 large eggs

4 tablespoons (1/2 stick) unsalted butter, melted and
    cooled to lukewarm

1 1/2 cups orange- or lemon-flavored seltzer

1 cup maple syrup

1/4 cup fresh orange juice

1 teaspoon fresh lemon juice

A pinch of salt

Grind the pecans with the flour, sugar, baking powder, salt, and nutmeg or mace in a food processor fitted with the metal blade or in a blender until the mixture is as fine as possible. Add 2 teaspoons of the grated orange rind and pulse a few more times. Transfer everything to a big bowl.

Whisk together the eggs and cooled butter in a small bowl. Add this to the flour-pecan mixture, then whisk in the seltzer.

Do whatever you have to do with your waffle iron and the batter. Meanwhile, gently heat together the maple syrup, orange juice, lemon juice, the remaining $1/2$ teaspoon orange rind, and the salt. Serve with the waffles.

Serves 4.

Sausage and Cheese Strata Soufflé

O f course this could be a supper dish as well, but it's awfully handy to have ready to pop into the oven in the morning. It would make a great Christmas breakfast with some kind of fruit. Many thanks to Gretchen Farmer.

1/2 pound bulk sausage

8 slices bread, de-crusted and cut into 1/2-inch cubes

12 ounces Monterey Jack or cheddar, grated (about 3 cups), divided

4 large eggs, beaten

1 1/2 cups milk

1 teaspoon Dijon mustard

1/2 teaspoon Worcestershire sauce

A pinch of cayenne***

3 tablespoons unsalted butter, melted and cooled

Brown the sausage in a skillet, breaking it up, and transfer it to paper towels to drain.

Brush a 2-quart soufflé dish with some of the fat from the skillet. In the dish, arrange layers as follows: one-third of the bread, one-third of the cheese, and all of the sausage, then another one-third of the bread, one-third of the cheese, and the remaining bread. Press the contents of the dish down firmly.

Whisk together the eggs, milk, mustard, Worcestershire sauce, and the optional cayenne in a small bowl; pour this mixture over the strata. Top the dish with the remaining cheese and drizzle the top with the melted butter. Chill the dish, covered, for at least 1 hour, or overnight.

Let the dish stand at room temperature for 45 minutes

before you bake it. About 10 minutes before you are ready to start baking, preheat the oven to 350 degrees.

Put the soufflé dish into a baking pan; fill the pan with enough hot water to come halfway up the sides of the soufflé dish. Bake the strata for 1 to 1¼ hours, or until it's golden brown and puffy. Serve immediately.

Serves 6.

Ultimate Oatmeal

God, I love this recipe. It always reminds me of *Eight Cousins*, by Louisa May Alcott—a book that is infinitely more worthwhile than *Little Women*, though still pretty dorky. Poor little heiress Rose comes to live with her uncle and turns up her nose at the porridge he serves her. "People are always telling me it's good for me, and that makes me hate it," she says (in my words). Uncle Alec tells her she can't be a good Scot without porridge, so Rose gives in and eats it. But if he'd served her *this* porridge, he wouldn't have had any trouble.

McCann's Steel Cut Irish Oatmeal is the only kind you're allowed to use. (You can easily find it in the oatmeal shelves of the cereal aisle at most supermarkets.) It has 1,000 percent more character than regular rolled oats, though the latter certainly has plenty of uses in cooking. Besides, the McCann's tin is more fun to read than any cereal box, though those certainly have plenty of uses in giving cranky children something to do at the breakfast table. The McCann's tin tells you, among other things, that the oats won an award for "Uniformity of Granulation" (signed CHAS. KEITH, Individual Judge).

If you can find Grade B maple syrup, you should buy it as well. It tastes stronger (and is usually cheaper) than pallid amber-colored Grade A.

It Happens To Everyone

I once babysat for some kids whose father told me they liked Quaker Oatmeal packets plain— dry and uncooked. When I gave them each a bowl of the dry oatmeal, they turned into farm animals. They stuck their heads into the bowls and began to snort like pigs, getting the oatmeal all over their faces and up their noses.

—Leah Chapin

3 1/2 cups water

1 teaspoon unsalted butter

A pinch of salt

1 cup heavy cream

1/4 cup maple syrup

1/4 cup light brown sugar, packed

1 cup McCann's Steel Cut Irish Oatmeal

1/2 cup dried cranberries

1 tablespoon sugar

1/4 teaspoon cinnamon

1/4 teaspoon nutmeg

Bring the water, butter, and salt to a rolling boil in a small saucepan.

Meanwhile, whisk together the cream, maple syrup, and brown sugar in a small bowl until the sugar dissolves and the mixture is smooth. Set aside.

Add the oats gradually to the boiling water. Reduce the heat to low and let the mixture simmer for 1/2 hour, stirring frequently. After the first 20 minutes, stir in the cranberries, sugar, and spices.

Serve the oatmeal immediately, with the reserved sweetened cream.

Serves 3 to 4.

Baked Applesauce

This is a lot better than canned applesauce, or I wouldn't take up your time with it. You can use it as a breakfast, a side dish, a dessert (vanilla ice cream or yogurt are nice "go-alongs"), or a topping for waffles and pancakes.

6–8 baking apples, peeled, cored, and sliced

$1/2$ cup sugar

$1/4$ cup raisins

$1/2$ teaspoon cinnamon

$1/2$ cup water

2 tablespoons ($1/4$ stick) unsalted butter

Preheat the oven to 250 degrees. Grease a nonreactive baking dish that will hold 2 quarts.

Put all the ingredients into the baking dish and toss them together. Cover with foil and bake for 2 hours, stirring occasionally. Take off the foil and bake for another hour—or longer, if you want the apples even softer. Serve warm or cold.

Makes about 2½ cups; serves 4 to 6.

One more thing about breakfast. Nothing is more daunting than trooping downstairs bright and early to find a sinkful of dirty dishes that you didn't wash before you went to bed. If, the night before, you have a premonition that that's going to happen to you, move all the dishes out of the sink and onto the stove. (Give the sink a cursory cleaning, if you have time.) Cover the dishes with a nice garbage bag or brightly colored towel. The sink will then be free for your breakfast needs, and you won't notice the dishes quite as much.

If you think you'll need the stove more than the sink, then keep all the dishes in the sink and cover them up there. We have a bathroom with a tub in it near our kitchen. When we first moved into the house, I could stash dirty dishes in the tub if I had to, but now we have a turtle living in there who wouldn't understand.

The point is: *get the dirty dishes out of sight until you have the strength to deal with them.*

Then tiptoe up to bed.

A Few Worthwhile Appetizers

The Recipes

R are is the child who needs to be served an appetizer. Let's say that somehow you're hosting a gathering where there are both appetizers and kids: perhaps a big cocktail party where you've (insanely) asked people to bring their families. In that case, most of the kids will be perfectly happy—*happier*—with various bowls of chips. The few children who actually like grown-up hors d'oeuvres can fend for themselves, slithering in and out of the grown-ups to grab fistfuls of blinis and caviar.

Sometimes you want to make slightly more effort, though—or at least to seem to have made more effort. At a big holiday dinner, for instance, it's kind of shabby to give the kids stale Goldfish crackers while you and the other adults wolf down lobster-stuffed filo. And while we're on this topic: anyone who's ever in charge of refreshments at a church or synagogue or post-piano-recital reception is *a total pig* if they don't make something just as nice for the kids as for the adults. What kind of message does it send a child if all the grown-ups at church have nice homemade cookies and the kids' table has nothing but some old crackers? Get with the program, coffee-hour planners across the land!

Now, back to appetizers. Here are a few that will impress the kids without taking up your whole day.

Garlic Pretzels

I first tasted these at a friend's shrimp boil. Right away, I took the bowl into protective custody, fending off all comers until I was sure I'd eaten enough. Then I called the pretzels' creator, Sally Cornell, and begged her for the recipe. I don't know what I would have done if she hadn't shared it with me.

1 cup vegetable oil

1 1-ounce envelope ranch salad dressing mix

1 teaspoon lemon pepper

1 teaspoon dried dill

1 teaspoon garlic powder

1 16-ounce box hard "beer" pretzels, broken into pieces
   (I use Snyder's sourdough pretzels)

Preheat the oven to 325 degrees.

Mix everything except the pretzels in a large bowl. Add the pretzels; toss and stir to coat thoroughly. Spread the pretzels evenly on a rimmed cookie sheet and bake them for 10 minutes, stirring occasionally.

Cool the pretzels on a brown paper bag (or a few thicknesses of paper towel) to absorb any excess oil. Store them in an airtight tin. They'll keep for 2 months, but keeping them for half that long would require superhuman restraint.

Makes 1 pound.

 **It Happens
To Everyone**

When my son Nat was three, I was sitting there in the living room drinking Dewar's on the rocks. He expressed an interest in it, and I thought, "Oh, yeah? Fine. This'll learn ya." I let him have a taste. He took a big gulp—and he liked it!

Oh, and he was the one who, upon taking his first taste of ice cream, cried. It was too cold. Sensitive? Don't ask.

—Ellis Wiener

Fiesta Dip

My friend Denise always makes this for her two girls. It's beautiful and, like so many beautiful things, popular. It's a milder version of those Mexican seven-layer dips, which makes it perfect for children.

"Serve with Fritos Scoops," says Denise. "Other chips aren't strong enough to hold this dip."

1 8-ounce package cream cheese, at room temperature

1/2 cup mayonnaise

1 jar "medium" salsa

1 red bell pepper, chopped

1 yellow bell pepper, chopped

1 small red onion, minced***

1 bunch scallions, chopped***

1 small tomato, halved, deglopped, and chopped

1–2 cups shredded mozzarella or Monterey Jack

A few sliced black olives***

Beat together the cream cheese and mayo in a medium bowl until smooth. Spread the mixture across a platter or serving dish that's about 9 inches across, and chill for at least 1 hour.

About 1 hour before serving, spread the salsa across the cream cheese mixture. Scatter the peppers, the optional onion and scallions, and tomato over the salsa. Sprinkle the cheese over the top. Add the olives last of all, if you're using them, and serve.

Makes one 9-inch-round plateful.

Taco Thing

This is much more than the sum of its parts. If it were up to me and no one was watching, I'd eat it with a spoon. Thanks, Jean.

1 8-ounce package cream cheese, at room temperature

1 15-ounce can Hormel No-Bean Chili

8 ounces Monterey Jack, grated (about 2 cups)

Tortilla chips

Preheat the oven to 350 degrees.

Spread the cream cheese across the bottom of a small baking dish. Pour the chili over it and put the Monterey Jack over that. Bake for 20 minutes, or until heated through. (You can also microwave this, but I'm not going to get specific about the timing, because microwaves vary so much.) Serve with tortilla chips, dipping way down to get all three layers.

And speaking of chips, children are very impressed when you serve them *hot* potato chips. Hot as in "heated in a 350-degree oven for 10 minutes," I mean. It makes the chips seem all novel and sophisticated.

Makes one dish that is roughly 9 x 11 inches, or something comparable.

apple Wedges with Dragon Dip

Your life as a parent will go much more smoothly once you start thinking of apples as vegetables. This *mildly* spicy dip elevates them to what a lesser writer might call "party fare."

1 3-ounce package cream cheese, at room temperature

4 ounces cheddar, grated (about 1 cup)

1/4 cup milk

1 teaspoon Worcestershire sauce

1/4 teaspoon dry mustard

1 teaspoon grated onion***

3 drops Tabasco

6 bacon strips, cooked until crisp, and crumbled

4–6 apples, quartered and cut into eighths

Beat together all the ingredients except the bacon in a medium bowl. Put them into the top of a double boiler, over simmering water, and stir constantly until they're smooth and creamy. *Then* add the bacon.

Serve the dip hot, with the apple wedges.

Makes about 1 1/2 cups dip.

 **I Can't Believe
I'm Doing This**

Often a baby in a high chair finishes eating and wants to wriggle away before the rest of the family has even put their napkins in their laps. A good way to trap Baby a little longer is to give her a few toy cars—or plastic animals—and let her drive—or walk—them through the food on the tray.

Toasted Pita Wedges

I hesitate to include such a simple recipe, even in a book of kid food. But no matter how many of these you make, there are never enough. Their only drawback as an appetizer is that they're so last-minute; their only drawback as a main-course bread is that they seem kind of flimsy and unsubstantial despite all the butter.

6 6-inch pitas

8 tablespoons (1 stick) unsalted butter, melted

Lemon pepper*** (for adults)

Sesame seeds or grated Parmesan (for children)

Preheat your broiler and set the rack in the middle of the oven.

Slice each pita around the perimeter and gently pull it in half, making two flat rounds. Brush the "cut" sides of the rounds lavishly with melted butter, then sprinkle lavishly with lemon-pepper seasoning, sesame seeds, or grated Parmesan. Cut each round into 6 wedges. Place the wedges on cookie sheets, being sure none overlap.

Broil the wedges one sheet at a time until lightly browned and bubbling. Watch them constantly; they'll be done in less than 90 seconds, and they burn easily. Pile the wedges into towel-lined baskets—one for adults, one for children—and serve immediately.

Makes 6 dozen wedges.

Stab-Your-Own Meatballs

You've had this a million times, but kids haven't. It's worth introducing them to—even though (or, perhaps, especially because) it has jelly in it. They will appreciate your providing them with those fancy toothpicks that have little frills at one end. Class with a capital K, but that's what children *like*.

Meatballs

1 pound bulk sausage

1 pound lean ground beef or ground turkey

2 large eggs

2/3 cup fine dried bread crumbs

1 teaspoon sage

1/2 teaspoon pepper

Sauce

1 1/2 cups ketchup

3/4 cup grape jelly

2 tablespoons balsamic or cider vinegar

1 tablespoon Worcestershire sauce

1/4 teaspoon ginger

Salt and pepper to taste

For the meatballs: Mix all the ingredients together with your hands in a large bowl. Mold *small* meatballs, an inch in diameter or so. Working in batches, fry them in a large dry skillet until done—about 5 to 8 minutes—and stash them on a dish, draining off the fat as needed.

For the sauce: Once all the meatballs are done, drain the skillet again. Put all the sauce ingredients into the skillet and

**It Happens
To Everyone**

We were in an Italian restaurant with the girls when they were about three. I ordered the wrong drink for one of them, and when she realized it, she screamed out, "Mommy, you wicked rat!"

—Cathy Helm

stir to combine. Return the meatballs to the skillet and simmer them in the sauce for 20 minutes.

Serve hot, with toothpicks. Remind the children that toothpicks are not weapons.

Makes many little meatballs, enough to feed perhaps 10 kids as an appetizer, and maybe even fill them up enough not to require dinner . . .

ALWAYS use clothespins to close snack bags.
Clothespins are cheaper than those plastic clamps that are sold for the same purpose, they can be used for a lot of other jobs, and they work much better than frail little twisty-ties on that stiff, crackly plastic that so many snacks are bagged in.

"It Tastes Like Chicken!"

Poor chicken. It's always being used to trick kids into trying new foods. What if people went around saying, "Oh, you'll like Ann Hodgman. She's just like Jane Doe"? And the thing is, not as many foods taste like chicken as everyone claims. This is not because modern chickens are tasteless, as food writers are always claiming; it's because different kinds of protein have markedly different textures from chicken, and kids notice texture almost as much as they do flavor. Rattlesnake, for instance, tastes and feels like raw turkey in your mouth. If you tried to trick kids into eating rattlesnake, you'd put them off chicken for the rest of their lives.

What's impressive about chicken is not that so many other meats taste like it, but that it can be cooked to take on so many other flavors. Your toddler likes french fries? Then she'll almost certainly like chicken fingers. Tomato sauce? Cook the chicken in tomato sauce and call it "pizza chicken." Candy? You might not want to go that far, but there are certainly many ways of making chicken sweetish.

You want to keep experimenting, because once you've got the kids hooked on chicken, you can gradually up the ante. Chicken McNuggets evolve into homemade breaded chicken fingers with a little minced garlic in the breading. Pizza chicken grows up into chicken cacciatore. Chicken in

The Recipes

orange sauce becomes chicken in wine sauce. Chicken in cream sauce becomes chicken in mustard sauce becomes *salmon* in mustard sauce.

Or at least this is the rock I cling to.

Perfect Broiled Chicken

I recently made a broiled chicken that had some kind of marinade on it. My eleven-year-old son said, "Okay, you can give me some, but only pieces that have *no flavor.*" I rushed to write that down. Perfect Broiled Chicken does have lots of flavor, but not the bad, complicated kind that scares children. When you can't get outside to grill your chicken, this is the recipe to use.

3–3½ pounds chicken pieces

2 tablespoons fresh lemon juice, divided

1 teaspoon paprika

1 teaspoon salt

½ teaspoon pepper

4 tablespoons (½ stick) unsalted butter, melted, divided

1 tablespoon sugar, divided

Preheat your broiler. If you're lucky enough to have a second oven that's not connected to your broiler, preheat the oven to 425 degrees. Otherwise, you'll just turn off the broiler and turn on the oven when you need it.

Put the chicken pieces, skin side up, into a broil-able pan. Brush them with half the lemon juice. Mix together the paprika, salt, and pepper in a small bowl and rub half this mixture evenly over the chicken. Brush the chicken with half of the melted butter and sprinkle evenly with half the sugar. Flip over the pieces and repeat the process: first the lemon juice, then the seasoning mixture, then the butter, then the sugar.

Leaving the chicken skin side down, broil it as close to the heat as possible for 5 minutes. Turn it over and broil it for 8 minutes. It's skin side up now, and will stay that way.

Turn the oven down to 425 degrees (if you don't have a second oven), set a rack in the middle of the oven and put the broiling pan on *that*, and bake the chicken for 20 to 25 minutes, or until it's well browned. Serve immediately, or wait until it's room temperature, or even chill it until the next day. It's great any way you choose.

Serves 4.

 **It Happens
To Everyone**

When Charlie was little and we went to the McDonald's drive-through, he always got McNuggets. But he only liked the white-meat ones. He'd hold each one up to the window, and if he saw that it had dark meat, he'd throw it out the window.

—Anne Owen

Chip Chick

It's not hard for homemade chicken fingers to be better than McNuggets, which taste like dog meat. But this recipe is *much, much* better—and much, much easier than driving a cranky bunch of children to McDonald's. Despite its simplicity, and despite the fact that crushed potato chips have been coating chicken for at least 50 years, it's the kind of thing people always want the recipe for.

I read once about some incredibly *haute* New York City chef using instant mashed-potato flakes as a breading for fish. I've never tried that, but it would probably work almost as well as potato chips.

1 1/2 pounds boneless chicken breasts

1 large egg

1/4 cup milk

1/4 teaspoon pepper

2 6-ounce bags any-flavor potato chips
   (lately, I've gotten really evil and started using Lay's
   "The Works")—you won't need them all, but you
   want a nice deep layer of them to work with

Preheat the oven to 400 degrees. Select a cookie sheet and, ideally, cover it with parchment paper, or grease it.

Cut the chicken into fingers or nuggets. Beat together the egg, milk, and pepper in a medium bowl, and soak the chicken in the mixture while you prepare the chips. Open the potato chip bags a teeny bit at one corner; then, with a rolling pin or skillet or unopened Coke can, or whatever you have on hand, crush the chips as fine as you can. Pour the crushed chips into a shallow baking dish.

A few at a time, flop the chicken fingers around in the chips until they're well coated. Put them on the cookie sheet and bake them for 10 minutes. Turn them and bake for about 10 more minutes. They should be nice and brown. Serve with a dipping sauce—such as the one on page 76—if you want.

Serves 4. Leftovers are good cold.

Note: My daughter makes a variation of these in which she uses low-fat chips and mixes 1 tablespoon each ketchup and barbecue sauce into the milk-and-egg mixture. Those are good too.

"Dump-and-Do" Chicken

Through the darling, darling Internet, I met a distant cousin named Dick Hodgman, who lives with his family in the same town (Prairie Village, Kansas) as my parents-in-law. What are the odds? Anyway, Dick's wife, Lynne, and I instantly began e-mailing each other about feeding our kids, who are exactly the same ages and genders. What are the odds?

"I make about two dinners a week that I *think* they'll eat and hope for the best on the rest," Lynne wrote. "My sister and I specialize in 'dump-and-do' recipes, like the following standards (even my kids will kind of eat them) for chicken."

I give you the technique exactly as Lynne gave it to me:

3–4 pounds chicken parts

Choice 1 (to be served with pasta)

1 28-ounce jar of your favorite spaghetti sauce

4–8 ounces cheddar, Monterey Jack, or other favorite cheese, grated (1–2 cups)

Choice 2 (to be served with rice)

1 cup bottled plum sauce

1/4 cup fresh orange juice

2–4 tablespoons soy sauce

Choice 3 ("a '70s favorite, I think," also to be served with rice)

1 1-ounce envelope onion soup mix

1 12-ounce jar apricot jam

1 8-to-12-ounce bottle chili sauce

ALWAYS use a big, strong, office-supply-store-type accordion file for your recipes. Don't waste your money on one of those cute files with a picture of a kitten wearing rain boots. The bottoms tear out of those before you know it. An ugly brown file will last much longer, and besides, it allows you to alphabetize your recipes more easily. You can, say, put Desserts in D and Cookies and Cakes in C and Xmas in X, Y, Z. You can even put Vegetables and BeVerages together, which is what I had to do because the "B" slot in my file was all filled with Beef and Bread.

Preheat the oven to 350 degrees. Line a 9-x-13-inch pan with foil for easy cleanup.

Place the chicken in the pan in a single layer.

For choice 1, pour the spaghetti sauce over the chicken and top with the cheese. For choices 2 and 3, mix together the topping ingredients and pour them over the chicken. Bake for 1 hour, or until the chicken is cooked through. Serve.

Serves 4.

"Practical Palate" Oven-Fried Chicken

Fried chicken is so good, but SO MUCH TROUBLE. Is it even worth it? I can only stand to make it about once every 18 months. That's why I'm always happy to come across a good oven-fried recipe.

Now, this recipe, adapted from one from my friend Kris Creighton (page 38), is very, very good. But I should note that the children in my family prefer that I dip their chicken in plain old Bisquick baking mix. I mention this in case you have some Bisquick in the house and feel like setting up a contest between the two recipes.

1/2 cup corn oil

8 tablespoons (1 stick) unsalted butter

1 1/2 cups flour

2 teaspoons pepper

2 teaspoons paprika

1 teaspoon garlic salt

1 teaspoon dried marjoram

1 teaspoon salt

1/2 teaspoon Ac'cent (optional, but I use it)

1 cup milk

1 large egg

8 chicken pieces (perhaps 4 half-breasts and 4 thighs)
   or—my own favorite—16 wings

Preheat the oven to 350 degrees.

Put the oil and butter into a 10-x-15-inch pan. (You need a pan big enough that none of the chicken pieces will touch one another.) Heat the pan in the oven until the butter is melted, and swirl the oil and butter together to blend. Set the pan aside somewhere that the dog can't get at it.

Combine the flour and seasonings in a large paper or plastic bag. Beat the milk and egg together in a shallow bowl. Dip the chicken pieces into the milk mixture and drop them, two at a time, into the bag. Shake the bag until the chicken pieces are thoroughly coated. As you finish the pieces, set them on a sheet of waxed paper.

Meanwhile, return the pan to the oven to preheat the oil mixture a little.

When all the chicken pieces are coated, place them skin side down in the buttery, oily pan. Bake them for 45 minutes; then turn up the heat to 400 degrees. Using tongs so that you won't pierce the crust, turn each piece over and bake for 10 more minutes, until well browned.

Serve the chicken hot or cold. Ideally, it shouldn't be refrigerated before serving, if you're serving it the same day—but you didn't read that here.

Serves 4 to 6.

"Sixteen"
(Crunchy Chicken Tenders)

This is a recipe for chicken tenders—not people who tend chickens, but those little strips of meat in chicken breasts that are also sometimes called tenderloins. Some grocery stores, like mine, do not sell chicken tenders; some do. If yours doesn't, you can achieve the same effect by cutting 1½ pounds of boneless chicken breast into 16 strips.

You wouldn't know *what* the recipe was supposed to be for if all you'd had to go on was my friend Ruth's handwritten version. On the orange Post-It note she handed me, she had merely written "16" as the first ingredient—not "16 chicken tenders." Her recipe also called for "1¼ cups crackers buttery," which translates to one "sleeve" of Town House crackers, crushed into crumbs. Things like this are what make my life so difficult.

Ruth's two daughters ask her to make this dish when they have friends over—and if that's not proof that kids like it, what is? Her daughters like the dipping sauce she serves with it, even though it's flecked with green. Maybe yours will too; in any case, *you* probably will.

Dipping Sauce

¼ cup mayonnaise

¼ cup sour cream

2 tablespoons dill pickle "chopped way fine," Ruth says

¾ teaspoon dried dill

Chicken Tenders

16 boneless chicken strips (totaling 1½–2 pounds)

¼ cup vegetable oil

1¼ cups "buttery" cracker crumbs, such as Town House
  or Ritz

½ cup grated Parmesan

¼ teaspoon garlic powder

Preheat the oven to 375 degrees. Set a rack in the lower third of the oven and grease a cookie sheet.

For the dipping sauce: Stir all the ingredients together in a small bowl and refrigerate while you prepare the chicken.

For the chicken tenders: Put the chicken strips in a medium bowl, drizzle with the oil, and flip them around with your fingers until they're coated. Combine the dry ingredients in a shallow pan or larger bowl. Press each chicken strip into the crumb mixture and place it on the cookie sheet.

Bake for 20 to 25 minutes, or until well browned. Serve with the dipping sauce.

Serves 3 to 4. Ruth always plays it safe and at least doubles the recipe: "I've never made just one batch of this," she says.

Stuffing-Fried Chicken

I n which we prove that stuffing works just as well on the outside of a chicken as on the inside.

3½-4 pounds chicken parts

1 cup creamy garlic salad dressing (I use Marie's)

1²/₃ cups stuffing mix (I use Pepperidge Farm), crushed fine

1 teaspoon pepper

Toss the chicken with the dressing in a large bowl (or do what I do: mush the chicken and dressing together in a large zipper-lock bag). Refrigerate the chicken, covered, for 2 hours (or do what I do and stick the sealed bag in the fridge overnight).

When you're ready to cook the chicken, preheat the oven to 400 degrees. Either line a 9-x-13-inch pan with a piece of parchment paper or grease the pan well.

Put the pulverized stuffing and pepper in a pan or on a plate and stir well. Flop each piece of marinated chicken around in the stuffing mixture until all the pieces are well coated. Press any remaining stuffing onto any remaining bare spots with your fingers.

Put the chicken into the prepared pan in a single layer. Bake the chicken for 1 hour, or until it's crisp and golden. Serve hot.

Serves 4.

Kid Wings

Of course there are many ways to make Buffalo wings, which are probably the best chicken wings on earth. Alas, they're often too spicy and vinegar-y for kids. This kind should work much better.

If you buy whole chicken wings, it's important to segment them. Cut off the tips and throw them out, or save them if you're the stock-making type. Then, using a cleaver, a big, heavy knife, or a dangerous pair of kitchen shears, cut each wing into two "drummettes." They're way, way better like that, and also easier for children to eat.

Marinate the chicken for at least 8 hours before cooking.

1/3 cup soy sauce

1/4 cup honey

2 tablespoons vegetable oil

2 tablespoons prepared chili sauce

1 teaspoon salt

1/2 teaspoon ginger

1 garlic clove, crushed

1/4 teaspoon cayenne***

3 pounds chicken wings, cut up as described above

At least 8 hours ahead, thoroughly combine all the ingredients except the chicken; add the chicken and stir to coat the wings. (This is done most easily if you pour the marinade into a large zipper-lock bag.) Refrigerate for up to 24 hours.

Preheat the oven to 325 degrees. Line a baking dish with foil.

Dump the wings and their marinade onto the baking sheet. Bake for 1 hour, turning the wings twice and basting them frequently with the marinade. Serve hot.

Serves 4.

If you are a homemade-stock maker—and there are some of us out there—ALWAYS reduce your stock down to a syrupy consistency, which is called demi-glace. It will take up much less space in your freezer. Then you can dilute it to the strength you want. Even more important, you can use blobs of it full strength in all kinds of sauces and instantly (though subtly) improve them about a million percent.

Fried Chicken Wings

I love fried chicken wings because there's such an excellent percentage of fry on them. They're simpler to panfry than other cut-up chicken, because they're so uniformly sized. And frying wings is a little easier than other methods, because you don't have to cut them into "drummettes"; you can just cut off the wing tips. Whenever I go to Roy Rogers—and I know where all the Roy Rogers rest stops are on the Mass Pike—I always get a couple of their fried chicken wings in lieu of one large, boring piece.

This recipe is really good for you. It provides extra insulation to keep you warm. But you need to start it a day before you want to serve it.

3 pounds chicken wings

1 cup plus 2 tablespoons coarse or kosher salt, divided

2 onions, thinly sliced

3 cups buttermilk

2 cups flour

2 teaspoons pepper

1/4 teaspoon cayenne***

2 cups vegetable oil, divided

8 tablespoons (1 stick) unsalted butter, divided

Cut off the wing tips and save them to make stock (uh-huh, right). Arrange the wings in a single layer in a 9-x-13-inch nonreactive baking dish. Sprinkle them with 1/2 cup of the salt. Turn them over and sprinkle them with 1/2 cup more salt. Refrigerate the wings, covered, for 2 hours.

Rinse the wings *thoroughly* and drain them well; pat them dry with paper towels. Rinse out and dry the pan they were sitting in, and put them back into it. Spread the onions over the

 It Happens To Everyone

It seems to me that there are more and more *adult* picky eaters around. Like my husband's cousin who won't eat bread and my sister-in-law who still will not eat anything "if it's touching each other." I once went out with a fellow (and I stress *once*) who wouldn't eat garlic, black pepper, pasta, or anything spicy.
—Ruth McGregor

wings; pour the buttermilk over the onions. Cover the dish with plastic wrap and refrigerate for 24 hours.

Drain the wings in a colander, but don't rinse them this time. Throw out the onions. Stir together the flour, the remaining 2 tablespoons salt, the pepper, and the optional cayenne in another 9-x-13-inch pan. One at a time, flop the wings around in the flour until they're thoroughly coated. (You can also put the flour mixture into a bag and shake the wings in it, a few at a time.) Arrange the wings on waxed paper and let them stand there, dreaming of flight, for 15 minutes. Sprinkle the rest of the flour mixture over them and pat it down. Let the wings stand for 15 more minutes.

Cover a cookie sheet with several thicknesses of newspaper and top the newspaper with paper towels. Put 1 cup of the oil and 4 tablespoons of the butter into each of two heavy skillets, preferably 10-inch cast iron. Heat over medium-high heat until the butter melts. Put half the wings in each skillet with their flat sides down. Cook, covered, for 10 minutes, or until dark golden brown. Turn the wings and continue to cook them, uncovered this time, for 8 minutes more, until dark golden brown on *that* side. Drain on the paper-towel-covered newspaper and serve immediately.

Serves 4.

Chicken Mahogany

This is a good glaze to know about. It's the brownest, shini-
est, sweetest one you're ever likely to try, and it works on
any form of chicken: individual pieces, wings, a whole roaster,
or boneless breasts.

It's best to use just one size of chicken piece for this recipe. I
use breasts. (If you use wings, you'll need to cook them for a
shorter time; if you use boneless breasts, for even less time. Legs
or thighs, of course, will take a bit longer.) And it's definitely
best to use a "light"—i.e., mild—molasses, or the chicken will
be too intense.

6 tablespoons bottled teriyaki sauce

1/4 cup mild-flavored molasses

1/4 cup water

1–2 large garlic cloves, crushed***

3 1/2 pounds chicken pieces

Thoroughly combine the sauce, molasses, water, and garlic in a
large, heavy skillet. Add the chicken pieces and flip them
around a few times to coat them in the sauce. Bring the mixture to a boil. Lower the heat so that the chicken is just simmering. Cover the skillet and cook the chicken for 10 minutes,
turning each piece halfway through the cooking time.

Now uncover the skillet and cook the chicken over low
heat, turning it frequently, for 30 minutes, or until it is cooked
through and the sauce has formed a nice glaze. Serve with rice.

Serves 4.

Three Easy Chicken Glazes

Because you can never have too many. Serve a child orange-glazed chicken one night and honey-glazed chicken the next night, and the child will believe she is being served two entirely different meals.

Glaze the First
This is one recipe in which I actually think garlic powder works better than fresh garlic. With fresh, the glaze gets too bumpy and the bits of garlic sometimes brown irregularly on the chicken, or even overbrown. This mars the shininess—the glaziness, if you will.

2/3 cup fresh orange juice

1/4 cup fresh lemon juice

2 tablespoons A-1 or other steak sauce

2 tablespoons Worcestershire sauce

1 teaspoon garlic powder

1 cup brown sugar, packed

4 tablespoons (1/2 stick) unsalted butter

Stir everything together in a medium saucepan and cook over medium heat until the butter is melted. Bring the glaze to a simmer and simmer away for 5 minutes, stirring frequently.

Glaze the Second
1/4 cup honey

1/4 cup soy sauce

4 tablespoons (1/2 stick) unsalted butter

Whisk everything together in a small saucepan over low heat until the butter is melted and the glaze is smooth.

Glaze the Third

   1/4 cup chicken broth

   2 tablespoons (1/4 stick) unsalted butter, melted

   1 tablespoon Worcestershire sauce

   1 tablespoon fresh lemon juice

Whisk everything together in a small saucepan over low heat until the butter melts.

For All Glazes

   3–4 pounds chicken pieces

Preheat the oven to 300 degrees. Line a 10-x-15-inch pan with foil.

   Place the chicken skin side down, in a single layer, in the pan and paint each piece with your chosen glaze. Bake for 1/2 hour. Turn the pieces of chicken over and paint them again. You'll keep them skin side up from now on.

   Bake the chicken for 2 to 2 1/2 hours more, basting it frequently—perhaps every 10 minutes. If the glaze gets used up, you can switch to basting the chicken with the pan juices. After 2 1/2 hours (including the 1/2 hour in which the chicken was upside down), test for doneness. The chicken should be practically falling off the bone when you serve it.

Serves 4.

ALWAYS buy many, many cheap magnetic bottle-openers and keep them on the side of your refrigerator. They'll gradually disappear, of course, but at least you'll usually have *one* where you can find it.

Honey-Baked Curried Chicken

This recipe, from *The Practical Palate* newsletter (see page 38) is a way to sneak in some curry. But you shouldn't be tempted to reveal this magic ingredient even if your children do like it. Once they hear the word "curry," they may decide they didn't like the chicken so much after all, and reject it the next time you offer it. Better to keep them ignorant for as long as you can.

4 tablespoons (½ stick) unsalted butter

¼ cup honey

1 tablespoon Dijon mustard, or plain old yellow if that's what it takes to get the recipe past your kids

1 teaspoon good curry powder

1 teaspoon salt

3 whole chicken breasts, halved (or a 3½-pound fryer, cut up)

Preheat the oven to 350 degrees.

Melt the butter in the oven in a 9-x-13-inch baking pan and add the honey, mustard, curry powder, and salt. Mix well.

Add the chicken pieces to the pan and turn to coat them on all sides with the butter mixture. Place them skin side down in ANOTHER baking pan (alas, the first one would get too "baked-on" and sticky if you used it). Bake uncovered for 30 minutes. Turn the pieces over and bake for another 20 to 30 minutes, basting occasionally, until the chicken is cooked through and nicely browned.

Serve with rice or noodles.

Serves 4—or 1, or 2, if your kids hate it. But they shouldn't have TOO much of a problem with this tiny amount of curry, should they?

Mom's Chicken I — Nora's

Nora is my friend who—when her kids ask what's for dinner—says, "We're having Yuck, I Hate It." But they do like
this. "Everyone wants the recipe!" says Nora.

6 tablespoons (³/₄ stick) butter

2 2-to-3-pound broilers, cut up

8 bacon strips, finely diced

1 large onion***

2 tablespoons flour

1 tablespoon curry powder (or less)

1 cup beef broth

¹/₄ cup orange marmalade (the original—but I use
 apricot preserves)

2 tablespoons ketchup

2 tablespoons fresh lemon juice

Preheat the oven to 400 degrees.

Melt the butter in a large skillet. Remove from the heat and
dip each piece of chicken in the butter, rotating to coat all sides;
put the chicken in a large baking dish. (You won't need the
butter again.)

In another pan, stirring often, brown the bacon and optional
onion; gradually add the flour, stirring constantly. Add the
remaining ingredients and simmer the sauce for 15 minutes.

Pour half the sauce over the chicken and bake it for 20 minutes. Add the remaining sauce and bake for another 20 to 25
minutes, or until the chicken is cooked through. Serve hot.

Serves 6.

Apple-y Roast Chicken

The woman I got this recipe from said that it's the only thing besides corn her two sons agree on.

1 12-ounce can frozen apple juice concentrate, thawed

1/2 cup ketchup

2 tablespoons cider vinegar or balsamic vinegar

2 teaspoons dried thyme

Up to 8 garlic cloves, peeled

2 small onions, quartered

1 tablespoon vegetable oil

1 3-pound roasting chicken

Stir everything except the chicken together in a large bowl.

Rinse the chicken under cold running water and pat it dry with paper towels. (I assume you've taken out the giblets and cooked them for your cat.) Put the chicken into the bowl and turn it a couple of times to coat it with the marinade. Slap some marinade inside the chicken as well. Cover the bowl and refrigerate it for at least 2 hours and up to 24, turning the chicken whenever you happen to think of it.

Preheat the oven to 350 degrees.

Put the chicken into a roasting pan, breast side up. (Hang onto the marinade; you need it in the next step.) Put the chicken into the oven, uncovered.

Once the chicken is in the oven, put the marinade into a heavy saucepan. Stirring frequently, bring it to a boil; lower the heat and simmer the marinade for 15 to 20 minutes, or until it is thickened.

Bake the chicken for 1 1/2 hours in all, or until tender, basting it with the marinade every 10 to 15 minutes. Serve hot.

Serves 4.

Roast Chicken Teriyaki

Marinating chicken is one of my favorite activities because it's so effective and yet so effortless. The chicken can sit there in the refrigerator for hours and hours—even days—while I smugly imagine it soaking up more and more flavor. And all I had to do was pour something over it and stick it in a bowl!

Or, in my case, into a large zipper-lock bag that then goes into a bowl. Flipping a plastic bag over every couple of hours is even easier than turning the chicken over with a fork.

Marinade

1/2 cup soy sauce

1/2 cup dry sherry (you can use fresh orange juice instead of sherry, though most kids won't detect the dreaded "wine" taste)

2 tablespoons sugar

2 garlic cloves, minced

1 tablespoon grated fresh ginger or 1 teaspoon ground

1 teaspoon sesame oil

3 pounds chicken pieces (I use breasts and thighs)

For the marinade: Stir the ingredients together until the sugar has dissolved.

Pour the marinade over the chicken pieces, cover, and refrigerate the chicken for at least 2 hours and up to 48, turning the pieces when you happen to think of it.

When you're ready to cook the chicken, preheat the oven to 400 degrees.

ALWAYS refuse to answer the phone from the time you start cooking supper until the time the kids are in bed. This gives you and the rest of the family a little oasis when no one can reach you, making for nicer meals and smoother bedtimes. Let the machine get it, for God's sake—and if it's really important, you can always call right back. It's probably just a telemarketer or some kid who wants your son to give him the homework assignment. If you have a family member who insists on answering phone calls during family time, like my husband ("It might be someone offering me a better deal on a long-distance carrier!" he actually said once), make it clear that s/he will have to take a message for you.

Don't go on and on about this to your family and friends, though. People are unaccountably insulted when you loftily announce, "I don't take calls during family time."

Put the chicken skin side down into a baking dish. Hang onto the marinade; you'll need it. Bake the chicken, uncovered, for 15 minutes. Turn the pieces over and bake for another 15 minutes.

Reduce the oven heat to 350 degrees. Pour the hung-onto marinade over the chicken and bake for another 20 minutes, or until cooked through, basting the chicken with the marinade every 5 minutes.

Serve, obviously, with rice.

Serves 4 to 6.

What to Do with Those Deli Chickens

"Little white bites," they used to be called in my house. (We actually stole the name from some nephews, who refuse to eat anything except little white bites.) The phrase means "pieces of chicken that are entirely free of seasoning, sauce, or grill marks."

White bites are generally what the children I know prefer. For a while, the only kind of *non*-white-bite chicken my kids liked was the hot-off-the-spit kind that comes preroasted from the deli or grocery store. "You got chicken!" my son still cries ecstatically when he smells it—as if it were the only kind of chicken on earth. Which is unfortunate, since I also love deli-roasted chicken and would prefer that the children leave me most of it. If it were up to me, one deli chicken apiece would be the preferred serving size, so that I'd get the full amount of skin.

What do they do to make those store-bought chickens so good? Probably we don't want to know. Plenty of paprika, is my guess, plus lots more salt and MSG than one normally cooks with at home. The point is that they *are* really good, and really easy, and adults like them just as much as kids—hey, what's the problem?

Well, deli chickens are way too small—that's one of only two problems I can think of. I always have to buy two for my family of four because it seems pointless to serve a roast chicken if you don't get a couple of sandwiches out of it the next day. The other problem is that one might, in time, get sick of eating plain roast chicken—not that we ever have in my house, but I suppose it *could* happen, maybe.

If you do somehow want to Do Something More with a deli roast chicken than just stab at it with your fork, God knows you have plenty of choices. After all, you're lucky enough to have a whole chicken to work with, and it will yield big, beautiful, thick slices—not the little dabs and flecks of leftover meat one usually ends up picking off a chicken carcass. Your main task is slicing off all the meat the minute you get the chicken; once it's cooled off, it will be harder to cut.

Then try one of the following recipes, each of which will serve 4. They're not really recipes, actually—more like "treatments." The point of a preroasted chicken is to make your life easier, after all.

Upscale Chicken Pizza

O bviously your children would rather have their pitas topped not with this mustardy stuff but with tomato sauce. For heaven's sake, go ahead and use tomato sauce on theirs. I just wanted *you* to have this recipe.

1/2 cup Dijon mustard

2 tablespoons soy sauce

1 tablespoon sesame oil

A pinch of ground ginger or a few gratings of fresh

4 pitas (sourdough or onion-flavored work well for adults)

1 deli roast chicken, meat sliced off and cut into bite-sized pieces

6–8 ounces mozzarella, Monterey Jack, or fontina, grated (1 1/2–2 cups)

Preheat the oven to 500 degrees.

Whisk together the mustard, soy sauce, sesame oil, and ginger in a small bowl until smooth. Divide this mixture among the pitas; top with the chicken and then—you guessed it—with the grated cheese. Place on a baking sheet. Bake the pizzas for 10 minutes, or until browned and bubbling. Serve hot.

Serves 4.

Sunrise Chicken Salad

This chicken salad is really easy and really pretty—which may make your kids more willing to try it. (Just don't tell them there's mayonnaise in it.) It "plates" attractively with some kind of green salad alongside. For summer lunches I always serve a couscous salad as well, made by preparing instant couscous and mixing it with a vinaigrette, some chopped toasted almonds, and a few minced scallions. Sighing heavily, I leave the children's portions of couscous plain.

1 deli roast chicken, meat sliced off and cut into bite-
    sized pieces
2 red bell peppers, julienned
1 cup mayonnaise
1 tablespoon grated orange rind
2–4 tablespoons tomato paste
2–4 tablespoons fresh lemon juice
2–4 tablespoons fresh orange juice
Salt and pepper

Toss together the chicken and red peppers in a medium bowl. Stir together the mayo, tomato paste, orange rind, and other ingredients in a small bowl, starting with 2 tablespoons each tomato paste, lemon juice, and orange juice and adding more until you've achieved a balance that tastes right to you. Add salt and pepper to taste. Stir the dressing into the chicken gradually; you probably won't need all of it. There you go!

Serves 4.

Sliced Chicken with Tangy Sauce

This Chinese-inspired dish goes well with rice and a stir-cooked vegetable of some kind. All you have to do to the chicken is slice it; the sauce is the big deal here. The great thing is that you can simply leave the sauce off your kids' pieces of chicken and have it all for yourself. I haven't starred the chilies, because I assume *only* grownups will be eating the sauce.

Liquid Ingredients

1 tablespoon peanut butter, whisked with 1 tablespoon boiling water

3 tablespoons soy sauce

1 tablespoon red wine vinegar

1 tablespoon sesame oil

2 teaspoons sugar

Seasoning Ingredients

3 tablespoons vegetable oil

1 scallion, minced

1 tablespoon grated fresh ginger

1 large garlic clove, minced

2 small fresh chili peppers, seeded and minced

Salt and pepper

1 deli roast chicken, meat sliced off

For the liquid ingredients: Whisk together all the ingredients in a small bowl until they're smooth and the sugar is dissolved.

For the seasoning ingredients: Heat a small skillet until very hot, add the vegetable oil, and swirl it around for a few seconds. Add the scallion, ginger, garlic, and chili peppers. Stir-fry for 10 seconds. Pour the contents of the skillet into the liquid ingredients, whisking until well blended. Add salt and pepper to taste.

Pour the sauce over the sliced chicken and serve.

Serves 4.

Your Own Deli-Style Chicken

Homemade "deli" chicken isn't quite as good as the spit-roasted kind you can get at the supermarket. "Good" being a relative term here, of course. I mean it in the same sense that homemade potato chips, though delicious in their own right, don't taste as "good" as store-bought. But this is still a great way to do a roast chicken when you want to pat yourself on the back for not buying *all* your kids' foods ready-made. And it does taste—and look—a lot like the kind you get at the store.

I can't stress enough how much it improves a roasting chicken to brine it before you cook it. I feel silly even mentioning this technique. I know: you already don't have any time, so how can you possibly brine a chicken 24 hours in advance of the time you cook it?

Well, of course you don't have to brine it. But it's not at all hard if you *do* have the time to plan (and enough space in your refrigerator). Promise me you'll try it once, anyway. Brining immensely improves a chicken's (or a pork tenderloin's, or a turkey's, or a shrimp's) texture and flavor. It makes the meat juicy and well seasoned without oversalting it at all. I predict that in a decade, it will be a standard household chore for anyone who's still cooking at home.

Brine (optional, but please try it)

1/4 cup salt

2 quarts water

1 3-to-3 1/2-pound roasting chicken

1 tablespoon sugar

1 tablespoon paprika

1 tablespoon garlic powder

1 tablespoon Ac'cent (optional)

More salt

 **It Happens
To Everyone**

I cooked up a big roast chicken with mashed potatoes and corn bread. "Gee, Mom," my son Teddy said, with dripping scorn, "what are you, some kind of mother from the 1950s?"

—Sarah Stuart

The day before you plan to cook the chicken, prepare it for brining. Remove the giblets. (Toss them unless you're going to cook them for the dog—not the neck, of course, because that has a bone in it.) Rinse the chicken inside and out with cold water.

For the brine: In a bowl big enough to hold the chicken and the water, stir the salt and water together until the salt's dissolved. Put the chicken in this brine, cover it, and chill it overnight. (If you have only a couple of hours for the process, double the salt—but really, doing it overnight is better.)

The next day, rinse the chicken thoroughly and pat it dry with paper towels. Preheat the oven to 375 degrees.

Mix together the sugar, paprika, garlic powder, and Ac'cent in a small bowl. Rub this mixture all over the chicken, coating it inside and out. Shake some salt over the outside of the chicken as well, but not too much; remember, it's been soaking in salt-water all night.

Put the chicken on a roasting rack in a roasting pan and roast it for 1/2 hour. *No,* you're not done. Turn down the heat to 200 degrees and bake it for 1 hour, basting it occasionally with the pan juices. No, not yet. Turn the heat up to 400 degrees and roast the chicken for a final 15 minutes. Now you're done.

Serves 4.

"Flat Tire" Chicken

C hicken, bacon, and cheese baked in a pizza crust. It doesn't *exactly* look like a flat tire, but it's flattish and roundish, and sometimes these funny(ish) names are alluring to children.

If you're not fond of making bread, you can, of course, use half a pound of purchased bread or pizza dough, though it's sometimes hard to roll out. If you have a bread machine—one of this decade's greatest appliances, though I never, ever actually bake bread in it—you can make the dough in that and take it through one rising.

Filling

2 large eggs, beaten

8 ounces Swiss cheese, grated (about 2 cups)

2 cups diced cooked chicken

8 bacon strips, cooked until crisp and crumbled (turkey bacon works okay here)

Optional add-ins, depending on your family:
    sliced black olives, sliced scallions, chopped red bell pepper, a minced onion, 1–2 minced garlic cloves

Salt and pepper to taste

Dough

1 envelope (2¹/₂ teaspoons) active dry yeast (does any recipe ever call for *in*active dry yeast?)

1 teaspoon sugar

²/₃ cup lukewarm water

2¹/₄ cups flour, plus more if needed

1 teaspoon salt

2 tablespoons vegetable oil

Egg Wash

1 large egg, beaten

1 tablespoon water

1 teaspoon poppy seeds or 1 tablespoon sesame seeds

For the filling: Combine the ingredients in a bowl, cover them, and stick 'em in the fridge.

For the dough: Dissolve the yeast and sugar in the lukewarm water in a small bowl and let sit for 10 minutes, or until foamy.

Combine the flour and salt in a large bowl. Stir in the yeast mixture and the oil. The dough should be medium-stiff; you can add a little more flour if necessary. Knead the dough on a floured surface for 5 minutes, or until smooth. (You can do this in an electric mixer that has a dough hook.)

Put the dough into a greased bowl and flip it around a few times to grease its entire surface. Cover and let rise in a warm spot until doubled—about 1 hour.

Preheat the oven to 400 degrees. Grease a large baking sheet that has a rim or a 12-inch pizza pan.

Punch the dough down and divide it in half. On a floured surface, roll each dough half into a 12-inch circle. Put one of the circles on the prepared pan.

Top this circle with the refrigerated chicken mixture, leaving a 1-inch dough border all around. Dip your forefinger into water and run it over this border. Place the other circle of dough on top. Pinch the edges well to seal them, and flute them with a fork if you feel like it.

Make a few slashes in the top crust with the point of a sharp knife. Cover the, uh, tire with foil and bake it for 45 minutes. The dough should not be brown; don't worry, you're about to brown it.

For the egg wash: While the pie is baking, mix together the egg and water.

After 45 minutes, brush the top of the pie with the egg mixture. Sprinkle on the poppy seeds or sesame seeds. Bake, uncovered, for another 15 minutes, until golden brown. Serve immediately.

Serves 4 to 6.

ALWAYS use a seatbelt on a grocery bag that contains eggs or other fragile foods. If your baby's carseat happens to be empty, belt the bag into that.

Chicken Packets

When you have noneating kids, you tend to rely on Pillsbury refrigerated-dough products a lot. They taste good to everyone except snobs. Kids also love to peel open the paper on the tube and let the dough pop out.

1 3-ounce package cream cheese, at room temperature

2 tablespoons (¼ stick) unsalted butter, at room temperature

2 tablespoons milk or chicken broth

2 cups shredded, cooked chicken

Salt and pepper to taste

2 tablespoons chopped chives or minced onion***

1 8-ounce tube Pillsbury crescent dinner rolls

Preheat the oven to 350 degrees. Have a cookie sheet ready.

Mash together the cream cheese and butter in a medium bowl. Beat in the milk or broth; add the chicken and seasonings and stir gently until everything is well combined.

Pop out that dough and gently unroll it into a sheet. Separate the sheet into 4 rectangles, pinching the "dotted lines" together to seal them. (You want to avoid as much leakage as possible during baking.) Set one-fourth of the chicken mixture in the middle of each rectangle. Then gather up the corners of each rectangle and bring them together over the center of the chicken mixture. Twist the corners up like a hobo's "bindle." You don't have to go the next step and actually knot them, but try to get them well pinched together.

Now you have 4 little packets, which you must put onto the (ungreased) cookie sheet and bake for 20 to 25 minutes, or until golden brown.

Serves 4.

Chicken Saté

This is a fancy name for chicken dipped into peanut sauce—Indonesian-ish peanut sauce, as opposed to the Chinese-ish sauce on page 186. (The sauce is good on raw vegetables too.) Kids will like it more if you cook the chicken on skewers, but I don't know what your household weapons policy is. There are some children for whom not jabbing a sibling with a skewer is an impossible task.

Chicken and Marinade

1/4 cup soy sauce

1/4 cup fresh orange juice

1 tablespoon honey

1 tablespoon vegetable oil

1–2 garlic cloves, crushed

1 teaspoon sesame oil

1 1/2 pounds boneless chicken, cut into 1-inch cubes

Saté Sauce

3/4 cup chicken broth

1/4 cup fresh orange juice

1 tablespoon soy sauce, or to taste

1 garlic clove, crushed

1 tablespoon sugar

1/4 cup smooth peanut butter

2 scallions, chopped***

For the chicken and marinade: Whisk all the marinade ingredients together in a medium bowl. Add the chicken cubes, turn to coat, cover, and marinate in the refrigerator for at least 2 hours and up to 24. (The sauce can be made ahead too and chilled for the same amount of time.)

Preheat the oven to 500 degrees.

Thread the chicken onto skewers, if you're using them, or just put the pieces on a foil-lined pan. If you plan to use bamboo skewers, be sure to soak them in water for an hour beforehand. Bake for 10 minutes, or until the chicken is cooked through.

Meanwhile, for the saté sauce: Whisk together the broth, orange juice, soy sauce, garlic, and sugar in a small saucepan until the sugar has dissolved. Over low heat, whisk in the peanut butter (it will be messy at first) until smooth. Whisking constantly, heat the sauce until it's thickened—about 10 minutes. Add the optional scallions.

Serve the sauce as a dip for the chicken, along with any cut-up raw vegetables your children will also want to dip.

Serves 4.

Chicken Fajita Linguine

To enjoy this supper, in which fajita-seasoned chicken is served *over* pasta instead of *in* tortillas, your children will obviously have to like chicken, chicken fajitas, linguine, and the idea that it's okay for linguine to taste like fajitas instead of tomato sauce. But it's not much of a stretch, really. You're just taking ingredients they already like (if they *do* like them, I mean) and recombining them. You're not, say, telling the kids, "But you *like* linguine!" and then covering it with eels.

8 ounces dried linguine or spaghetti

2 tablespoons vegetable oil

1 pound boneless chicken breasts, cut into $1/2$-inch slices

1–2 garlic cloves, minced***

1 1.25-ounce envelope fajita seasoning mix

$1/3$ cup water

1 red bell pepper, cut into strips

1 yellow bell pepper, cut into strips

$1/4$ cup diced onion***

2 medium tomatoes, halved, deglopped, and chopped***

Salt and pepper

2 tablespoons chopped fresh cilantro***

Cook the linguine or spaghetti in boiling salted water according to the package directions. Drain it well.

Meanwhile, heat the oil in a large, heavy skillet until it's sizzling. Add the chicken and optional garlic. Cook over medium heat, stirring frequently, for about 10 minutes, until the chicken is browned and a cut-open piece is no longer pink inside.

Whisk together the fajita seasoning and water in a small bowl. Add this mixture, the bell peppers, and the optional onion to the chicken. Cook, stirring frequently, until the vegetables are soft—7 to 10 minutes. Stir in the optional tomatoes and toss well. Add the cooked linguine to the pan and toss it gently but thoroughly until it's coated with the sauce and the chicken and vegetables are evenly dispersed throughout. Season to taste and serve immediately, adding the optional cilantro at the table.

Serves 4.

ALWAYS wash the family toothbrushes in the dishwasher at least once a week. Why shouldn't a toothbrush be as clean as a fork? They both go in your mouth. And it's not as if all your toothbrush germs are lightly covering all your dishes and glassware. The dishwasher *rinses,* too—remember?

Stir-Fried Chicken with Peanuts

Whenever I make this, we all go back for thirds.

Chicken (must be started at least a few hours ahead)

2 pounds boneless chicken breasts, cut into 1-inch chunks

1 large egg white, beaten

1 tablespoon cornstarch

1 tablespoon vegetable oil

Sauce

2 large garlic cloves, crushed

1 teaspoon grated fresh ginger

2 large dried chili peppers***

6 tablespoons soy sauce

1/4 cup sherry

2 tablespoons red wine vinegar

1 tablespoon sesame oil

2 tablespoons plus 2 teaspoons sugar

4 teaspoons cornstarch

1/4 teaspoon salt

1/4 cup vegetable oil

1–1 1/2 cups salted peanuts, or more

For the chicken: A couple of hours before you'll be cooking the chicken, or up to 24 hours before, put it into a small bowl with the egg white and cornstarch. Stir until the chicken is well coated with this odd mixture. Cover and refrigerate the chicken for at least 1 hour.

Up to an hour before you start stir-frying, bring a large pot of water to a gentle simmer. Add the oil to the water. Stir in the chicken. Cook, stirring constantly, for 2 to 3 minutes, or until all the chicken pieces have turned white. Drain the chicken in a colander and set it aside.

For the sauce: Put the garlic, ginger, and the optional chili peppers on a plate so that they'll be easier to scrape into the pan. Mix together the rest of the sauce ingredients in a small bowl.

Heat a wok or large, heavy skillet until a drop of water bounces off its surface when you flick it on. Add the vegetable oil and swirl it around; then scatter in the garlic, ginger, and optional chili peppers and stir them for a couple of seconds while they hiss and spit. Lower the heat to medium and add the chicken; stir-fry it for 5 minutes, or until a cut-open piece shows that it's completely cooked through.

Stir the remaining sauce ingredients one more time and add them to the chicken. Cook, stirring constantly, until all the chicken is coated with sauce. Stir in the peanuts.

Serve with lots of rice. If you added them, fish out the dried chili peppers before serving, especially if you don't want the children to know you used them.

Serves—well, it *shouldn't* serve only 4, but that's the way it works in my house. Technically, 2 pounds of chicken in a recipe like this should serve 6.

Mom's Chicken II — Martha's

"This will become a family/company standby," said Martha Fairbairn when she contributed this recipe to our nursery school cookbook years and years ago. "It freezes beautifully and can be increased for a crowd."

It was this recipe, nonetheless, that my three-year-old daughter refused to eat *even one bite of* at Martha's house when we went there for supper, *even after I washed the sauce off under the faucet.* I was so embarrassed to see Martha's two pre-schoolers gobbling it down that I ridiculously said, "Laura, if you don't try this, we have to go home right now, without dessert." She didn't, and we did, and unfortunately we had made and brought the dessert ourselves.

Maybe it's the fact that in Chicken Divan, foods *definitely* touch other foods. When my friend Lisa Lasagna was three, her mother made a version of this dish that so upset Lisa that she walked back and forth across the dining room, crying and pretending to be blind so she wouldn't have to see the loathsome substance.

But I know *plenty* of other kids, well, not plenty but a few, well, Martha's anyway, who *love* this chicken, as well they should.

1 10-to-11-ounce can condensed cream of chicken soup

1 8-ounce container sour cream

1 cup Hellman's or Best Foods mayonnaise

3 tablespoons fresh lemon juice, or more to taste

2 teaspoons curry powder, or more to taste

1 large bunch broccoli, steamed lightly and chopped

3 whole boneless chicken breasts (about 2 pounds),
  cooked and cubed

4 ounces extra-sharp cheddar, grated (about 1 cup)

1 cup fresh bread crumbs, for topping

Preheat the oven to 350 degrees.

Stir together the soup, sour cream, mayonnaise, lemon juice, and curry powder in a large bowl. Add more lemon juice or curry powder to taste. Spread a thin layer of the sauce across the bottom of a 9-x-13-inch baking dish. Then spread all the broccoli across the sauce and cover it with half of the remaining sauce. Top that with the chicken and the rest of the sauce; scatter the cheese over the top, and dust the cheese with the crumbs.

Bake for 30 to 40 minutes, or until browned and bubbling. Serve hot.

Serves 6 to 8.

ALWAYS ask people if they have any special food problems—dislikes, weird diets, allergies, and so on—before you have them over for a meal. Do this even for kids. You may not feel like accommodating your guests' needs, but at least you should be prepared when they say, "Mommy says I can't have anything with white flour in it."

Turkey Sloppy Joes

"**M**y sister developed this recipe for the San Diego paper," writes my friend Danica Kombol. "She obviously had to do something low-fat and low-sodium. She says you are welcome to use it as is. Personally, I'd put the fat back in!"

But you know what? Just this once, I'm going to leave it low-fat, because this recipe is a great example of how to "lean up" a standard. (I'm putting the salt back in, though. I bet you don't use low-sodium ketchup at your house.)

1 pound ground turkey

1/2 cup diced onion

3 garlic cloves, minced or pressed ***

3 tablespoons chicken broth

3/4 cup unsweetened applesauce

1/3 cup ketchup

1/4 cup tomato sauce

1 tablespoon Worcestershire sauce

1 tablespoon balsamic vinegar

2 teaspoons Dijon mustard

1 teaspoon fresh lemon juice

4 teaspoons brown sugar, packed

A pinch of paprika

Salt and pepper

4 hamburger buns or hard rolls, toasted

Coat a large nonstick skillet with nonstick cooking spray (or a tablespoon of vegetable oil). Add the turkey, onion, optional garlic, and chicken broth to the skillet and cook over medium heat until the meat is no longer pink—6 to 8 minutes—breaking up the clumps with your spoon as you stir.

Whisk together the applesauce, ketchup, tomato sauce, Worcestershire sauce, vinegar, mustard, lemon juice, brown sugar, and paprika in a large glass measuring cup or bowl. Stir this mixture into the turkey and continue to cook over medium heat for 10 to 15 minutes, or until the mixture thickens. Season to taste with salt and pepper. Divide the mixture among the rolls.

Serves 4.

"It Doesn't Taste Like Chicken!"

The Recipes

What can I say? Not all main courses do. Some of these recipes taste like—and are—meat, or even fish, and may be hard to slip past certain children. As of this writing, my son, John, still eats fish the way most people take pills—by holding his nose, taking a bite, and washing it down with lots of liquid.

Children seem to shun meat in a bigger variety of ways than any food group except vegetables. My daughter eats no red meat at all. John has always liked hamburgers, but he only started liking steak when he was ten, and he hates beef in any other form—even "easy" forms like Sloppy Joes and meat loaf. Once, when he was in kindergarten, I made pork tenderloin for supper. John took a reluctant bite and shouted, "I LIKE PORK!" in amazement.

Ever since then, though, he *hasn't* liked pork. He hates ham, too, and forget about lamb. I don't serve veal (and neither should you, until veal calves are raised more humanely), but John would hate it if he had the chance.

I'm sure your children have their own preferences, or—to be more accurate—nonpreferences. All you can do is keep trying. I tend to serve "easy" main courses the day after I've served "hard" ones that no one has liked, and I often alternate meatless suppers with meaty ones. It's my way of showing the kids either that life isn't fair or that rewards await those who take on challenges.

Still, may I take this opportunity to point out that I loved fish when I was a child? I just want it on the record.

Very Easy, Very Kid-Pleasy Meat Loaf

This recipe for a mild and unthreatening meat loaf comes from my friend Cindy Kane. Not only do both Cindy's kids like it, but her daughter Dale—who, as of this writing, is ten years old—has been making it herself for several years.

1 1/2 pounds lean ground beef

2/3 cup evaporated milk

1 tablespoon Worcestershire sauce

1 teaspoon minced or grated onion

1 large egg

1/2 cup cracker crumbs ("We use Saltines," says Cindy, "and Dale puts them in a big zipper-lock bag and squishes them with her fingers.")

1 1/2 teaspoons salt

1 teaspoon dry mustard

1/4 teaspoon pepper

Preheat the oven to 350 degrees.

Mush all the ingredients together by hand in a large bowl. Pat them into a 9-x-5-inch loaf pan and bake for 1 hour, uncovered. Let stand for 5 minutes before slicing.

Serves 4 to 6.

Cheesy Meat Loaf

I'm always on the lookout for new meat loaf recipes, and this is a great one because of all that cheese. If you want, you can cook it in a covered grill over low heat. Baked or grilled, it makes great sandwiches, and it freezes very well.

3 pounds lean ground beef

1 cup fresh bread crumbs

1 8-ounce can tomato sauce

8 ounces Swiss cheese or extra-sharp cheddar, grated
   (about 2 cups)

1/4 cup milk or beef broth

2 large eggs, slightly beaten

2 tablespoons Worcestershire sauce

2 tablespoons minced onion***

1 teaspoon dried basil

1 teaspoon dried oregano

1 teaspoon salt

1 teaspoon pepper

3 tablespoons tomato paste***

Preheat the oven to 350 degrees. Line a baking sheet that has a rim or 9-x-13-inch baking dish with a couple of thicknesses of foil (for easier cleanup).

Mush all the ingredients except the tomato paste together in a large bowl until well mixed. Mold the meat loaf mixture into a large, flattish mound in the center of the prepared pan. "Ice" the top with the optional tomato paste if you want; I always do.

Bake the meat loaf for 1¹/2 hours, or until it is browned and cooked through. Serve it hot the first day and cold, in sandwiches, thereafter—that would be my recommendation, anyway.

Serves 8.

Good, Good Goulash

My friend Denise (she of the Fiesta Dip on page 59) has two daughters who both played ice hockey in high school. Whenever the girls had their hockey team over for supper, Denise would make this goulash. It's simple but effective, and the guests would shovel it in. Later, when one of Denise's daughters became a vegetarian, Denise began substituting 2 cups of cooked kidney beans for the ground beef. Still, the guests continued to shovel it in—as did I, when Denise served me this for lunch so that I could test it.

1 pound lean ground beef

1 small onion, chopped

1 small green bell pepper, chopped

8 ounces elbow macaroni, cooked and drained

2 10-to-11-ounce cans condensed tomato soup, undiluted (Denise uses Campbell's)

Salt and pepper to taste

Sauté the ground beef, onion, and green pepper together in a large skillet over medium heat until the meat is browned and cooked through—about 10 minutes. Stir in the other ingredients and heat the mixture thoroughly.

That's it! "Don't you have to bake it or something?" I asked Denise. "You can," she said. "You can put everything together ahead of time and bake it when you need it. It's just that I'm the last-minute type."

Serves 4 to 6.

It Happens To Everyone

My youngest, when she was maybe eight, was served some kind of stew and urged to try it. "It's yucky," says she. "How do you know until you've tasted it?" says I. "My imagination is telling me how bad it tastes," says she.

—Marialisa Calta

BBQ Hambies

This is a good winter dish, when you don't really feel like standing outside at the grill hip-deep in snow. Before you start, though, make sure there are hamburger buns in the house. Hamburger buns have a way of not being there when you need them.

Hambies

1¼ pounds lean ground beef or ground turkey
(if you use turkey, adding a teaspoon of Kitchen
Bouquet will make the meat less pale)

2 slices bread, softened in ½ cup milk

1 large egg

1 teaspoon salt

1 teaspoon pepper

1 tablespoon grated horseradish***

2 garlic cloves, minced

Barbecue Sauce

1 small onion, minced

2 tablespoons vegetable oil

¾ cup ketchup

6 tablespoons cider or balsamic vinegar

1 tablespoon Worcestershire sauce

1 tablespoon brown sugar, packed

1½ teaspoons chili powder

Salt and pepper to taste

Preheat the oven to 350 degrees. Grease a casserole or a 9-x-13-inch pan.

For the hambies: Mush the ingredients together in a bowl and mold them into patties. I'm not going to tell you how big or flat the patties should be. That's a personal decision. But if you use turkey—and especially if you don't add Kitchen Bouquet to it—I recommend making the patties quite flat. Tall, pale hamburgers don't look nice.

Bake the hamburgers in the prepared dish for ¹/₂ hour, or until no longer pink inside, draining off the fat as necessary.

Meanwhile, for the sauce: Sauté the onion in the oil in a small skillet for about 5 minutes, until translucent. Add the other ingredients and bring to a boil, stirring frequently. Cook the sauce for 1 minute.

Pour the sauce over the hamburgers and continue baking for another ¹/₂ hour.

Serves 4.

Beef (Burger) Stroganoff

My friend Cindy's brother Mac used to temporarily abandon vegetarianism whenever his mother served this dish. Hamburger Stroganoff has a pleasantly '50s-ish quality (the decade, not the age) and has always been a favorite of mine as well. It deserves to be resurrected.

The dish is about 75 percent less good without the onion and garlic, though, so do try to include at least some if you think your children can possibly bear it. The mushrooms really can be left out, but if you include them, you might like to leave them in big enough pieces that *certain young people* can navigate around them easily without seeming rude.

1 pound lean ground beef

1 onion, minced

1/2 teaspoon dried thyme

1 cup thick-sliced mushrooms***

1 tablespoon flour

1 tablespoon tomato paste

1/4 cup beef broth

2–3 garlic cloves, minced***

1 8-ounce container sour cream

2 tablespoons minced fresh parsley***

Salt and pepper

Hot cooked rice or noodles

ALWAYS remember that a child's diet does not have to be balanced at the end of the day. It can balance out over the course of a few days. This is true for you too.

Brown the beef with the onion over medium heat in a large, heavy skillet. Drain off all but a tablespoon or so of fat, add the thyme and the optional mushrooms, and cook until the mushrooms give up their liquid. (If you're not going to add the mushrooms, drain off all the fat before adding the thyme.) Sprinkle the flour over the contents of the skillet and stir it in; when that's done, stir in the tomato paste, beef broth, and optional garlic. Cook the mixture over medium heat, stirring constantly, for 5 minutes, until thickened and amalgamated. Turn the heat down to low and whisk in the sour cream, the optional parsley, and salt and pepper to taste. Don't let the mixture boil, or the sour cream might curdle.

Serve immediately with rice or noodles.

Serves 4.

One-Pot Spaghetti

Of course you have your own way of doing spaghetti, but I can pretty much guarantee that this recipe will be easier. Also, for some reason, my children actually prefer it to "regular" spaghetti and tomato sauce.

When you think about it, why can't all pasta-and-sauce recipes be done in this one-pot way? There's already an oven-cooking method for pasta, where you put the pasta and the sauce in one of those oven bags, but *this* is even easier than *that* because it doesn't call for precooking the pasta at all. Let's start lobbying Congress or something.

Obviously this recipe can be dolled up to the degree that your kids will be able to bear it. Some crushed red pepper or a cup of sliced mushrooms sautéed with the meat; a few chopped dried tomatoes cooked along with the sauce; a handful of chopped parsley or torn-up fresh basil added just before serving—you get the idea, don't you? My own kids wouldn't tolerate these additions, of course. I'm just building castles in the air here . . .

2 tablespoons corn oil

1 onion, minced, or 2 garlic cloves, minced

1/2 pound lean ground beef, turkey, pork sausage, or
    turkey sausage

1 teaspoon dried basil

1 teaspoon dried oregano

1 14-ounce jar spaghetti sauce

1 8-ounce can tomato sauce

Salt and pepper

8 ounces dried pasta (I use fusilli, just to pretend the
    dish is fancier than it actually is)

2 cups water

Grated Parmesan, to pass at the table (optional)

Heat the oil in a large, heavy pot and sauté the onion until translucent. (If you're using garlic instead, add it at the same time as the meat.) Add the meat and herbs and cook slowly, breaking up the lumps of meat with a spoon, until the meat is browned and cooked through. If you feel like it, drain off the fat. (I never do, because I use ground turkey with this recipe and there's never enough fat to drain off.)

Add the spaghetti sauce and tomato sauce and cook, stirring, for a couple of minutes. Add salt and pepper to taste. Now add the pasta and the water. Stirring steadily, bring the mixture to a boil. Lower the heat, cover the pot, and simmer for 1/2 hour. Stir the pot frequently to make sure it doesn't scorch on the bottom. If the mixture looks as if it's really too dry, add up to 1/2 cup of water—but you're unlikely to need it.

After 1/2 hour, the pasta will be cooked through and the sauce will have thickened appropriately. Give the mixture a final stir and serve with grated Parmesan at the table, if that is the way of your family.

Serves 4.

Bacony Tomato Sauce

S trange as it may seem, you may not always want to make One-Pot Spaghetti (page 122). When you don't, this spaghetti sauce is an extremely worthwhile change of pace.

4 ounces sweet Italian sausage (about 2 links), squeezed out of the casing

6 thick-sliced bacon strips, diced

1 medium onion, diced

1 teaspoon dried basil

1 teaspoon dried oregano

1–2 "shakes" of cayenne***

1–2 large garlic cloves, minced

1/2 cup red wine (or juice from the canned tomatoes)

4 cups canned tomatoes (I use Redpack), drained and coarsely chopped

Salt and pepper

Cook the sausage and bacon together in a large, heavy skillet over medium heat. Stir often, breaking up the sausage with the edge of the spoon, until the bacon is crisp and the sausage is thoroughly cooked, 5 to 10 minutes. Drain the fat from the skillet, swearing under your breath as you try to keep the meat from falling out. Add the onion, herbs, and the optional cayenne. Cook over low heat until the onion is browned—yes, *browned*. Stir in the garlic and cook for another minute or two.

Add the red wine or tomato juice and cook for a couple of minutes, stirring constantly and scraping the bottom of the skillet. Add the tomatoes and salt and pepper to taste. Over low heat, cook the sauce uncovered, stirring frequently, for 1/2 hour, or until it's thick. Serve hot over pasta.

Makes 4 cups; enough to sauce 1 pound of pasta.

"More"

This is from my friend Martha Fairbairn, also known as Marph. I thought it sounded too plain, but no, her kids scarf it down. If you can get it past your kids, you'll have the advantage of saying, "There! See? You like *casserole*!" Then you can try to sneak a seafood casserole past them next time.

1 pound lean ground beef

8 ounces dried pasta, cooked and drained
   (Marph uses rotini)

1 can Healthy Request tomato soup

1 large garlic clove, crushed***

Salt and pepper to taste

4 ounces cheddar, grated (about 1 cup), for topping
   (Marph uses low-fat)

Preheat the oven to 350 degrees. Grease a 2-quart baking dish.

Cook the beef in a large skillet, stirring, until browned and cooked through, breaking up the lumps of meat with the spoon as you stir. Drain off the fat. Add the cooked pasta, the soup, and the optional garlic. Season liberally with salt and pepper.

Put the mixture into the baking dish and top with the cheese. Bake it for 1/2 hour, or until the cheese is melted and the mixture is bubbling. Serve hot.

Serves 4.

Pasta alla Pizza

Those "refrigerated fresh" filled pastas—ravioli, tortellini, tortelloni, and so on—are one of the world's greatest decent-tasting time-savers. They cook up in about 6 minutes, literally; you can freeze them and then boil them without even thawing them; and they come in such a wide range of stuffings that you have *no choice* but to find one your children will like. Here, you use sausage-filled ravioli to make a pasta that— as its name suggests—is strongly reminiscent of pizza. And you don't even have to scrounge up a tip for the pizza deliverer.

To make "cheese pizza ravioli," just substitute—you guessed it!—cheese-filled ravioli and leave out the pepperoni. To make "cheese pizza tortellini,". . . I think you can figure it out.

1 9-ounce package refrigerated fresh sausage ravioli

2 tablespoons vegetable oil

2 cups red bell pepper strips

1 cup sliced mushrooms***

1 garlic clove, minced***

6 ounces mozzarella, grated (about 1 1/2 cups)

1/4 cup grated Parmesan (about 1 ounce)

3/4 cup prepared pizza sauce

2 ounces pepperoni slices (about 1/2 cup)

Preheat the oven to 350 degrees.

Cook the ravioli according to the package directions. (With the brand I use, the ravioli boils for 6 to 7 minutes.) Drain and set aside.

Heat the oil until hot in a large, heavy, ovenproof skillet (I use one that's made of cast iron). Add the bell peppers, the optional mushrooms, and optional garlic and cook over medium heat, stirring frequently, until the peppers are softened, about 5 minutes. If you are using the mushrooms, continue to cook until all the liquid is absorbed. Meanwhile, in a small bowl, toss together the two cheeses until they're blended.

Take the skillet off the heat and carefully stir in the ravioli. Pour the pizza sauce over the skillet ingredients and toss gently; sprinkle the pepperoni slices evenly over the top. Now cover the pepperoni with the two cheeses.

Bake the ravioli for 5 to 10 minutes, or until it is heated through and the cheeses have melted. Serve immediately.

Serves 4.

**It Happens
To Everyone**

My brother wouldn't eat anything red.

—Lisa Diamond

Taco Salad

There are about 900,000 different recipes for taco salad, which we call Mexicali Sally in our house. I'm giving you this in case you just moved to Earth and don't have your own version yet.

I don't bother with those salads where everything is served in a bowl made of a taco shell. Shaping taco shells into bowls is not my idea of fun, and besides they're almost impossible to eat. So I add crushed tortilla chips—much easier.

My son still doesn't like tomatoes, so I leave them in pretty big chunks for easy fishing out.

1 pound lean ground beef or turkey

1 tablespoon vegetable oil (if you're using very lean beef or ground turkey)

1 medium onion, diced***

1 1-ounce envelope taco seasoning

1 large head romaine lettuce, slivered

3 tomatoes, halved, deglopped, and chopped

8 ounces extra-sharp cheddar, grated (about 2 cups)

1 15-ounce can red kidney beans, rinsed and drained (optional)

2 tablespoons minced red onion***

2 tablespoons taco sauce

2 tablespoons sour cream

Salt and pepper to taste

1 5- or 6-ounce bag tortilla chips, crushed

Cook the ground beef or turkey (in the oil, for turkey) with the optional onion in a heavy skillet, stirring frequently, until the meat is browned and cooked through. Drain the meat if necessary. Add the taco seasoning and however much water the package calls for, and cook according to the directions on the package. Set aside to cool.

Toss together the cooled meat mixture, lettuce, tomatoes, cheese, and the optional beans and optional onion in a large salad bowl. Whisk together the taco sauce and sour cream in a teensy bowl; stir them thoroughly into the salad. Season to taste, though I doubt you'll want to add salt. Chill the salad for at least 1 hour.

Stir in as many crushed chips as you want to just before serving; you may not want to add them all.

Serves 6.

Taco Bake

For those times when you want a supper that's *even easier* than tacos.

1 pound lean ground beef or turkey

1 1-ounce envelope taco seasoning

1 cup water

1 16-ounce can refried beans (optional)

1 cup salsa of your choice

1 8-ounce container sour cream

1 pound cheddar, grated (about 4 cups)

Tortilla chips

Preheat the oven to 350 degrees. Grease a 9-x-13-inch baking dish.

Cook the meat thoroughly in a large skillet over medium heat. Drain off any fat. Add the taco seasoning, water, and beans (if using) to the meat. Reduce the heat to low and cook, stirring for 5 to 10 minutes, or until the mixture thickens.

Spread the meat mixture in the baking dish. Combine the salsa and sour cream in a small bowl; spread this mixture over the meat. Top with the grated cheese.

Bake for 20 to 25 minutes, or until bubbly. Serve with tortilla chips.

Serves 6.

Tamale Pick-Me-Ups

another thing you could call these very-slightly-Mexican bites would be Supper Cookies. The novelty of that name might win over a few children. The dish itself is simplified simplicity, South-of-the-border meatballs, with an enchilada sauce/dip that the children are *more* than welcome to skip.

2 cups crumbled corn bread (it's fine to use a mix)

1½ pounds lean ground beef or turkey

1 garlic clove, minced***

1 8-ounce can tomato sauce

3 ounces Monterey Jack, grated (about ¾ cup)

½ teaspoon pepper

¼ teaspoon salt

1 10-ounce can mild enchilada sauce

Preheat the oven to 375 degrees.

Mix together the crumbled corn bread, meat, the optional garlic, tomato sauce, cheese, pepper, and salt in a large bowl. Mold the resulting "dough" into balls about 2 inches in diameter. Bake the balls in an ungreased shallow, rimmed pan for 25 to 30 minutes, or until they're browned and cooked through.

Meanwhile, heat the enchilada sauce in a small saucepan over low heat.

Serve the Pick-Me-Ups hot, with the enchilada sauce as a dip. Giving each kid a small bowl of sauce on the side is a good way to cut down on the potential mess.

Serves 4.

Barbecups

ah, those Pillsbury refrigerated biscuits. Where would modern culture be without them? This recipe won the Pillsbury Bake-Off in 1968. A kid who won't touch meat loaf will eat Barbecups.

3/4 pound lean ground beef, cooked and drained

1/2 cup barbecue sauce

2 tablespoons grated onion***

1 tablespoon brown sugar, packed

3 ounces cheddar, grated (about 3/4 cup), plus more for topping

1 8-ounce tube Pillsbury refrigerated biscuits

Preheat the oven to 400 degrees.

Stir together the beef, barbecue sauce, the optional onion, brown sugar, and cheddar. Separate the biscuits and press each one into a muffin-tin cup, making sure that the dough reaches all the way to the top of the cup.

Fill each Barbecup with the beef mixture, and sprinkle on some more grated cheddar. Bake for 10 to 12 minutes, and serve right away.

Serves 2 to 3.

Dogfood (Sloppy Joe Dip)

Yes, it's a dip—but I think it's more fun to serve it as supper. (It's also more fun for kids to call it Dogfood than its real name.) Or lunch, on a rainy Saturday. Red bell pepper strips for a vegetable, and you're all set.

1 pound lean ground beef or ground turkey

1 tablespoon vegetable oil (if you're using very lean beef or ground turkey)

1 6-ounce can tomato paste

1 1.5-ounce envelope Sloppy Joe mix

1 8-ounce container sour cream

Salt and pepper to taste

Chopped onion for the grown-ups

Corn chips or taco chips

Cook the meat thoroughly in a large skillet. Drain it if you need to. Add the remaining ingredients—except the onion, which should be kept in a separate dish for anyone brave enough to use it. Mix well, and cook gently until heated through. Season to taste. Serve with many, many chips.

Serves 4 to 6.

ALWAYS freeze little blobs of leftover tomato paste to put into soups and stews. I know you won't actually do this, but now that I've started doing it (after many years of putting it off), I can tell you for sure that it's a good idea.

Hearty Soup

We call this "Hamburger Soup" in my family. Of course it could also be called "Turkey Soup" if you use ground turkey, but you might get sued for misrepresentation if people are expecting a chicken-noodle-type thing. This is more like a stew.

"The canned soup is embarrassing these days," wrote my friend Charmaine Babineau when she sent me this. No, it's not—not in this context, anyway. If it bothers you, you could always substitute some canned tomatoes or tomato puree.

1½ pounds lean ground beef or ground turkey

2 tablespoons vegetable oil

2 large onions, diced

1 small red or green bell pepper, diced

2–3 garlic cloves, minced

1 pound mushrooms, sliced and sautéed***

2 cups grated carrots

1 46-ounce can tomato or V-8 juice

2–4 cups canned or cooked pinto or kidney beans, drained

2 10-to-11-ounce cans condensed cream of mushroom soup

2 tablespoons chili powder, or more to taste

1 tablespoon dried basil

1 teaspoon paprika

1 teaspoon cumin

1 teaspoon pepper

Salt to taste

Grated cheddar or Parmesan or Velveeta chunks , to pass at the table (optional)

Coat a large nonstick skillet with nonstick cooking spray (or a tablespoon of oil) and sauté the meat until brown, breaking up the clumps with a spoon. Drain off any fat. Set aside.

Heat the 2 tablespoons oil in a large kettle or pot, and sauté the onions, bell pepper, and garlic, stirring frequently, until the onions are translucent. Add the rest of the ingredients except for the salt and optional cheese. Bring the soup to a boil, lower the heat to a simmer, and cook the soup for 1 hour, stirring it frequently. Taste it for seasoning. (You probably won't need to add salt, what with those "embarrassing" canned soups.)

If you like, you can add grated cheese or Velveeta chunks at the table. "Yes, we did that," says Charmaine, referring to the Velveeta. You go, girl!

Serves 6 to 8.

Not-Too-Spicy Marinated Sirloin

I know steak restaurants are coming back into style, but I bet—with absolutely no evidence except my gut instincts—that steak isn't served at home nearly as much as when I was a child. Which may be just as well, because most supermarket beef is graded Choice, not Prime; restaurants use most of the Prime beef in this country. (Of course Choice is better for our hearts, but I'm talking taste here.) Supermarket steak is worth dressing up a bit when you do serve it.

For any children who prefer their steak untouched by vile seasoning, you can just cut off a piece before you marinate the rest of the meat. But this is quite a mild, teriyaki-ish marinade, and the chances are good that most children will like it.

You'll need to start marinating the steak at least 8 hours ahead of serving time.

1 1/2 teaspoons dry mustard

3/4 teaspoon ginger

1 large garlic clove, crushed***

6 tablespoons soy sauce

3 tablespoons fresh lemon juice

1 tablespoon vegetable oil

2 pounds sirloin, porterhouse, or T-bone steak

Mix together the mustard and ginger in a small bowl. Whisk in the garlic, soy sauce, lemon juice, and oil until the mixture is smooth. Pour the marinade over the steak and cover it. (I use a 1-gallon zipper-lock plastic bag for this.) Refrigerate for at least 8 hours and up to 24.

An hour before cooking, take the meat out of the refrigerator to bring it to room temperature. Grill or broil in accordance with your family's custom. Serve right away.

Korean Bulgogee, aka Fire Beef, aka Sticky Steak

My college friend Elizabeth Rinehart, who lives all the way out in Montana, sent me this recipe. Her daughters normally "won't eat things with more than two ingredients," but they love fire beef.

"You really need to be eating right by the grill so you can keep cooking while you eat," says Elizabeth, because the meat only cooks for a few seconds. You need to cut the slices very, very thin before cooking—"like thick-cut bacon." Freezing the meat for an hour or so before slicing it will help make that easier.

1/4 cup soy sauce

1/4 cup dry sherry

3 tablespoons vegetable oil

1 tablespoon sesame oil

2 tablespoons sugar

2 chopped scallions

1 large garlic clove, crushed

1 1/2 pounds boneless sirloin tip or rib-eye steak, sliced
   very thinly against the grain

Whisk together the liquid ingredients, sugar, scallions, and garlic in a large bowl. Add the meat slices and let marinate, covered and chilled, for at least 2 hours and up to 24.

Grill the meat slices over very hot charcoal for just a few seconds on each side. "Koreans eat it with rice, but it's good on a bun too," says Elizabeth.

Serves 4.

Chili Pie with Cornmeal Crust

Chili is a very personal matter. This is one of the mildest, most kid-ish versions available, but you should feel free to make adjustments to my recipe as your family leanings require. If your children are bean-averse, you can leave out the beans and use more meat. I've even been known to leave out the tiny, tiny amount of chili powder this recipe calls for.

It comes from Rebecca Briccetti, who is my daughter, Laura's, godmother. She made this for David and me right after we came home from the hospital with Laura. Laura didn't want any, but then she was only three days old. It's been one of our favorites ever since.

Filling

1 pound lean ground beef or turkey

2 garlic cloves, crushed

1/3 cup chopped red bell pepper

1 tablespoon vegetable oil

2 cups canned tomatoes

1 tablespoon chili powder

1 teaspoon cumin

1 teaspoon dried oregano

1 teaspoon salt

1/2 teaspoon pepper

Cayenne to taste

2 1/2 cups canned pink or red kidney beans, rinsed and
    drained well

ALWAYS set a timer if you, like me, live on the edge and dry your cast-iron frying pans by putting them over direct heat. This really *is* the best way to keep a just-washed iron pan from rusting, but it's also the best way to burn down the house if you forget what you're doing. Once I took the dog out while I was drying a skillet on the stove, and the dog chased a cat into the neighbor's yard, and so on. . . . Set the timer and *don't leave the kitchen until it goes off* (and until you've turned off the stove, of course).

Pastry

1 cup flour

1/2 cup yellow cornmeal

1/2 teaspoon salt

8 tablespoons (1 stick) unsalted butter, chilled and cut into thin slices

1/4 cup ice water

For the filling: Brown the meat with the garlic and bell pepper in the oil in a large skillet over medium heat, breaking up the meat with your spoon as you stir. Add the tomatoes and seasonings and cook for 5 minutes, or until the mixture has thickened slightly. Turn the heat to low, add the drained beans, and cook for 5 more minutes, stirring frequently. Put the mixture into a casserole and let it cool while you prepare the crust.

Preheat the oven to 400 degrees.

For the pastry: Sift together the flour, cornmeal, and salt into a medium bowl. Cut in the butter until the mixture looks like, well, coarse meal. Add the water and toss the dough lightly with a fork until it begins to come together. Lightly gather it together some more, then press it into a disk. On a floured surface, roll it out until it's about 1/4 inch thick and slightly larger than your casserole.

Place the rolled-out pastry on top of the casserole, as you would for a pie. Trim the edges, leaving a 1/2-inch overhang, turn them under, and flute them. Cut several large slits into the crust to let the steam escape. If you're up to it, you can also decorate the crust with any pastry scraps.

Bake the pie for 30 minutes, or until the crust is well browned. Serve hot.

Serves 4.

Greek Beef Stew

another treasure from my friend Lisa Lasagna. It may look a little scary on first reading, what with the onions and wine and such, but her kids love it. And the *really* scary additions—the walnuts and feta, which to me are what make this recipe so great—get added at the table, so squeamish children can avoid them entirely.

1 tablespoon vegetable oil

2 pounds lean boneless beef, cut into 1-inch cubes

24 small white pearl onions, peeled
   (kids can avoid these if they want, but you do need to
   add them, and they do need to be fresh—not frozen)

2 tablespoons unsalted butter

1 teaspoon sugar

1^1/$_2$ cups water

^{1}/$_2$ cup red wine

1 tablespoon red wine vinegar

1 6-ounce can tomato paste

1 garlic clove, crushed

1 2-inch cinnamon stick

2 bay leaves

^{1}/$_2$ teaspoon pepper, plus more to taste

1 tablespoon brown sugar, packed

Salt to taste

2 tablespoons cornstarch, mixed with 3 tablespoons
   water (optional)

^{1}/$_2$ cup coarsely chopped walnuts, to pass around at the
   table

^{1}/$_4$ pound feta, coarsely crumbled, to pass around at the
   table

Heat the oil in a large pot over medium heat until it smokes. Drop in some of the beef cubes and spread them over the bottom. Don't crowd them. Stir the beef with a wooden spoon until it's browned on all sides, about 4 minutes. Remove with a slotted spoon and set aside; repeat until all the meat is browned.

While the meat is cooking, place the onions in a small saucepan of cold water. Bring to a boil and immediately drain the onions.

When all the meat is cooked, drop the butter into the pot and add the onions. Sprinkle them with the teaspoon of sugar —this helps caramelize them—and sauté them over medium heat until they're golden brown, stirring frequently. Then take 'em out of the pot with that same slotted spoon and set them aside. You won't need them again—no, silly, of course you will! You'll need to add them after the stew has cooked for 1 hour.

Return the meat to the pot. Add the water, wine, vinegar, tomato paste, garlic, spices, and brown sugar. The liquid should barely cover the meat; add more water if necessary. (You may also have to add small amounts of water from time to time during the cooking to maintain that level.) Bring the liquid to a boil, reduce the heat, and simmer the stew, covered, for 1 hour.

Add the onions. Continue to cook the stew for another 1/2 hour or so, until the meat is tender. Taste for seasoning; Lisa adds 1 teaspoon of salt at this point. Fish out and discard the bay leaves and cinnamon stick.

If you like a thick stew, add the cornstarch paste to the pot, bring the stew to a boil, and boil it for 1 minute, stirring constantly.

The nuts and feta cheese may be added at the table.

Serves 4 to 6.

Best Beef Stew

This is practically the only recipe I'm stealing from myself—my earlier two cookbooks, that is. I put it into my first cookbook because it really is the best stew recipe there is. I put it into my second because it had become harder to find Campbell's Tomato Bisque soup, and some readers appeared frightened to try regular Campbell's Tomato without my permission. I'm including it here as well, in case there's anyone left in America who hasn't tried it yet.

As I said in both earlier books, I've made an honest effort to upgrade the tomato soup part of this recipe with various tomato pastes and canned tomatoes, but tomato soup really does work best. Use it without shame.

> ALWAYS save those flat open cartons that cases of soda and beer come in. They're your best friend when you have to transport bake sale items (cupcakes, especially) or take a dish to a potluck.

    2 pounds suitable-for-stew beef, cut into 1½-inch cubes

    6 carrots, cut into thick slices

    2 large onions, coarsely chopped

    1 large baking potato, diced (no need to peel it)

    1 bay leaf

    1 teaspoon dried oregano

    1 teaspoon salt

    ½ teaspoon pepper

    1 10-to-11-ounce can Campbell's Tomato, Cream of
        Tomato, *or* Tomato Bisque Soup

    ½ soup can water

Preheat the oven to 275 degrees.

In a heavy, lidded casserole that holds about 2½ quarts, combine everything and stir until well mixed. Cover the casserole first with a tight layer of foil and then with the lid.

Bake the stew for 5 hours. (At this low oven temperature,

everything takes awhile.) After the first 2 hours, check it every ½ hour or so to make sure there's enough liquid. There probably will be, but you can add a little more water if you think it's indicated. Serve hot.

Serves 6.

Batter-Up Beef Stew

The prerequisite for this recipe is that your kids like stew. Also, you have to have some leftover stew hanging around. Those two things accomplished, this is a good change of pace. The cheese batter sort of puffs up around the stew in a nice way as it bakes.

4 tablespoons (1/2 stick) unsalted butter

1 1/2 cups flour

1 tablespoon sugar

2 teaspoons baking powder

1 teaspoon salt

4 ounces cheddar, grated (about 1 cup)

1 1/2 cups milk

3 cups or so leftover beef stew

Preheat the oven to 350 degrees.

Melt the butter in the oven in an 8-inch square baking dish. While it melts, stir the dry ingredients in a bowl; toss in the cheddar until well mixed, then stir in the milk.

When the butter is melted, pour the batter over it. Now gently spread the stew on top of the batter. *Do not stir.* The batter must remain a separate entity for this recipe to work.

Bake for 1 hour. The batter should be puffed and brown. Serve immediately.

Serves 6.

Paul's Pot Roast (Don't Knock It till You've Tried It)

When Paul's mother, Renie, told me about this recipe, she assured me that Paul is a very good cook and would never like a recipe with all these premade ingredients if it weren't worth it. Oh, Renie, we all know *that*.

  2 tablespoons vegetable oil

  3 pounds beef brisket

  5 large onions, sliced

  1 40-ounce squeeze bottle ketchup

  1 ketchup bottle of water

  1 1-ounce envelope onion soup mix

  1 16-ounce can whole cranberry sauce

Preheat the oven to 300 degrees.

Heat the oil in a large, heavy pot and brown the meat on all sides. Stir in the rest of the ingredients. Cover the pot tightly and cook the meat, covered, for 3 to 4 hours, stirring occasionally. (Turn the meat a couple of times while cooking if it's not all submerged.) Uncover and cook for 1/2 hour more.

Remove the pot from the oven and let the meat stand for 15 minutes. Slice it across the grain and serve with the sauce.

Serves 6.

Ann's Pot Roast

Everyone I've ever made this pot roast for has loved it, although one reader made it for herself and wrote me, "Your pot roast—what a joke!" Anyway, my *kids* love it, even though it has wine in it. But then one day I got another recipe from my friend Paul Sax (page 145), and my husband almost literally raved about Paul's Pot Roast (as I cleverly named it). So I'm including them both, and you can do your own taste test.

Both recipes benefit from being made a day early, skimmed of fat, and reheated the next day. Actually, Ann's Pot Roast demands it.

5 pounds beef brisket, trimmed of all visible fat

Lots of pepper

1/4 cup vegetable oil

8 onions, thickly sliced and separated into rings

6 carrots, cut into thick chunks

3 garlic cloves, minced

2 bay leaves

1/4 cup tomato paste

Salt to taste

1 16-ounce can tomatoes, with juice

1 cup dry red wine

Preheat the oven to 300 degrees.

Cover both sides of the brisket with lots of pepper. Heat the oil in a large, heavy casserole and brown the brisket over medium heat. Set the meat aside and cook the onions in the same oil for 15 minutes, scraping up and incorporating the browned bits. The onions should be golden and soft. Stir in the carrots, garlic, and bay leaves.

Turn off the heat and place the brisket on top of the veggies. Coat the meat on both sides with the tomato paste; then re-pepper it and add a little salt. Pour the tomatoes and red wine over all.

Cover the casserole tightly with foil, then with the lid. Bake the pot roast for 4 to 5 hours, or until thoroughly tender. (You can add a little beef broth or water if it starts to get dry.) Let cool; refrigerate overnight.

The next day, skim off any congealed fat. Reheat the pot roast and vegetables either on the stovetop or in a 300-degree oven.

Slice the meat across the grain and serve with the pan juices and vegetables spooned over. You'll probably want to add more salt at the table.

Serves 8.

Oven-Barbecued Beef

Perfect for a winter day, this is a gorgeous shredded-beef thing that you serve on some kind of roll. It does take a while to cook—up to 7 hours. But you can make it yesterday and serve it today, if you see what I mean.

2 tablespoons vegetable oil

1 3-pound chuck roast, trimmed of all visible fat

1 large onion, chopped (or minced to invisibility, if that's what your children require)

2 garlic cloves, minced

2 cups ketchup

3/4 cup water

1/4 cup vinegar

3 tablespoons Worcestershire sauce

2 tablespoons brown sugar, packed

2 tablespoons chili powder

1 tablespoon Dijon mustard

Salt and pepper to taste

12 buns or hard rolls

Heat the oil in a large pot and brown the beef on all sides. Dump the rest of the ingredients into the pot and bring them to a boil, stirring gingerly around the big hunk of meat. As soon as the liquid boils, turn the heat down to a simmer, cover the pot, and never let it boil again.

Cook the beef gently for at least 2 hours and up to (or even past) 3. Turn it several times in its bath.

When the meat is tender enough, use two forks to pull it apart into shreds. Continue to cook, uncovered, until the shredded meat is incredibly tender. This may take up to 4 hours in all, so be patient and *keep the heat low.* The meat won't soften properly if it's cooked at too high a heat.

When the shredded beef is tender enough to suit you, serve it on the buns.

Serves 12. This recipe is not easy to halve (it's hard to find little chunks of chuck), so you might want to freeze half of it if you have a small family.

Sausage "Polenta"

This is another recipe that uses Jiffy corn muffin mix (that's the "polenta" part), and a useful thing it is too. I make it with turkey sausage, to please the non-red-meat eater in my house. Any kind will do, though; the friend who gave it to me, Jean Chapin, uses sweet Italian links cut into pieces. You could even buy pregrated Monterey Jack, though I grate my own so I'll feel more housewifely. On the other hand, I use a 28-ounce jar of spaghetti sauce instead of the canned tomatoes and tomato paste Jean uses. I won't tell anyone if you do this too.

Polenta

1 8½-ounce box Jiffy corn muffin mix

½ cup grated Parmesan (about 2 ounces)

½ cup milk

1 large egg

Sausage

1 tablespoon vegetable oil

1 large onion, chopped***

1 garlic clove, chopped***

1 15½-ounce can tomatoes, drained (save ½ cup of the liquid) and chopped

6 tablespoons tomato paste

½ teaspoon dried oregano

Salt and pepper to taste

1 pound sausage of your choice, squeezed out of the casing, cooked, and crumbled (or sliced, or in links)

½–1 pound Monterey Jack or fontina, cut into cubes

Preheat the oven to 375 degrees. Grease a 2-quart baking dish or oblong pan.

For the polenta: Stir the muffin mix, Parmesan, milk, and egg together in a medium bowl. Spread the batter evenly over the bottom of the baking dish or pan.

For the sausage: Heat the oil in a large skillet and sauté the optional onion and optional garlic until translucent, about 5 minutes. Add the canned tomatoes and the $1/2$ cup of their liquid, the tomato paste, and seasonings. Cook for about 5 minutes, stirring frequently, until the sauce thickens. Remove from the heat.

Arrange half the cooked sausage over the cornmeal batter. Spread this evenly with the tomato sauce, and top with the remaining sausage. Bake for 15 minutes. Top with the cheese and bake for 10 minutes more, or until the cheese is bubbling. Serve immediately.

Serves 6.

Ham-and-Cheese Roll-Up

I just love this. It's basically like a ham and cheese sandwich, but much more show-offy. Actually, it's a ham and cheese strudel, with nothing in it to frighten a child except the word "strudel." ("Roll-up" is more user-friendly.)

1 cup (2 sticks) unsalted butter, divided

1 large onion, finely chopped***

3/4 cup raw rice

1 1/2 cups chicken broth

Pepper to taste

2 tablespoons minced fresh parsley***

10 sheets frozen filo dough (read the box carefully for
   defrosting instructions)

4 ounces thin-sliced ham (or smoked turkey), cut into
   fine strips

4 ounces Swiss cheese, grated (about 1 cup)

4 ounces cheddar, grated (about 1 cup)

Preheat the oven to 375 degrees. Lavishly grease a cookie sheet or (preferably) cover it with parchment paper.

Melt 1 tablespoon of the butter in a large saucepan. Add the optional onion and cook for about 5 minutes, until it's translucent. Add the rice and chicken broth. Bring to a boil and cook for 15 minutes, or until the rice has absorbed all the broth. Cool to lukewarm, then season to taste with pepper and stir in the optional parsley.

Meanwhile, melt the rest of the butter in a small saucepan. Put 1 filo sheet in front of you and brush it lavishly with melted butter. Repeat this process, stacking the sheets and using plenty of butter, until all the sheets have been used.

Carefully spread the cooled rice over the filo sheets, leaving

**It Happens
To Everyone**

A short list of what I wouldn't
eat as a child: hot dogs, pizza,
and sandwiches. And that means
any kind of sandwiches. I liked
to eat my food "separately"—
which eliminated any meals that
combined meat with bread.
At mealtimes, I ate all the meat
at once, then ate the vegetable,
then the rice—I never skipped
around. I grew up to be a normal
adult, and now I eat everything
with gusto, in full combinations.
(Except if it has cilantro in it.
Hate cilantro.)

—Lynn Snowden

a 2-inch border all around. Top the rice with the ham and the
ham with the cheeses.

Slide your hand under a short end of the filo stack and lift
up approximately 3 inches of it. Fold this over once, as if you
were making the first fold in a business letter. Fold the long
sides over to seal the filling. Continue folding/rolling until the
strudel is all rolled up.

Place the strudel on the cookie sheet seam side down. With
a sharp knife, make several slashes in the top to let out the
steam.

Bake for 35 to 40 minutes, or until the strudel is well
browned and crisp-looking. (Some of the filling may leak out
onto the pan, but don't worry about that.) Let the strudel stand
for 5 minutes before you slice it with a sharp knife.

Serves 6.

Apricot-Orange Pork Tenderloin

You *really* don't need to worry about serving this recipe in front of outsiders. It's good from a grown-up point of view too.

Usually pork tenderloins are packaged two to a—well—package. If you can find a single tenderloin that weighs about a pound and a half, go for it.

Ideally, the meat should marinate for up to a day before you cook it.

1 6-ounce can frozen orange juice concentrate, thawed

1 juice can water

3 tablespoons apricot preserves

2 tablespoons brown sugar, packed

2 tablespoons soy sauce

1 garlic clove, minced

1/2 teaspoon ground ginger

2 pork tenderloins, totaling approximately 1 1/2 pounds

The day before you're going to be cooking the pork (if possible), stir together the juice concentrate, water, preserves, brown sugar, soy sauce, garlic, and ginger. Slice the pork into 1-inch-thick medallions and marinate them in this mixture in the refrigerator for at least 2 hours, or overnight.

When you're ready to cook, bring the meat and marinade to room temperature. Preheat the oven to 500 degrees. (This *is* the correct temperature.)

Put the meat and marinade into a baking dish. Bake the pork for 20 minutes, turning each medallion once after 10 minutes. If you want them browner before serving, put them under the broiler for a minute or so.

Serve the medallions with the sauce. My standard accompaniment is instant couscous (cooked in chicken broth) with currants and chopped toasted almonds stirred in; the grown-ups at the table also add chopped scallions.

Serves 4.

How to Make Pork Tenderloin 100 Percent Better
(and it was already pretty good)

Pork tenderloin is a great cut—a manageable size and easy to cook. Practically any recipe that calls for boneless chicken breast can be made with pork tenderloin instead.

The only drawback to this cut is that it's so low in fat that it can be dry. Brining the tenderloin not only makes it juicy without adding fat, it also adds flavor all the way through, unlike just salting the outside of the meat.

Any recipe that calls for pork tenderloin will be improved if you brine it first. What you do is this. Take 2 pork tenderloins, which together should weigh about 1 1/2 to 2 pounds. Stir 1 1/2 tablespoons of salt into 2 cups of water, then pour over the pork. Cover and chill for 24 hours, turning occasionally. Then go ahead with your recipe—say, the one on page 156.

Brining the tenderloins and then slicing them 1 inch thick and grilling them with any kind of barbecue sauce is delicious. Not as good as steak—let's not go overboard here—but much better than *plain* grilled pork.

Pork Tenderloins with Apple Stuffing

Everyone who knows me is tired of hearing how great I think Pepperidge Farm stuffing is, but let me just say it one more time: it's great. It is one of my ancestral foods. In this recipe, it's especially great because you prepare it with apple cider instead of boring old water.

For maximum succulence, you should brine the pork tenderloins according to the method on page 155. But since you'll be topping them with bacon, you can omit that step if you need to save time.

Note that you will need skewers or some other sharp, pointy implements to hold the tenderloins together. Either that, or you can fasten them with kitchen twine or unflavored dental floss.

1 1/3 cups apple cider, divided

2 tablespoons (1/4 stick) unsalted butter

2 cups Pepperidge Farm herb stuffing mix

3/4 cup chopped apples (I use Golden Delicious)

1/2 cup minced onion***

2 pork tenderloins, each weighing 3/4-1 pound

Salt and pepper to taste

4 bacon strips, cut crosswise in half

Preheat the oven to 350 degrees.

Bring ⅓ cup of the cider and the butter to a boil in a medium saucepan over medium heat. Remove from the heat and stir in the stuffing mix. Stir in the apples and the optional onion and mix well.

Rinse each tenderloin under cold water and pat it dry with paper towels. With a sharp knife, slice each tenderloin lengthwise about three-quarters of the way through. In other words, don't separate the loins into two separate pieces—just "butterfly" them. You want each tenderloin cut enough so that you can flatten it, though.

Are you still with me? Sprinkle the tenderloins with salt and pepper. Flatten one so that the cut side is up, and cover it with the apple stuffing. Press the other tenderloin on top of the stuffing so that you have a big "sandwich." Either skewer the two pieces of meat together in several places, or tie them together, keeping the meat as flat as possible.

Place this rather cumbersome object on a rack in a shallow roasting pan. Pour the remaining 1 cup cider over the meat. Arrange the bacon evenly across the top.

Bake for 1 to 1½ hours, basting occasionally with the cider, until the meat is cooked through and brown on top. Discard the bacon; it's done its job. Transfer the meat to a platter.

If you want to serve the pan juices, use a bulb baster to remove the fat; then whisk the juices together and pour them into a small bowl or gravy boat. "Gravy boat," "tureen": where do they come up with these names? Serve hot.

Serves 6 to 8.

Cider Pork Chops with Only a Teeny, Teeny Bit of Mustard

I don't see how anyone's kids could spot the Dijon in this, but if you think that's really a risk, by all means omit it. This is a rich dish, and if your children don't eat their share, you'll end up finishing *their* chops and getting way too full. It's another treasure from *The Practical Palate* (see page 38).

4 pork chops, approximately 1 inch thick

2 tablespoons (¹/₄ stick) unsalted butter

¹/₂ cup apple cider

1 teaspoon Dijon mustard

¹/₂ cup heavy cream

Salt and pepper to taste

2 tablespoons minced fresh parsley***

Fry the chops in the butter in a covered skillet over low heat for 15 minutes, turning frequently.

Add the cider and cook the chops, covered, for 10 more minutes. Remove them to a platter and add the remaining ingredients to the skillet. Whisk the sauce—for behold, it *is* a sauce now!—over low heat until slightly thickened. Pour the sauce over the chops and serve them with noodles.

Serves 4, unless you have an unusually hungry family—in which case you should multiply the recipe accordingly.

Teriyaki Pork Chops

You know that we no longer have to cook pork until it's stiff and gray, right? It's perfectly safe to leave the center pink. Not rare, just pink. Rare would probably also be safe, but who eats rare pork?

2/3 cup soy sauce

1/4 cup sherry

3 tablespoons cider vinegar

3 tablespoons light brown sugar, packed

2 tablespoons grated fresh ginger

2 large garlic cloves, crushed

4 pork chops, approximately 1 inch thick

2 tablespoons vegetable oil

Bring the soy sauce, sherry, vinegar, brown sugar, ginger, and garlic to a boil in a small, nonreactive saucepan, stirring constantly until the sugar is dissolved. Cool the marinade to room temperature. (If you want to hasten the process, you can put the saucepan into a 9-x-13-inch pan filled with ice water.)

Arrange the chops in a single layer in a baking pan and pour the marinade over them. Marinate them at room temperature for 1 hour, turning them a couple of times; you can also marinate them, chilled and covered, for up to 24 hours. But bring them to room temperature before you cook them.

Drain the marinade off into a small, nonreactive saucepan. Bring the liquid to a boil over medium heat; then lower the heat and simmer for 5 minutes.

Meanwhile, heat the oil in a large, heavy skillet and cook the chops for 6 to 8 minutes on each side, or until they're cooked through but still pink. Drizzle the hot marinade over them and serve right away.

Serves 4.

 **It Happens
To Everyone**

I was great at hiding food in my
pockets. My mother once opened
the washing machine and found
a hot dog floating in the water.
                    —Patty Marx

The Dog Show

(In which, as a service to my readers, I taste-test many, many brands of hot dogs)

When my sister, Cathy, was about three, my mother took her to the pediatrician for a checkup and mentioned that Cathy didn't like to eat much. The doctor bent down and said, "I bet you like hot dogs, don't you?"

Yes. Most kids do. Actually, most *people* do, especially my aunt Gail. No matter where you take Aunt Gail for lunch, she always orders a hot dog. Aunt Gail won't even be happy if you drag her someplace fancy. She'll spend the whole time looking nervously for the exits, as if a hot dog might be waiting outside if she could just make a dash for it.

I see her point, though I plan to be a much more expensive lunch date when *I'm* 90. Hot dogs never let you down. You have to trick up a hamburger with piles of cheese and other glop, but a hot dog tastes good on its own. Sure, all those nitrates are probably pickling you—but at a barbecue, who cares? Be sensible another time, I say.

Not that I was even one bit sensible when I tested some of the leading hot dog brands for this book. Though no one was forcing me to do more than *taste* each brand, I always managed to finish the whole dog—even unto the ninth in a row. Such thorough testing enables me to state with confidence that although Nathan's and Hummel are my favorite brands and Ball Park Franks are my son's favorite, most hot dogs taste fine. (Except for Tofu Pups, which are an insult to tofu, hot dogs, and vegetarians.) True, there's a lot of variety out there. Hot dogs can have natural casings or a skinless exterior; spicy seasonings or mild; and chewy meat or a more processed fleshiness. Adults will probably prefer the more challenging brands, children the blander ones. My daughter won't care, as long as there's no red meat in her hot dog. And of course Aunt Gail will love them all.

Now, let's say you want to add a little trouble to what is usually a trouble-free meal. In that case, you might want to serve . . .

Heroic Mustard

E ven the most basic supermarket mustards are better than homemade—except for this one. It's very hot, very sweet, very easy to make, and very easy to eat plain off the end of a knife when no one's looking.

1/2 cup Colman's dry mustard (no other brand will work)

1/2 cup distilled white vinegar (no other type will work)

A pinch of salt

1/4 cup sugar

1 large egg, beaten

Whisk together the mustard, vinegar, and salt in a nonmetal bowl until smooth. Cover and let stand for at least 8 hours, or overnight.

Transfer to a nonreactive saucepan. Whisk in the sugar and egg and cook over low heat, whisking constantly until the mixture reaches a full boil. Cool before serving.

Makes about 3/4 cup, which can be stored in the fridge for up to a month.

Five Easy Extras

a couple of different people suggested that I include a few adult-pleasing condiments in this book so that children and their parents could be satisfied at the same meal. The kids eat their boring, boring hamburgers and chicken without any bothersome "ingredients," you see, and the parents sprinkle on, or brush on, or dip into, little ramekins of some kind of intensely flavored condiment that makes life worth living. Heroic Mustard (opposite) is one example of this kind of thing. Here are a few more.

The Most Basic Dry Rub

1/4 cup lemon pepper

2 tablespoons garlic powder

2 tablespoons brown sugar, packed

1 teaspoon salt

1/2 teaspoon cayenne

Combine everything thoroughly. Store airtight and use to rub over the adults' pieces of chicken, pork, beef, or spareribs before cooking.

Makes about 1/2 cup.

Sweet Pepper Glaze

1/2 cup mild honey

2 tablespoons *mild* hot pepper sauce (I use Durkee Red Hot), plus a few drops *hot* hot pepper sauce if you want

1 tablespoon fresh lemon or lime juice

1 tablespoon unsalted butter, melted (optional)

1/4 teaspoon salt

1/4 teaspoon pepper

Stir the ingredients well in a small bowl. Brush over grilled meats just before serving; you can't heat this sauce, or too much of the taste will dissipate.

Makes about 3/4 cup.

The Pantry Mustard

The Pantry is a wonderful gourmet store in my town. Everyone who lives around here should buy their own Pantry mustard (which is mandatory with ham); you're only allowed to make your own if you don't live here.

1/4 cup coarse-grained mustard

1/4 cup Dijon mustard

1/4 cup dried basil

1/2 cup vegetable oil

Blend the mustards and basil in a food processor until smooth. Keep the machine running as you slowly add the oil; process until the mixture is smooth. The mustard will keep indefinitely in the refrigerator, but it should be covered tightly so it won't darken.

Makes about 1 cup.

ALWAYS waive all your junk-food rules when you're taking the family on a long car or plane trip. The stricter you are during the rest of the time, the more delighted your kids will be when you let them buy huge, forbidden boxes of Jujyfruits from the highway rest stop.

Vinegar-Soy Dip

1/2 cup soy sauce

1/2 cup cider vinegar or balsamic vinegar

1/4 cup sesame oil

4 teaspoons sugar

4 scallions, chopped

Whisk the liquids together in a small bowl, then whisk in the sugar and scallions. Paint pork or chicken with the sauce while grilling or serve as a dip for vegetables, especially snow peas.

Makes about 1 1/3 cups.

Secret Sauce for Meat or Poultry

Not the McDonald's kind, but the kind you don't want anyone to know you make. When will society accept Lipton's onion soup mix for the marvel it is? Even some children may like *this*.

6 tablespoons apricot preserves

1 cup French dressing

1 1-ounce package dry onion soup mix

Melt the preserves in a small saucepan over low heat, stirring constantly. Add the French dressing and onion soup mix and stir until thoroughly combined. Serve as a sauce for meat or poultry.

Makes about 1 1/2 cups.

Paintbrush Stuff

Says Jacki Prindle, in AOL's Moms Online, "This is an excellent marinade and great as a sauce on meat. My nieces poured it onto everything they ate, including vegetables. It got its name because when my sister-in-law first put it on the table in a jar, her daughter said, "That looks like the stuff Daddy uses to clean paintbrushes!"

It's a fairly respectable mixture, actually. Too respectable (meaning "good") for some kids, probably.

1/2 cup olive oil

1/4 cup fresh lemon juice

1/4 cup Worcestershire sauce

Up to 5 garlic cloves, crushed

1 1/2 teaspoons liquid smoke

1 teaspoon salt

1/2 teaspoon Ac'cent (optional)

Mix all the ingredients in a blender until smooth. Store in the refrigerator for up to 1 week. Use as a dip, a marinade, or a sauce for meats and vegetables.

Makes about 1 cup.

Pizza'd Shrimp

I never used to understand why some children don't like shrimp. Shrimp look awful, admittedly, but they're so mild-mannered! Then I made friends with a Bosnian family who'd moved here and who also hated shrimp (and, in fact, all fish). Thus I realized that shrimp have an innately hateful quality that I'd somehow never noticed. I still love them, though.

Usually, disguising a hated ingredient doesn't work. In this recipe, it does. Not that you still can't tell you're eating shrimp—but you need have no qualms about forcing your children to eat a couple of bites. The pizza sauce *absolutely neutralizes* the main ingredient.

1½ pounds peeled large shrimp

1 16-ounce jar pizza sauce

4–8 ounces mozzarella or "pizza cheese," grated
   (1–2 cups)

Preheat the oven to 350 degrees.

Put the shrimp into a baking dish. Pour the sauce over them. Put the cheese on top. Bake for 25 minutes, until the cheese is melted and bubbling.

Serve with rice or noodles, and remember that these shrimp can't possibly offend anyone. Oops!—unless your child hates pizza.

Serves 4 to 6, depending on how many shrimp eaters are at the table.

Oven-Barbie'd Shrimp

For reasons that must have to do with chemistry—a subject about which I know nothing—different kinds of heat in food strike the palate in different ways. I can enjoy almost any amount of heat made by hot peppers, but very hot mustards are harder for me to take; they sting my nose too much. Maybe I haven't worked as hard to build up my mustard tolerance as I have my pepper tolerance, but every time I try a hot mustard, my sinuses always seem to react as if they'd never *heard* of mustard before. It helps me be more sympathetic toward kids and their dainty, undeveloped palates.

Children, of course, tend to tolerate hot foods less well than adults, at least in the Western Hemisphere. But they too seem to do better with "barbecue" heat than, say, mustard or curry heat. Maybe that's because many barbecue sauces contain a big wallop of sugar—in the form of ketchup or out-and-out sweeteners like molasses—to help the medicine go down.

Although the sauce in this recipe is not notably sweet, it's rich and flavorful and not frighteningly spicy, and the heat is easy to adjust. I wouldn't waste the dish on a child whom you know won't touch shrimp, but for any fence-sitters out there, this presentation may tip them over the edge. Of the fence, you see. The fence of liking shrimp, that is.

You'll need to start this recipe 4 to 6 hours before cooking it to give the shrimp time to marinate in the barbecue sauce.

3 pounds jumbo shrimp, peeled and deveined

1 cup (2 sticks) unsalted butter

1 cup vegetable oil

1 cup bottled chili sauce

1/4 cup fresh orange juice

3 tablespoons fresh lemon juice

3 tablespoons Worcestershire sauce

A few drops of Tabasco

2 large garlic cloves, chopped***

2 tablespoons chopped fresh parsley***

2 teaspoons paprika

2 teaspoons dried oregano

1/2–1 teaspoon black pepper

1/2 teaspoon salt

1/2 teaspoon dried thyme

1/2 teaspoon dried rosemary

1/4 teaspoon (or up to 2 teaspoons) cayenne***

2 large lemons, sliced very thin

French or Italian bread, on the side

Rinse the cleaned shrimp and dry them carefully with paper towels. Spread them out in a 9-x-13-inch baking dish.

Heat the butter, oil, chili sauce, orange juice, lemon juice, Worcestershire, Tabasco, the optional garlic, optional parsley, paprika, oregano, pepper to taste, salt, thyme, rosemary, and the optional cayenne over low heat in a large saucepan, whisking often, until the butter has melted and the sauce is well mixed. Stir in the sliced lemons. Pour the sauce over the shrimp and put the baking dish into the refrigerator. Refrigerate for 4 to 6 hours, stirring every 1/2 hour.

About 20 minutes before you plan to bake, preheat the oven to 300 degrees.

Bake the shrimp for 1/2 hour, stirring every 10 minutes. Serve the shrimp and their sauce in bowls, allowing your children to freely dip and swish their bread around in the sauce as well.

Serves 6 to 8.

Sugar-Baked Shrimp

Don't worry that this recipe is like putting jam on shrimp. The sugar adds crunch and sweetness, but it's not syrupy. It's more like a sophisticated sweet-and-sour coating than anything else.

1 cup!!!!! sugar

2 tablespoons flour

1 teaspoon salt

1/2 teaspoon pepper

1/4 teaspoon cayenne***

1/4 teaspoon allspice

1/4 teaspoon cumin

1 large garlic clove, crushed

1 tablespoon minced fresh ginger

24 jumbo shrimp, peeled and deveined but with
    tails left on

Fresh lime wedges

Preheat the oven to 500 degrees. Grease a baking sheet or (better) cover it with parchment paper.

Stir everything except the shrimp and lime together in a large bowl.

A few at a time, roll the shrimp in the sugar mixture and set them on the baking sheet. Bake for 10 minutes, or until the sugar has started to caramelize in spots.

Take the shrimp out of the oven and turn them over on the baking sheet. Squeeze the lime juice over them and serve right away.

BBQ Salmon

I used to make this with swordfish, but as of this writing, swordfish is being overfished, and we're not buying it in my house. So I switched to salmon. Of course the recipe would also work with tuna or halibut or any other "meaty" fish. (Including swordfish, if the boycott is ever lifted.)

1½–2 pounds salmon steaks

2 tablespoons soy sauce

2 tablespoons fresh orange juice

2 tablespoons ketchup

1 tablespoon vegetable oil

1 teaspoon grated orange rind

1 tablespoon fresh lemon juice

1 large garlic clove, crushed

1 teaspoon sugar

1 teaspoon sesame oil

½ teaspoon dried oregano

½ teaspoon pepper

Put the salmon in a large baking dish. Whisk the remaining ingredients together in a small bowl and pour them over the salmon. Marinate at room temperature for 45 minutes, or in the refrigerator for 2 hours.

Grill or broil the salmon for about 8 minutes a side, or until it's as done as you like it. Serve immediately.

Serves 4.

It Happens To Everyone

Jessie's half-brother Eric, about five years old, was very pleased and excited to be taken to a real adult restaurant with his parents and big sister Jessie. He carefully studied the menu, only needing a little help, and proudly ordered swordfish. When it was served, he started to cry and cry. "What's wrong, Eric?" asked his parents. He sobbed out, *"Where's the sword?"*

—Elaine Hopkins

Tuna Sesame

α t my house, this is another recipe that used to use sword-fish. Until the swordfish boycott is over, I'll make it with tuna, halibut, or monkfish. You could also use sea scallops, which are so sweet and mild that *all* children would gobble them down if they had any sense . . .

1 cup sesame seeds
1/2 teaspoon salt
1/2 teaspoon pepper
1/2 cup ranch dressing
11/2 pounds tuna fillet, cut into 11/2-inch cubes

Preheat the oven to 300 degrees. Line a large baking dish with foil.

Bake the sesame seeds in a shallow pan for about 10 minutes, stirring occasionally, until they're golden brown. Take them out, put them in a small dish to cool, and turn the oven up to 500 degrees.

Stir the salt and pepper into the sesame seeds. Place the ranch dressing in a shallow dish and gently flip the fish cubes around in it until they're coated. Roll them in the sesame seeds until they're coated with *them.*

Spread the fish cubes out in the baking dish. Bake for 10 minutes, or until the fish is just cooked through.

Serves 4.

Ritz Fitz (Oven-Fried Fish Fillets)

I bet you were hoping for a lot of good fish recipes in this book, but for the most part, fish is a lost cause where picky eaters are concerned. I've basically given up, and am waiting for peer-group pressure to coerce my children into appreciating The Bounty of the Sea.

But they don't mind this recipe too much. They eat three bites, and David and I eat the rest.

4 tablespoons ($^1/_2$ stick) unsalted butter

$^2/_3$ cup crushed crackers (I use Ritz)

$^1/_4$ cup grated Parmesan (about 1 ounce)

$^1/_2$ teaspoon dried basil

$^1/_2$ teaspoon dried oregano

$^1/_4$ teaspoon garlic powder

1 pound sole, scrod, perch, or other mild-tasting fish
    fillets

Lemon wedges

Preheat the oven to 350 degrees.

Melt the butter in a 9-x-13-inch pan in the oven. While it melts, combine everything else except the fish and lemon wedges in a pie pan.

Slop the fish around in the melted butter, dip each piece in the crumb mixture, and return it to the baking pan.

Bake the fillets for 20 to 25 minutes, or until the fish flakes with a fork. Serve with lemon wedges, and good luck to you.

Serves 4.

I Can't Believe I'm Doing This

"I made some frozen fish squares for Ian for dinner, and burned them black. But did I throw them away? No. I simply told him they were FISH CRISPS. It worked like a charm!"

—Roz Chast

Tuna-ghetti

I wouldn't venture to try this with children who don't like tuna or garlic, but for those who do, it can be a wonderful introduction to pasta that doesn't come with tomato sauce on it. You have to use the tuna packed in oil for this, but remember you're doing it for a good cause.

1 pound dried pasta (I use spaghetti)

2 6-ounce cans solid albacore tuna packed in oil

1 large garlic clove, minced

Salt and pepper to taste

Minced fresh parsley to add at the table***

Grated Parmesan to add at the table (optional)

Cook the pasta according to the package directions; drain, but save ¹/₂ cup of the pasta water.

Meanwhile, plop the tuna into a small bowl and flake it with a fork. Add the garlic and toss well.

Slither the hot pasta into a serving bowl, and toss it well with the tuna mixture and the ¹/₂ cup pasta water. Season to taste.

Pass the optional parsley and Parmesan at the table, and don't listen to rude grown-ups who tell you that cheese shouldn't be served with fish sauces. We are not at a fancy restaurant.

Serves 4.

"It Doesn't Have to Be Meat, You Know"

In the olden days, children used to have bread and milk for dinner. In my house, we sometimes have onion rings. That's right: WE SOMETIMES HAVE ONION RINGS FOR DINNER. (With vegetables, of course. I'm not *trashy*.) When I go to all the trouble of making onion rings, I want them to be the star of the meal.

The same goes for my World's Best Bread, which takes almost as much labor to produce as a—well, not a human baby, perhaps, but *some* kind of baby. On the nights I've made this peasant-style bread, we have it with carrot sticks and red pepper strips, and a glass of milk. Maybe some cheese, maybe not. It's no different from having pancakes for supper—which we also sometimes do.

Not every supper needs a big, sullen hunk of protein as its centerpiece. Nutritionally speaking, there's no need for it; if your children are getting enough calories, they're getting enough protein. From the cook's point of view, depending on meat all the time is a boring way to cook. And for children who tend toward vegetarianism, it's repellent.

If there's one area in which our kids are way ahead of us, it's two areas: computers and vegetarianism. Most families I know have at least one vegetarian child. I approve, though supper can get complicated when you have a kid who doesn't eat meat but doesn't like vegetables and

The Recipes

legumes. Some parents solve this problem by making the veggie child cook her own meals, but that often results in two cooks darting around getting in each other's way at the stove when there are only six minutes until dinner. In a "mixed" family—one with both vegetarians and meat eaters—an occasional carb-based dinner pleases everyone. With a glass of milk, it also provides plenty of protein.

The recipes in this chapter are all meant to be served as a "main course." In some, there's no meat at all. In some, meat (bacon, especially) is treated as a condiment that can be kept out of the vegetarian's portion. I have a whole pile of little ramekins that I use for my daughter's supper when we're having something with meat in it and she's not.

None of these recipes is vegan. In fact, everything I've just said falls apart if your kids go vegan instead of "regular" vegetarian. But let's assume they won't do that until they've moved out of the house.

MUST-Make-from-Scratch Macaroni and Cheese

W*hy must I? Is Stouffer's all that bad?*

No, no. But this is very much better, and it gives you a legitimate excuse to use Velveeta, which—because it's a plastic, not a food—is incredibly easy to work with. Since I'm not from France, I LOVE Velveeta. No one believes that; they think I'm just being perverse and retro. But every couple of months I buy a block of it and wolf down big hunks of it plain or on crackers. (Eight Ritz crackers takes care of the whole 8-ounce block.) We never had Velveeta when I was growing up, and I have to make up for lost time.

But you don't *have* to use Velveeta in this. Cheddar or Monterey Jack work fine, or you can use a mixture of all three.

12 ounces dried macaroni

2 tablespoons (¼ stick) unsalted butter

2 large eggs

1 12-ounce can evaporated milk

½ teaspoon paprika***

½ teaspoon dry mustard***

Salt and pepper to taste

12 ounces Velveeta or other processed "American" cheese, grated or chopped (about 3 cups); if you use "regular" cheese, grate it.

Preheat the oven to 350 degrees. Grease a 9-x-13-inch baking dish.

Cook the macaroni in a large pot of boiling salted water according to the package directions, but take it off the heat 2

 It Happens To Everyone

My daughter Miranda was very popular last year when she brought tofu cubes to school. I soak them in soy sauce and put them in Tupperware, and they really are delicious. One mother called and asked me if it was true I was sending "little pieces of futon" in Miranda's lunchbox.

—Danica Kombol

minutes early. Drain it well and return it to the hot pot. Stir in the butter.

Beat the eggs with the evaporated milk in a small bowl. Add the optional spices and salt and pepper. (Don't oversalt—the cheese will be salty.) Add the milk mixture to the macaroni.

Over very, very low heat (you don't want the eggs to scramble), stir the cheese into the macaroni until it has melted. Put the mixture into the baking dish and bake it for 20 minutes.

After 20 minutes, turn the oven up to 500 degrees. Bake the macaroni and cheese for 5 to 8 more minutes, or until it's beginning to brown and get crusty on top.

Serves 4.

Nonthreatening Cheese Fondue

K ids these days. I swear. When I was little, a nice box of prepared cheese fondue was good enough for *me*. But even
that is too "exotic" for my guys. Maybe it's the white wine and
kirsch, which all cheese fondue recipes seem to insist on. Why?
The fondue concept is so perfect for children—it's so nice and
violent, stabbing something with a fork and then drowning it
in a vat—that poisoning the cheese with wine is lunacy.

But this recipe wouldn't dream of doing anything silly like
that. This recipe *likes* children.

1 cup chicken broth

1 large garlic clove, minced***

1 pound Swiss cheese, grated (about 4 cups)

1/4 cup flour

1 11-to-12-ounce can condensed cheddar cheese soup
  (sorry 'bout that, Switzerland)

A 1-pound loaf crusty French or Italian bread, cubed

Simmer together the broth and the optional garlic in a fondue
pot or medium saucepan. Toss the cheese and flour together
until the cheese is thoroughly coated with the flour. Gradually
blend the floured cheese into the broth, stirring constantly
until all the cheese is added and melted. Blend in the (undiluted) soup. Stirring often, heat the mixture till it's nice and
smooth. Then start stabbing that bread.

You could probably sneak in a few vegetables for dipping, as
well—carrots or slightly steamed broccoli or red bell pepper
strips—or, failing that, you could at least try apple wedges.

Makes about 4 cups; serves 4.

Lazy Man's (or Lazy Mom's) Lasagna

*a*ll the flavors of lasagna with, comparatively, no work at all.

1 pound lean ground beef

1/2 cup minced onion***

1 garlic clove, minced***

1 teaspoon dried basil

1 teaspoon dried oregano

Salt and pepper to taste

12 ounces frozen (not thawed) cheese ravioli

1 14-ounce jar spaghetti sauce

8 ounces provolone, sliced

1/2 cup grated Parmesan (about 2 ounces), for topping

Preheat the oven to 350 degrees.

Brown the beef with the optional onion, optional garlic, herbs, and salt and pepper in a large, ovenproof skillet (I use one that's made of cast iron). When the meat is thoroughly cooked—it will take 8 to 10 minutes—drain off any fat and take everything out of the pan. Now put the still-frozen ravioli into the pan, breaking them up if they're clumped. Spread the ground-beef mixture evenly over the ravioli, and ladle the spaghetti sauce evenly over the ground-beef mixture. Over medium heat, without stirring, cook until the ravioli are heated through and beginning to brown on the bottom—about 10 minutes.

Take the skillet off the heat, lay the provolone slices over the ground-beef mixture, and sprinkle the whole thing with the Parmesan. Bake for 10 minutes, or until the cheese is melted. Serve hot.

Serves 4.

Baked Fettuccine

This is an upscale version of macaroni and cheese (see page 178)—richer, fancier, and easier. Just like upscale life itself.

2 tablespoons (¼ stick) unsalted butter, melted

1 pound dried fettuccine

4 ounces Parmesan, grated (about 1 cup), divided

4 ounces provolone or fontina, grated (about 1 cup)

4 ounces Gruyère or Swiss cheese, grated (about 1 cup)

4 ounces mozzarella, grated (about 1 cup)

2 tablespoons fresh bread crumbs

½ cup milk

½ cup heavy cream

Tomato sauce as a topping (optional)

Preheat the oven to 400 degrees. Grease a 2-to-3-quart casserole dish.

Cook the fettuccine in boiling salted water according to the package directions. Drain it well, put it back in the pan, toss it with the melted butter, and set aside.

Set aside 2 tablespoons of the Parmesan. Mix the remaining Parmesan and other cheeses together in the greased casserole. Toss together the reserved Parmesan and the bread crumbs in a small bowl. In yet another small bowl, blend the milk and cream.

Add the buttered fettuccine gradually to the cheeses in the casserole, tossing until well mixed. Pour the milk mixture over the pasta mixture. Smooth the top of the casserole, and sprinkle on the crumbs and Parmesan.

Bake the fettuccine for 20 to 30 minutes, or until it is heated through and bubbling. Cover with foil during the last

ALWAYS *taste* the water you're about to cook pasta in, to see if you've salted it enough. This two-second action will save many a meal from being dull. Pasta never tastes as good if you salt it after cooking. I always add enough salt to make the water as salty as chicken noodle soup. (Not, for instance, as salty as the ocean.) You'll need to experiment to learn what makes the pasta taste right to you, of course—but just passing a saltshaker over the surface of the water rarely accomplishes anything. About 1 tablespoon per gallon is recommended by many pros.

Also, ALWAYS follow the directions about how much water to use when you cook pasta, because you will always want to use less than you're actually supposed to. Measuring the water a few times will help you get the right feel for how much you should use, and how big a pot you need. It will also help you realize that it's actually no harder to use the correct pot size and water quantity than it is to use a much-too-small saucepan and end up with gummy pasta.

10 minutes so that the dish won't get too brown: it will taste creamier if it stays pale.

Serve the fettuccine hot, with warmed tomato sauce, if you want.

Serves 6.

Peas and Bow Ties
in Swiss Cheese Sauce

Of course you can use other pasta in place of the bow ties—which, as you probably know, are also called farfalle, or "butterflies." (Cooked butterflies! Gross!) I just happen to like the look of the tiny dots of peas and the ruffly bow ties together.

1 1/3 cups half-and-half

8 ounces dried bow tie pasta

1 cup frozen green "baby" peas, thawed

3 tablespoons unsalted butter

2 tablespoons flour

1/4 cup grated Swiss cheese (about 1 ounce)

1/4–1/2 cup grated Parmesan (1–2 ounces)

Salt and pepper

A pinch of nutmeg***

In a small saucepan, bring the half-and-half to a simmer. Turn off the heat, but leave the saucepan on the burner. Meanwhile, cook the bow ties according to the package directions. Drain them well, and stir in the peas. Keep warm while you make the sauce.

Melt the butter in a medium saucepan over medium heat. When it begins to bubble, lower the heat and whisk in the flour. Whisking constantly, cook the butter and flour together for 3 to 5 minutes, or until they have thickened. Add the heated half-and-half all at once and continue to whisk constantly until the mixture is smooth and reaches a full boil—about 5 minutes.

Take the saucepan off the heat and sprinkle in the Swiss cheese. Pour the sauce over the bow ties and peas, toss with the Parmesan for a few seconds, season to taste (add the nutmeg if you want), and serve immediately.

Serves 4.

It Happens To Everyone

My sister Julie would eat only unsauced spaghetti. My mother ordered plain spaghetti for her in a restaurant once, and it came with sauce on it. Julie said, "I HATE sauce!" and picked up the bowl and threw it backwards over her head into the next booth, all over the person sitting there.

—Cindy Kane

Spaghetti Sesame

This is just a silly name for noodles in sesame-paste sauce. I don't actually use sesame paste when I make this for kids; I use peanut butter.

This recipe is not strictly authentic. If your children like it, they may be shocked to taste sesame noodles in a Chinese restaurant. Still, it's a step in the right direction. Another step in the right direction: roasted peanut oil, which is new to my grocery store and which I sometimes use instead of sesame oil. It makes the peanut butter seem more legit.

8 ounces dried spaghetti or linguine

1/4 cup smooth peanut butter

2 tablespoons hot water

6–8 tablespoons soy sauce, or to taste

2 tablespoons sugar

2 tablespoons sesame oil

1 teaspoon vinegar

1 "shake" cayenne

1 garlic clove, crushed, and/or 4 chopped scallions***

1/2 cup shredded carrots

1/4 cup shredded cucumber

Cook the pasta in a large pot of boiling salted water according to the package directions. Drain in a colander and rinse it under cold water until it has cooled completely. Drain it again and set it aside while you make the sauce.

Whisk together the peanut butter and hot water in a large bowl. Whisk in the soy sauce, sugar, sesame oil, vinegar, cayenne, and the optional garlic and/or scallions. Toss the pasta and vegetables with the sauce. Serve.

Serves 4.

Cheese-ghetti

This is a very mild, very cheesy tomato sauce for, as they say, "the younger set." I think it might be a little too soothing for anyone older than, say, ten. On the other hand, I've been known to make it for myself at the end of a bad day, and to take it to bed with me. So maybe we should say it might be a little too mild for anyone more mature than, say, forty-three.

- 8 ounces dried spaghetti or linguine
- 1 15-ounce jar tomato sauce
- 1 6-ounce can tomato paste
- 8 ounces Longhorn or other mild cheddar, grated (about 2 cups)
- 2 tablespoons (¼ stick) unsalted butter

Cook the pasta in boiling salted water according to the package directions. Drain.

Meanwhile, stir the remaining ingredients together in a large saucepan over very low heat. Whisk constantly just until the butter and cheese have melted.

Toss the hot pasta with the sauce and serve immediately.

Serves 4.

Tortilla Towers

Layers of refried beans, cheese, red bell pepper, more cheese, and tortillas, all stacked up and baked.

12 small (6-inch) flour tortillas

About 1/4 cup vegetable oil, divided

1 cup chopped red bell peppers

1/2 cup minced onion***

1 16-ounce can refried beans

6 ounces Monterey Jack, grated (about 1 1/2 cups)

1 4-ounce can chopped mild green chilies, drained***

2 cups picante sauce

6 ounces extra-sharp cheddar, grated (about 1 1/2 cups)

1/4 cup sour cream***

1/4 cup sliced black olives***

Fry each tortilla in a little of the oil in a heavy skillet over medium-high heat until lightly crisp. Pat the tortillas dry with paper towels as they finish cooking.

In the same skillet, sauté the bell peppers and the optional onion together in the remaining 1 tablespoon oil, stirring frequently, until the vegetables are soft—about 5 minutes. Remove from the heat.

Preheat the oven to 375 degrees.

Spread each of 4 tortillas with one-fourth of the refried beans. Put the "beaned" tortillas onto a large, rimmed baking sheet and cover each of them with a second tortilla. Combine the bell peppers and onion, Monterey Jack, and the optional chilies and spread one-fourth of this mixture on each tortilla. Put a new tortilla on each stack and carefully pour 1/2 cup of the picante sauce over each tortilla stack. Finally, top each stack with one-fourth of the grated cheddar.

Bake the tortilla stacks for 15 to 20 minutes, or until they're heated through and the cheese is melted. With a broad spatula or pancake turner, carefully transfer one stack onto each eater's individual plate. Top the stacks with the optional sour cream and optional olives.

Serves 4 generously. For little kids or dieting teenagers or whatever, the stacks can be cut into wedges with a very sharp knife.

Gougère

"**M**om! We're having a good supper!" my four-year-old son once called out when I walked in from a late-afternoon meeting to see the rest of the family eating a meal I'd prepared earlier. Such an exclamation was rare for John at the time. He's just not an eaty kid, and as an infant used to shriek and twist with rage when I tried to put him in his high chair. The hungrier he was, the more he hated to be imprisoned in there.

So naturally I held on to the recipe, and made it so often that everyone got sick of it. Now it's your turn. Gougère is a wonderful cheese pastry that rises up in the oven like a giant cream puff, except that you don't fill it. Well, you could, but I don't. I do sometimes add chopped ham, crisp-cooked bacon, or browned onions to the dough before baking, though.

It's important that the eggs and Parmesan for this recipe be at room temperature before you add them to the pastry. Otherwise, the dough will cool down too much and not puff correctly when it's baked. So take the eggs out of the fridge at least 2 hours before you use them.

1 cup milk

4 tablespoons (1/2 stick) unsalted butter

1/2 teaspoon salt

1/2 teaspoon pepper

A pinch of nutmeg

3/4 cup plus 2 tablespoons flour

4 large eggs, *at room temperature*

4 ounces Parmesan, *at room temperature,* grated (about 1 cup, but you do need the correct weight here)

1 large egg, beaten with 1 teaspoon water, for brushing

Additional grated Parmesan (about 2 tablespoons), for sprinkling (optional)

Preheat the oven to 375 degrees. Grease a 9-inch pie pan.

Put the milk, butter, salt, pepper, and nutmeg in a large, heavy saucepan. Cook over medium heat, stirring frequently, until the butter has melted and the mixture comes to a full boil.

Take the saucepan off the heat and dump in the flour all at once, stirring hard with a wooden spoon. Return the pan to the heat. Stir vigorously and constantly for 2 to 3 minutes, until the mixture comes away from the sides of the pan. This recipe will give you good arm muscles. (There are recipes for making gougère in a food processor, but that involves quite a lot of sticky cleanup. A saucepan and spoon are actually easier in the long run.)

Take the pan off the heat again (this time, turn off the burner). Beat the eggs, one at a time, into the hot dough, stirring vigorously after each addition until the egg is completely incorporated and the dough is smooth. The dough will be very stiff and thick. Beat in the Parmesan.

Scrape/pour the dough into the prepared pie pan. Brush with the egg-water mixture and sprinkle with the extra Parmesan, if desired. Bake for 50 minutes without once opening the oven door. The gougère should be quite brown and puffy. Without taking it out of the oven, make a few slashes in the top with a sharp knife; this will let out some of the steam in the center and help the gougère stay puffy once it's out of the oven. Bake for 10 more minutes. Serve the gougère hot, at room temperature, or cold.

Serves 4 to 6.

White Pizza

I wouldn't presume to intrude on your family's pizza routines. I assume you've got them all worked out. But this is even easier to make than regular pizza—especially if you use a premade crust—and kids often appreciate the novelty of a nonred pizza. White pizza's as far as I go, though. I hate those "dessert" pizzas in catalogs, with all those candied cherries and chocolate spatters on them. Ick! Don't remind me!

1 12-inch prepared pizza crust

4 tablespoons (1/2 stick) unsalted butter, at room temperature

1 tablespoon mayonnaise

2 tablespoons grated Parmesan

1 large garlic clove, minced

1 teaspoon minced fresh parsley***

1/2 teaspoon dried basil

1/4 teaspoon dried oregano

8 ounces mozzarella or "pizza cheese," grated (about 2 cups)

Preheat the oven to 400 degrees.

Place the pizza crust on a large cookie sheet. Mix together the remaining ingredients except the mozzarella in a small bowl. Spread the mixture over the pizza crust and top with the mozzarella. (You may not want all the cheese.)

Bake the pizza for 15 minutes, or until the cheese is lightly browned and bubbling. Serve.

Makes one 12-inch pizza.

Apple Pizzas

 **I Can't Believe
I'm Doing This**

For anyone who's not sick of using refrigerated biscuits.

  1/2 cup light brown sugar, packed

  2 tablespoons flour

  1/2 teaspoon cinnamon

  5 apples, preferably Golden Delicious

  2 8-ounce tubes refrigerated buttermilk biscuits,
      separated but unbaked (20 biscuits)

  4 ounces mild cheddar, grated (about 1 cup)

  1 tablespoon cold unsalted butter

Preheat the oven to 350 degrees. Line two cookie sheets with foil or parchment paper.

Stir together the brown sugar, flour, and cinnamon in a small bowl. Peel, core, quarter, and thinly slice the apples. Roll or pat the biscuits into little flat circles about 3 inches in diameter and put them on the cookie sheets.

Sprinkle the cheese over the flattened biscuits. Dot each biscuit with a couple of flecks of butter; then divide the apple slices among the "pizzas." Top the apples with the brown sugar mixture.

Bake the pizzas for 20 to 25 minutes, or until brown and bubbling.

Makes 20 "pizzas."

"Spanakopita"

In quotes because this is made not with spinach but with broccoli—and also because it's a rather inauthentic treatment of the filo. Still, it's more authentic than the method of Someone I Won't Mention who used to take the filo out of the box and plunk a pile of it into a baking pan without buttering it. That was like eating baked tissue paper.

These are often served as an appetizer, but why not serve them as a main course?

2 cups cooked chopped broccoli, well drained

1 large egg

³/₄ cup crumbled feta (about 3 ounces)

8 ounces ricotta

¹/₂ cup grated Parmesan (about 2 ounces)

¹/₄ teaspoon pepper

8 tablespoons (1 stick) unsalted butter, melted

4–6 sheets filo dough (read the box carefully about how to defrost it)

Preheat the oven to 350 degrees. Butter a cookie sheet.

Stir together everything except the butter and filo in a bowl. If you were to add them to the bowl, it would *really* be inauthentic.

Spread out a sheet of filo on a cutting board and brush it lavishly with melted butter. (Keep the remaining filo covered.) Put another sheet of filo on top and lavishly butter that. With a sharp knife, cut the rectangle of double-filo into 4 squares. Place 1 to 2 tablespoons of broccoli mixture at one end of each square. Roll the dough over the filling, folding the ends in like an egg roll. As you finish each "egg roll," put it on the buttered

 It Happens To Everyone

I once lived next door to a couple who were complete health freaks. Organic everything. Sweet potato was their idea of dessert. Somehow they produced a little girl who wouldn't eat anything—even sprouts—unless it was drenched with ketchup.

—Julia Coopersmith

cookie sheet seam side down and brush it with, yes, more butter. Repeat this process until the filling is all used up.

If you don't want to bake the pastries now, you can freeze them, unbaked. (They'll be much better if you freeze them before baking rather than after.)

Bake the pastries for 20 minutes, or until they're brown and crisp. If you're baking them from the freezer, there's no need to defrost: just bake them for about 10 minutes longer. These are best served hot.

Makes 8 or more pastries.

Parmesan Aïoli on Grilled Country Bread

"*Oh, my God!*" That's what people always say when they try this for the first time. The recipe originated at the West Street Grill in Litchfield, Connecticut—where my husband and I have been unable to finish many an excellent meal because we've stuffed ourselves on this bread as a first course. I tried and tried to come up with the recipe on my own, but it was never right. When *New York* magazine ran the real version, I wanted to kiss the page.

Even kids who don't like garlic tend to love this (although you might not want to let them see you making it). We always serve it on Christmas Eve, along with a chef's salad. For the kids, I pick out some of the "good stuff"—chicken, bacon, cheese—and put it on their plates before I toss the rest of the salad. That way, they won't have to ruin their entire holiday season with horrible lettuce and salad dressing.

You'll need to prepare the aïoli a day before you plan to use it. You're actually supposed to make it with a mortar and pestle, but I can't stand to. So I've adapted it for a food processor.

3 large garlic cloves

A pinch of salt

1 large egg

2 tablespoons Champagne vinegar

1 cup corn oil

6 ounces Parmesan (real Parmigiano-Reggiano, not one of those flat, waxy triangles next to the yogurt in the dairy section), coarsely grated (about 1½ cups)

2 tablespoons finely chopped fresh parsley ***

1 tablespoon freshly ground black pepper

ALWAYS line the bottom of your toaster oven with foil, right from the very start. It will be much easier to clean that way. (There's no more maddening, finicky chore than trying to scrub the greasy bottom of a toaster oven.) And similarly, ALWAYS line the vegetable drawers of your refrigerator with paper towels.

1 loaf "country" bread—i.e., white but peasant-y, and not presliced (see page 204 if you want to make your own)

Turn on your food processor and drop in the garlic cloves. When they're minced, add the salt, egg, and vinegar. Process the mixture for a few seconds; then, leaving the food processor on, add the oil in a very, very slow stream. (If you haven't lost that oil-pouring cup that came with your processor, use it now.) Process until the mixture thickens to the consistency of mayonnaise.

Transfer what is now aïoli to a bowl. Stir in the cheese, parsley, and pepper. (You can't add the parsley to the processor, or it will turn the whole mixture green, which doesn't say "cheese" very clearly. You can, however, leave the parsley out entirely if your children hate green flecks. When will agriculture come up with a good-tasting strain of invisible parsley?) Cover the mixture and refrigerate it for 24 hours to meld the flavors and soften the garlic's impact.

When you're ready to go, preheat your broiler. Slice the bread; cut it into the "piece size" you want to serve, and either toast it or grill it briefly on both sides. Slather the aïoli on the grilled bread, broil it until it's golden and bubbly, and serve it immediately. If I were you, I'd forget about dinner, but maybe you have more self-control than I.

Serves 4 to 6 as an appetizer, 4 as a "main-dish bread" with salad alongside.

Monster Bread

Muenster, of course. I haven't tried this with other kinds of cheese, but I see no reason why *you* can't.

8 tablespoons (1 stick) unsalted butter

1 cup milk

4¹/₂ cups flour—bread flour works best—divided, plus a little more if needed

2 envelopes (5 teaspoons) active dry yeast

1 tablespoon sugar

2 teaspoons salt

¹/₂ teaspoon paprika

2 large eggs, beaten

2 pounds Muenster cheese, shredded (6–8 cups)

Milk to brush on the bread

2 tablespoons sesame seeds or 2 teaspoons poppy seeds, for sprinkling***

Melt the butter in the milk in a small saucepan. Cool the mixture to lukewarm if it's gotten warmer than that.

Stir together 1 cup of the flour, the yeast, sugar, and salt in a large bowl.

Add the milk mixture gradually to the flour mixture, then beat for 5 minutes. If your mixer has a dough hook, switch over to that and add the rest of the flour. If not, beat in as much flour as you can with the mixer; then continue to add the rest with your hands or with a wooden spoon.

Knead the dough on a floured surface for 10 minutes, either by hand (yuck! I hate kneading bread) or in the mixer with the dough hook. Add a little more flour as needed to make a stiff dough.

Grease a large bowl and place the dough in it, rotate it a few times to grease the entire surface, and cover the bowl. Leave the dough alone for 1/2 hour; it won't rise much during that time.

Stir the paprika into the beaten eggs; in a large bowl, stir *that* into the shredded cheese.

On a floured surface, roll and stretch the dough into a rectangle about 2 feet long and 6 inches wide. Don't get annoyed when the dough keeps bouncing back—you'll get there eventually. Mound the cheese-egg mixture down the center of the dough, like a mole track in a lawn.

Fold one long side of dough up over the other, "painting" the overlap with water to help seal the dough. Pinch the seam *hard*. Pinch the ends closed hard too.

Gently place the dough into a greased 9-inch round cake pan, coiling it to fit. Brush the loaf with milk and sprinkle it with the optional seeds. Let it rest for another 1/2 hour.

Meanwhile, preheat the oven to 350 degrees.

Bake the bread for 1 hour. Serve immediately.

Serves 6 to 8.

Homemade Soft Pretzels

Two ingredients are crucial when you make homemade pretzels: bread flour (available in most supermarkets and from the King Arthur Flour Baker's Catalog, page 22) and pretzel salt (available at some baking-supply stores and also from King Arthur). Kosher salt is only a feeble substitute for pretzel salt, and there's no substitute for the high-gluten flour you need to make good pretzels. True, you can shape them more easily with all-purpose flour, but I don't recommend using it. The pretzels won't have any soul.

When I make these, I serve them as one of those main-course breads I like so much. This is an involved recipe (although I use my bread machine to make and knead the dough, which saves me a lot of boring work), and I want to showcase it.

1 envelope (2½ teaspoons) active dry yeast

1 tablespoon sugar

2 cups lukewarm water

5½ cups bread flour, divided

1 tablespoon table salt (not pretzel salt)

2 tablespoons baking soda

Pretzel salt, for sprinkling the tops

Stir together the yeast, sugar, and water in a large bowl. Let the yeast sit for about 10 minutes, until foamy. Then stir in 2 cups of the flour. Only then should you add the table salt.

Knead in the remaining 3½ cups flour; then knead the dough for 10 minutes by hand on a floured surface or in an electric mixer fitted with a dough hook; or use the "knead" cycle in a bread machine.

Cover the dough, put it into an oiled bowl, and let it rise in a warm place until doubled in bulk—about 2 hours.

Punch the dough down and divide it into 16 equal pieces.

Okay, here's where you start swearing. You're supposed to roll each ball of dough into a 20-inch rope. With bread flour in

ALWAYS remember that if your children are getting enough calories, they're getting enough protein.

the dough, this is not easy. You have to keep stretching and stretching and *sssssstrrrrretching* the dough. But if you make the ropes shorter, you won't be able to get that traditional pretzel shape. On the other hand, no one's going to arrest you if you don't make traditional pretzel-shaped pretzels. Why don't you just roll the dough into the longest rope you can, and then make it into a ring? Or just roll it out into 12-inch ropes and tell everyone you were making pretzel rods? It's your call.

Whatever you make, put the dough shapes onto a cookie sheet that you've covered with waxed paper or plastic wrap. Let the pretzels rest for 1/2 hour.

Meanwhile, preheat the oven to 450 degrees. Cover a cookie sheet with parchment paper or greased foil, and get out a big nonreactive kettle or pot.

Put 6 cups of water and the baking soda in the kettle. As soon as the 1/2 hour is up, bring the water to a boil, stirring, and then lower it to a simmer.

More swearing is about to ensue. Gently slip 3 or 4 pretzels into the simmering water, keeping them far away from one another. Simmer them gently for 1 minute. With a slotted spoon (hold a towel in your other hand to catch the drips), carefully take them out of their bath and set them on the cookie sheet. Sprinkle them with pretzel salt. Keep on going until you've finished with all 16 pieces of dough.

Bake the pretzels for 12 to 15 minutes, or until they're medium brown and crusty-looking. Cool them on a rack.

Makes 16 pretzels.

Variation: If your store sells frozen pizza dough made by a bakery (as opposed to the refrigerated kind that come in tubes), you can make good pretzels from that too. The dough is so stretchy that you'll probably end up with something that looks more like hot dog rolls—and it may not brown as nicely—but that won't hurt anyone.

A Few Observations on Sandwiches

In *Bless This Food: The Anita Bryant Cookbook,* Ms. Bryant explains her philosophy about peanut butter sandwiches:

> "After spreading several thousand peanut butter sandwiches, I am convinced that a child's peanut butter sandwich preference is as much a part of his personality as his hair color.
>
> . . . A folded-bread man can *never* bite into a cut sandwich, and a cut-only man cannot *bear* the sight of a folded slice of bread."

Like so much of *Bless This Food,* this is sort of dopey and yet sort of true. Many kids do care an unbelievable amount about the way their sandwiches are fixed, and they hate it when "sandwich variety" is forced upon them. It does no good to point out that a folded sandwich tastes exactly the same as a sliced one and that cutting it in half diagonally isn't *morally* better than cutting it into two rectangles. For years the only sandwich my brother would eat, growing up, was "cream-cheese-and-jelly-whole-without-the-crusts." I hated anything sweet with my peanut butter, and still do. My dad never liked peanut butter at all. One of my nephews only likes a plain meat sandwich—and by "plain," I mean "with no bread." "I send the meat to school in the bread," says my sister-in-law, "but only as a container."

The aversion to crusts is puzzling too. It must be inborn, since even a toddler who's been isolated from other children for her whole life still leaves the crusts on her plate. Of course it's true that crusts do taste and look different from the rest of the bread, so they probably contain subtle toxins that only children can recognize.

Given the incredible rigidity with which children treat their sandwiches, it's probably futile for me to suggest anything new here. That's why I'm calling these "observations," not "instructions that you must carry out." I have *observed,* for instance, that:

Flour tortillas can make any sandwich more interesting. Just spread on the filling and roll up the tortilla. There's no reason the "wrap" concept shouldn't be just as popular with children as it is with adults.

A quick, easy quesadilla is made by spreading any cheese the child likes over one flour tortilla, topping it with another tortilla, wrapping the whole in foil, and baking it at 350 degrees for 10 minutes, or until the cheese has melted. With the addition of a little pizza sauce, this becomes a "pizza quesadilla."

There is no point in banning Marshmallow Fluff as a sandwich ingredient if you allow jam, jelly, and honey. All of these are basically sugar. If you deny your child the pleasure of a Fluffernutter but allow a PBJ, you're being inconsistent.

The above notwithstanding, you can sometimes get a kid to eat a PBB (peanut butter and sliced banana) — or a PBA (peanut butter and sliced apple) — or the other kind of PBB (peanut butter and bacon) — or a PBP (peanut butter and popcorn). All of these have slightly more nutritional value, or at least more fiber, than peanut butter and jelly.

Any sandwich becomes more interesting if you use cookie cutters to cut shapes out of the top piece of bread.

If you're really, really worried about vegetables, you can try grating some carrot into the peanut butter in a sandwich. I'm not saying your child won't notice, but you can try. Maybe you can claim you used crunchy peanut butter; in a way, you'll even be telling the truth.

World's Best Bread

If you like making bread, this *must* become a household staple. It's wonderful plain, without anything on it; it makes great sandwiches and peerless toast; and it's huge, so if you take it to a party you'll get maximum Brownie points.

I always make the dough in the bread machine and take it through its first rising there. Then I—well, I'll describe what I do with it in a little while.

I'm sorry this recipe has so much to say, but with this bread, there *is* a lot to say. And I'm sorry you have to make this bread over a 24-hour period, but it's worth it. And I'm sorry you need an instant-read thermometer to check its doneness, but that's something you should own anyway. In sum, I'm not all that sorry.

Sponge

1¼ cups bread flour (*not* all-purpose)

1 tablespoon whole wheat flour

1 tablespoon rye flour

1 tablespoon semolina flour

1 tablespoon rolled oats

1 tablespoon cornmeal

1 tablespoon wheat germ

⅛ teaspoon active dry yeast

1 cup chlorine-free water

Bread Dough

3¹/₂ cups bread flour

1 tablespoon coarse or kosher salt

¹/₄ teaspoon active dry yeast

1¹/₄ cups chlorine-free water

1 tablespoon honey

2–3 cups cornmeal for the cookie sheet

For the sponge: Put all the ingredients into the bowl of a bread machine or, if using an electric mixer, into a large bowl. Mix them thoroughly (for at least 5 minutes), until they form a thick, smooth liquid. Unplug the bread machine, if that's what you're using; if you're using a mixer, just cover the bowl. Let the sponge rest for 16 hours at room temperature.

For the bread dough: Stir the sponge down completely. Add all the dough ingredients to it. Put the dough through the Knead cycle on your bread machine. Or knead it for 15 minutes by hand on a floured surface or with an electric mixer fitted with the dough hook. Cover the dough and let it rest uncovered for ¹/₂ hour in a warm place.

While it sits, cover a large cookie sheet—preferably one with a rim—with the cornmeal. Make sure the cornmeal covers every bit of the cookie sheet. You don't know where the bread dough will choose to migrate as it rises, and you don't want it to stick.

After ¹/₂ hour, punch down the dough. Shape it into a ball and put it on the cornmeal, seam side down. Let it rise for anywhere from 2 to 4 hours, until it has doubled in bulk. (On a cold day, this may take even longer.)

Set a rack in the lower third of the oven and preheat the

oven to 400 degrees. Put a pan of boiling water on the oven floor.

With a sharp knife, slash the top of the loaf in ¼-inch-deep rows or crosshatches. Bake the bread for 30 to 35 minutes, or until the center registers 190 degrees on an instant-read thermometer. If you want the crust to be especially crisp, turn off the oven when the bread is done and prop open the oven door with a wooden spoon; then let the bread cool in the oven. If you don't feel like doing that, just transfer the bread to a rack to cool the way I do.

Makes enough bread to serve 16 people at a sitting, or a family for several days; I cut it up and freeze it in big chunks that I thaw and slice up as needed.

 **I Can't Believe
I'm Doing This**

Cheese Towers

My friend Andy Aaron's son, Will, was getting tired of American cheese served "plain," so Andy came up with a solution. See, you cut the cheese into little squares and use them to make towers! You can even make a bridge. And the funny thing is, a preschooler will actually believe that you're serving him a new dish.

Grilled Cheese Soup

 **I Can't Believe
I'm Doing This**

Now that I've got your attention, the soup isn't really grilled. But it's just as good for a child's lunch as grilled cheese would be.

1 10-to-11-ounce can condensed tomato soup

³/₄ cup milk

¹/₂ soup can water

8 ounces sharp cheddar, grated (about 2 cups)

Salt and pepper

Oyster crackers (optional)

Whisk together the soup, milk, and water in a medium saucepan over low heat until they're simmering. Turn the heat way down and whisk in the grated cheese *just* until it melts. Season to taste and serve immediately—with oyster crackers if you're my kind of person.

Serves 3.

Carrot Soup

"Kids don't like soup," my daughter said. "You can skip soup recipes." But is that really true? Aren't there some families out there for whom soup is a completely normal dinner? I just *know* there must be. For instance, the woman who gave me this recipe has children . . .

Don't denigrate orange juice concentrate. It's a very good source of flavor—*concentrated* flavor, get it? And it adds depth and body without adding fat.

4 tablespoons (½ stick) unsalted butter

1 small onion, minced***

3 cups thinly sliced carrots

4 cups chicken or vegetable broth

1 6-ounce can frozen orange juice concentrate, thawed

2 cups light cream or half-and-half

Salt and pepper

Ground cloves

Melt the butter in a large nonreactive pot and sauté the optional onion until translucent. Add the carrots and broth, bring to a simmer and simmer gently until the carrots are soft. Puree the carrot mixture in a food processor or blender. (If you use a blender, you'll need to do this in batches.) Add the orange juice concentrate and cream or half-and-half.

If you're serving the soup hot, return it to the pot and heat it thoroughly but don't allow it to boil; season to taste with the salt and pepper and cloves. If you're serving it cold, season it to taste and then chill it, remembering that chilling sometimes reduces the power of seasonings and that you'll want to try it again before serving it.

Serves 6.

Broccoli Vichyssoise

Because they're more novel, cold soups sometimes seem more edible to children.

> 1 bunch broccoli (2–3 large stems)
> 4 medium potatoes
> 2 medium onions
> 4 cups chicken or vegetable broth
> 3 cups milk
> 2 cups half-and-half
> Salt and pepper

Cut the broccoli florets off the stems, and chop the stems. Peel and dice the potatoes and onions. Put everything into a soup pot, add the broth, and cook until the vegetables are just tender.

Puree the vegetables, in batches, in a food processor or blender, in batches if necessary. Add the milk and half-and-half; season to taste. Chill the soup thoroughly and check the seasoning again before serving.

Serves 6 to 8.

Black Bean–Bacon Soup

This is an eeeeeeeeasy soup that relies on instant powdered dried beans—a product that tends to float throughout supermarkets. Sometimes it comes to roost near the produce section, sometimes near the canned dips, sometimes in the "exotic" aisle. It's well worth seeking out—not because it makes such great dip, but because as an *ingredient* it has so much flavor.

6 thick-cut bacon strips, diced

1 small onion, minced***

1 7-ounce box instant (powdered) black beans

4 cups water

1 15½-ounce can red kidney or pinto beans, rinsed and drained

Salt and pepper

Cook the diced bacon and the optional onion in a large, heavy saucepan over medium heat until the bacon is crisp. Don't drain it.

Take the pot off the heat and stir in the instant beans and water. Stir in the canned beans. Put the pot back on the heat and bring it to a boil; then lower the heat to a simmer and cook for 5 minutes, stirring frequently, until heated through. Season to taste. Serve.

Serves 4.

ALWAYS keep nail scissors, ChapStick, tissues, tweezers, Scotch tape, paper clips, and so on in **EVERY SINGLE ROOM** that has someplace you can stash them. If you stockpile all this stuff in the kitchen, people will come in and nag you for it all the time. Even worse, they'll take it away from the kitchen and lose it and then go on nagging you. Train your family to use the supplies in whatever room they happen to be in, and to *leave* them in that room.

Vaguely Mexican Soup

Not to be served if your kids don't like Mexican food. *To* be served, with extreme if not excessive ease, if they do.

4 cups water

1 7-ounce box instant (powdered) refried beans (see
   previous page)

1 11-ounce can "Mexican-style" corn

1 cup salsa, as hot as your kids can bear (I won't tell if
   you use mild)

Salt and pepper

Grated cheddar, chopped onions, and chopped red bell
   peppers, to be added at the table (optional, but they
   may make you feel as if you're a more accomplished
   cook)

Bring the water to a boil in a large pot. Stir in the beans and corn. Lower the heat and simmer for 5 minutes, stirring frequently, until heated through. Add the salsa. Season to taste. Serve with optional stuff. That's it.

Serves 4.

Berry Soup

This comes from my friend Lisa, who writes, "It's a favorite summertime supper for us, with rolls (Serving Suggestion)."

I suppose you could also make it in the winter, with frozen berries, but much would be lost. Besides, it just *seems* like a summertime recipe. Making it in the winter is a Non-Serving Suggestion unless you live in a place that's warm year-round.

1 quart orange juice, preferably fresh

16 ounces plain unsweetened yogurt

16 ounces sour cream (you can use more or less yogurt or sour cream, as long as you end up with a total of 4 cups)

1 tablespoon honey

2 tablespoons fresh lemon or lime juice

A pinch of cinnamon

A pinch of nutmeg

1½ pints fresh raspberries, blueberries, or strawberries, or whatever mixture of these you want

Whisk together everything except the berries in a large bowl. Taste for seasoning, adding more honey, lemon or lime juice, and/or spices if you want. Chill this mixture thoroughly.

Wash and drain the berries, slicing the strawberries if they're big. When you're ready to serve, divide the berries among individual serving bowls and ladle the soup on top.

Serves 4.

Cream-Cheesy Spinach

I've said it before and I'll say it again: if you buy frozen spinach, be sure that you always buy frozen *whole* spinach. The chopped kind gives you way too much green water for your money.

Since the spinach is going to be baked, and therefore will take on a "casserole-y" appearance, it can work as a vegetarian main dish. For the same reason, I see no reason to use fresh spinach in this recipe. Skip it and go right to the frozen kind. Whole.

2 10-ounce packages frozen whole spinach, thawed and drained

1 5-ounce package garlic-herb Boursin, at room temperature

Salt and pepper

1 cup grated Parmesan (about 4 ounces)

½ cup dried bread crumbs

Preheat the oven to 350 degrees. Grease a small baking dish.

You may think you've already drained that spinach, but believe me you're not there yet. Roll it up in several thicknesses of clean towel and squeeze it and squeeze it and squeeze it until it's all wrung out. Peel it off the towel, put it onto a cutting board, and chop it fine. (I didn't say using whole spinach was *easier* than using the chopped kind—just that it's better.)

Put the chopped spinach in a large bowl and stir in the Boursin until these two very unlike substances are thoroughly combined. Season to taste. Pat the spinach down into the baking dish. Toss together the grated Parmesan and bread crumbs in a small dish and sprinkle them over the spinach.

Bake the spinach for 20 minutes, or until it's heated through and the top is brown. Serve immediately.

Serves 2 to 3 as a main dish, 4 as a side dish.

Easy Cheesy Spinach

 **I Can't Believe
I'm Doing This**

You know, it's perfectly okay to use Stouffer's products once a week or so. They can't prosecute you for it except maybe in New York State and California. I bet you're *quite familiar* with the Stouffer's section in the frozen-food aisle, aren't you? *I* am. I hardly ever make plain old lasagna for my family anymore, Stouffer's does it so well.

Stouffer's Welsh Rarebit is also a good thing to have on hand in your freezer. When you're in a hurry, it's a great way to "synthesize" various unrelated ingredients—in this case, spinach, bacon, and French-fried onions—and turn them into a real meal. And it's so nice and orange, just like the cheese of one's childhood.

Obviously you'll want to use turkey bacon if you have a no-red-meater in your household, or omit the bacon entirely if you plan to serve this as a vegetarian dish. In the latter case, cooked mushrooms might be a good addition if your children tolerate them. I don't think bacon-flavored soy bits are worth the paper this book is printed on, but you can certainly use them if your kids like them.

Although most people secretly worship them, there's no getting around the fact that the "french-fried onions" are a little bit shameful. But the King Arthur Flour Baker's Catalog sells a good, upscale version that's not quite so embarrassing as the canned kind; see page 22.

2 10-ounce packages frozen whole spinach, thawed and drained

1 large garlic clove, minced***

4 thick-cut bacon strips, cooked until crisp, and crumbled (optional)

1 10-ounce package frozen Welsh rarebit, thawed

1 cup canned "french-fried" onions

Preheat the oven to 350 degrees. Grease a small baking dish, about 9 x 6 inches.

All frozen spinach must be drained incredibly thoroughly. Press the thawed spinach hard in a sieve or colander to extract as much water as possible; then, as with the other spinach recipes in this book, roll it up in a cloth towel and squeeze it hard, hard, hard.

Chop the spinach fine and spread it across the bottom of the prepared baking dish. Sprinkle the optional garlic and optional crumbled bacon evenly over the spinach, spread the rarebit over that, and sprinkle the onions over the cheese. Bake the cheesy spinach for 20 to 25 minutes, or until it's heated through and bubbling. Serve.

Serves 4 as a main dish.

ALWAYS remember the *edges*. Whenever you prepare a dish that needs to be sprinkled with something—salt, pepper, Parmesan, bread crumbs, streusel—make sure you cover the whole dish, not just the center. Yes, you'll have to clean up the counter afterward. Stop complaining! You want to make sure that *everyone* gets some of that nice crumb topping.

Spinach Superballs

How long has it been since you made these? And has it ever occurred to you that your children might like them? They were a big appetizer in the '70s; you couldn't go to a party without someone proudly brandishing a trayful of them. Let's reincarnate them, say I—this time, as a dish that a) contains spinach; b) spinach, that is, that your children will very possibly like; c) makes a novel main course; and d) gives you the chance to reminisce about your own third-grade days, when Superballs first came into style and everyone was boinging them all over their driveways and in their classrooms. How beautiful the unmarked gray-blue sheen of a new Superball, and how quickly it got scratched and chipped . . . like the equally beautiful lacquered wooden handles of a fancy jump rope I once got for my birthday, which a friend of mine dragged home from school *by the rope part*, so the handles scraped against the sidewalk and got ruined. As another friend once said, "I forgive, but I don't forget."

2 10-ounce packages frozen *whole* spinach, thawed, drained, chopped, and twisted in a clean towel to wring out as much moisture as possible

2 cups Pepperidge Farm herb stuffing mix, crushed

1 cup grated Parmesan (about 4 ounces)

8 tablespoons (1 stick) unsalted butter, melted

3 large eggs, beaten

1–2 large garlic cloves, crushed***

1/4 teaspoon pepper

ALWAYS save and freeze the leftover rind from your Parmesan cheese. A nice chunk of Parmesan rind is a great, enriching addition when you're making stock. (Naturally, you'll want to fish it out before making the stock into soup.) Even if you think you'll never make soup, why not save a couple of rinds in the freezer just in case you change your mind? They'll help you feel more like one of those people who run a well-ordered kitchen.

Mush everything together with your hands in a large bowl. Chill the mixture, covered, for at least 2 hours, or overnight.

When you're ready to bake the spinach, preheat the oven to 350 degrees.

With wet hands, roll the mixture into 1-inch balls and place them on a cookie sheet. Bake them for 20 to 30 minutes, or until browned on the bottom and cooked through. You can't really judge the doneness by appearance, though; you'll need to break open one of the balls and try it. Not a big problem.

Makes 3 dozen balls. If you don't feel like baking them all, you can freeze some of them unbaked.

Spinach Frisbees

I think that the best way to introduce these savory spinach-and-cheese patties to your children is to tell them how lucky they are that Popeye is no longer held up as a role model. Popeye always gave me the creeps when I was a kid, and the thought that he ate spinach—*canned* spinach! even I knew how wet that would taste!—was not an inspiration to me. Who wants to be strong if it makes you as scary and depressing as Popeye?

"*Now*," you can say to your kids, "*we can enjoy delicious, delicious spinach dishes without the specter of that horrible sailor hanging over our heads.*"

Anyway, these Frisbees work best as a main dish if you serve them with a couple of sides like rice, a salad, and some bread. Otherwise, they're a great side dish themselves, especially with roast chicken.

1 10-ounce package frozen whole spinach, thawed and drained

1–2 garlic cloves, minced***

1 large egg

1/4 cup seasoned bread crumbs, crushed stuffing mix, or cracker crumbs

1/4 cup grated Parmesan (about 1 ounce)

Salt and pepper to taste

A pinch of cayenne***

3 tablespoons Olive Oyl—I mean, vegetable oil

Drain the spinach exceptionally well: press out as much water as you can, then roll the spinach up tightly in a cloth towel to extract even more water. Chop the spinach fine. Combine the spinach with everything else except the oil in a medium bowl.

Preheat the oven to 200 degrees.

Heat the oil in a heavy skillet over medium heat until very hot. Drop the spinach mixture by the tablespoon into the hot oil. Cook until the bottoms of the Frisbees are firm; flip them over and cook them until *that* side is firm. Keep the finished Frisbees warm on a cookie sheet in the oven until all of them are cooked; then serve immediately.

Serves 4.

Broc Bake

You can make this up to 24 hours ahead. It's plenty sturdy. Don't even think of using frozen broccoli, though. Frozen broccoli's only use is feeding parakeets.

1 large bunch broccoli (2–3 large stems)

2 tablespoons (1/4 stick) unsalted butter

1 cup sliced mushrooms***

2 tablespoons minced onion

1/2 teaspoon dried thyme

2 tablespoons flour

1/2 cup milk

1/2 cup chicken broth

Salt and pepper

4 ounces extra-sharp cheddar, grated (about 1 cup)

1/2 cup fresh bread crumbs

1/4 cup grated Parmesan (about 1 ounce)

1/4 teaspoon paprika

Preheat the oven to 350 degrees. Grease a 9-x-13-inch baking dish.

Steam the broccoli just until tender, about 5 minutes. Rinse it under cold water to stop the cooking, then drain it and chop it into bite-sized pieces.

Melt the butter in a small skillet over medium heat. Add the optional mushrooms, onion, and thyme and cook until the onion is translucent. Sprinkle the flour over all and stir it in thoroughly for a minute or two. Add the milk and broth and cook, stirring constantly, until the mixture has thickened. Add salt and pepper to taste.

Spread the cut-up broccoli in the greased baking dish. Pour the sauce over it and sprinkle the cheddar over the sauce. Toss together the bread crumbs, Parmesan, and paprika and sprinkle them evenly over the cheddar.

Bake the casserole for 20 to 25 minutes, or until it's heated through and the top is browned. Serve hot.

Serves 4.

It Happens To Everyone

When I was two, my mother gave me a plate of broccoli as a snack. I sat in my high chair nibbling as my father washed his hair in the kitchen sink. My mother looked over to find that I had suddenly started rubbing the broccoli into my hair, mimicking my dad.

—Kelly L'Heureux

Barbecued Potatoes

I imagine that this recipe was originally meant as a side dish, but what are they trying to do? Kill us? It's so rich that I serve it as a main course—and only once in a while. A salad is all you need to, as they say, "complete the meal."

The original recipe called for the potatoes to be wrapped in foil, which probably got depressing when the foil ripped and the potatoes fell onto the coals. Using a foil pan (which is then wrapped in more foil) makes a lot more sense.

2 pounds russet or Yukon Gold potatoes, unpeeled

1 teaspoon salt

1 teaspoon pepper

1 pound thick-sliced bacon, cut into 2-inch pieces

10 ounces extra-sharp cheddar, grated (about 2½ cups)

2 tablespoons (¼ stick) unsalted butter

1 large garlic clove, minced***

1 8-ounce container sour cream

Prepare a fire in your grill.

Slice the potatoes as thin as possible. (You should end up with about 6 cups.) Toss them with the salt and pepper.

Spread about one-third of the bacon across the bottom of an 8-x-11-inch foil pan. Cover the bacon with a layer of sliced potatoes and cover them with one-third of the cheese. Cover the cheese with another layer of potatoes and dot *that* layer with one-third of the butter. Stir the optional garlic into the sour cream and spread one-third of THAT on top of the butter-dotted potatoes. Repeat the entire process twice more, making layers of the bacon, potatoes, cheese, more potatoes, butter, and the sour-cream mixture.

Wrap the foil pan tightly with foil. Place the wrapped pan

ALWAYS be passive-aggressive about ice-cube trays. If you're not the one who used up the ice, just let the tray sit there in the dish drainer. It's amazing how many husbands and children believe that empty ice-cube trays need a long interval of "draining" before they can be refilled. Unless you are an ice addict yourself, let the empty trays pile up until someone says, "Hey! Where's all the ice?" Then you answer sweetly, "The person who uses up the last cube of ice should be the person who refills the tray."

over hot coals and cover the grill. Cook for 45 minutes. If you're really worried about whether the potatoes have cooked enough, you can try to unwrap a little corner of the foil—but that can be messy, and you'd have to watch out for the hot steam. I'm sure they're fine.

With a sharp knife, slash the bottom of the foil in several places to let the fat drain out. Serve the potatoes right away.

Serves 4.

Tater Tot Surprise

 **I Can't Believe
I'm Doing This**

My next cookbook will be really fancy, and that will take away the shame of including the following (which is, nonetheless, kind of great):

1 32-ounce bag frozen Tater Tots, cut in half (or you can use the infinitely superior Crispy Crowns, which are already much thinner and don't need to be cut up)

1 10-to-11-ounce can condensed cream of chicken soup

8 tablespoons (1 stick) unsalted butter, melted

4 scallions, chopped***

1 8-ounce container sour cream

4 ounces cheddar, grated (about 1 cup)

4 cups corn flakes, crushed into crumbs

Preheat the oven to 350 degrees. Grease a 9-x-13-inch pan.

Mix everything except the crushed corn flakes in a large bowl. Spread in the greased pan, top with the corn flakes, and bake for 25 minutes, or until heated through. Serve hot.

Serves 6.

Corn Bread Casserole

My daughter, Laura, suggested giving this recipe a different name. "Kids won't think it sounds good." I'm at a loss, though. What could they possibly think sounds better? "Yellow Casserole"? Maybe "Spoon Corn Bread" would work; the recipe is, after all, basically a spoonbread.

"Everyone loves it," writes Kris Creighton (see page 38). "I try not to use packaged mixes, but this recipe works so well I don't mind. The person who shared this with me said that only Jiffy brand works, but I haven't tried any other."

This casserole serves a lot of people, and there's no easy way to halve it unless you weigh out 3 ounces of corn bread mix and measure (and then halve) the three beaten eggs. Or you could do the same thing by eye. You don't have to be too precise here.

3 tablespoons butter, divided

2 15-ounce cans "cream-style" corn

1 12-ounce bag frozen corn, thawed and drained

1 8½-ounce package Jiffy corn muffin mix

1 8-ounce container sour cream

3 large eggs

2 tablespoons minced onion***

2 tablespoons minced green or red bell pepper***

Preheat the oven to 350 degrees.

Melt the butter and use a bit of it to grease a large casserole. Combine the rest of the butter and the remaining ingredients in the casserole and stir well.

Bake for 50 to 60 minutes, or until set. Serve hot.

Serves 10.

Grammie's Cheese Grits

"You're putting grits into the book, aren't you?" asked my son, John. "Because I love grits." This was news to me. I'd always thought John was the one hold-out in our family of grit-lovers. Boy, you turn your back, and all of a sudden your kids are eating grits. Talk about time's winged chariot hovering near!

You don't have to use Velveeta—regular cheddar would also be fine—but you should. It's traditional.

3 cups water

1 tablespoon unsalted butter

1/4 teaspoon salt

1 small garlic clove, minced***

3/4 cup quick-cooking grits (Quaker is the brand I use)

8 ounces Velveeta, cut into small cubes

1 large egg, beaten

1/2 teaspoon paprika

Salt and pepper

Preheat the oven to 350 degrees. Grease a 9-inch square baking dish.

Bring the water, butter, salt, and the optional garlic to a boil in a heavy saucepan and gradually stir in the grits. Reduce the heat to low and cover the pan. Cook the grits, stirring frequently, for 5 to 7 minutes, or until they're thick. (Make sure not to let the bottom of the pan scorch as the water gets absorbed.) Add the cheese and stir it in as it melts.

When the cheese is all melted, take the saucepan off the heat and stir in the egg and paprika. Season to taste. Scrape the mixture into the prepared pan. Bake for 20 to 25 minutes, or until the grits are beginning to brown. Serve immediately.

Serves 4 to 6.

"I Lost My Pea!"

That's what my brother Ned once said at the dinner table when he was about three. Like many children, he knew that peas would kill him. My parents didn't believe him, and the rule was that he had to "try" one pea. I don't remember what happened to the one he lost. Maybe the dog got it, or maybe it just rolled away. In any case, Ned's little ploy didn't work.

But he still grew up to be big and strong, and this is what we need to keep in mind when we try to force vegetables down our reluctant children's gullets. The amount of vitamins contained in . . . oh, let's pull an example out of the air . . . in one pea is not going to save a child's life. He'll learn that peas won't kill him, and isn't that enough for now? Maybe later he'll grow up to like peas, or broccoli, or something green. Maybe he won't. At least he probably won't live at home for the rest of his life, so you won't have to watch him refuse to eat every member of the vegetable kingdom until he dies of beriberi.

Vegetables would be less of a problem if adults admitted that we, too, don't like them as much as other foods. Check anyone's recipe file—hell, check this book!—and you'll find far fewer vegetables than any other category. So we may seem less convincing about the deliciousness of "nice fresh vegetables" than we'd like. It's more honest simply to

The Recipes

order a child to eat one smidgen of vegetable per supper. And I don't see any reason to try to trick him into eating the vegetables, either. What's the point of something like zucchini bread? By the time it's finished baking, any nutritional value the zucchini once had is long gone. And the hidden message — "zucchini is so disgusting that I had to turn it into greenish cake" — is counterproductive.

Salads are worth fighting for, though. In one form or another, they're one of the most important foods you can persuade your child to like. Nutrition apart, salads are very useful — especially in restaurants and school dining halls. Saying "I'll just have the salad" is still one of the best one-uppers there is. Ordering a salad can delay a child's hunger pangs while she waits for her yucky and disappointing main course, and a vegetarian who's trapped at a steak house for someone's birthday can always find something edible at the salad bar. I know a vegetarian family who actually thought Sizzler restaurants were famous for their salads.

Until I went to college, however, I thought green salad tasted like grass with vinegar on it. If I squint my palate, so to speak, I can still see what I meant.

When you're dealing with children, you may have to stretch your concept of what a salad should be. One reason I thought salads tasted like vinegared grass was that we

always had classic French salads when I was growing up—
oil and vinegar, lettuce and tomatoes fresh from the garden
(I can still remember the teeny, teeny slugs that sometimes
came inside on the lettuce—really, they were almost cute),
no "bought" dressings, no raisins, no croutons, nothing but
pristine salad. I admire my parents for their purism, but if a
child doesn't like lettuce or vinegar, she won't find much to
like about a traditional green salad.

I'm not saying that Jell-O and canned pears count as
salad. Still, adding kid-friendly ingredients to the salad bowl
can be a good way to lure in more tentative eaters. If a kid
eats something that's only very mildly saladlike (say, raw
red pepper strips dipped in a mild dip, which you've re-
christened Dip Salad) and thinks, "Hey, this isn't so bad!
Maybe I *do* like salad after all!", you've gained a great deal.
There's a huge gulf between the thought "I don't like salad"
and "I don't like *this* salad." Remember, your goal is not to
force your children to eat sophisticated vinaigrettes: it's to
give them confidence. *Every time a child can add a new food to
his repertoire, he'll feel more confident.*

With one or two likable salads under their belts (so to
speak), kids can more easily be induced to branch out. "This
is that poppy-seed dressing you like, only it's on lettuce this
time . . . See? Mandarin oranges! You like *them*! . . . Okay!

Okay! Stop screeching. Leave the tomato on your plate and eat the other stuff."

Another good thing about salads: they make plain cooked vegetables seem much tamer. How hard can it be to eat a green pea once you've mastered *salad*?

Here are a few recipes for mildly dressed-up vegetables and mildly welcoming salads.

Double Sesame Asparagus

J ust one more recipe from Kris Creighton's *Practical Palate* (see page 38), and then I'll stop, I promise. This recipe also works beautifully with broccoli, but you should steam it for a minute or so before you stir-fry it.

1 1/2 pounds fresh asparagus

1 teaspoon cornstarch

1 teaspoon soy sauce

1 teaspoon dry sherry

1 tablespoon vegetable oil

1 garlic clove, minced

1 teaspoon grated fresh ginger

1/4 teaspoon salt, or to taste

1/4 cup chicken broth

1 teaspoon sesame oil

1 tablespoon sesame seeds, toasted at 300 degrees for
   10 minutes

Wash and trim the asparagus and slice it diagonally into 1-inch pieces. Mix the cornstarch with the soy sauce and sherry in a small bowl.

Heat a large, heavy skillet until hot. Add the oil, heat *it* until hot, and add the garlic and ginger. Cook for a few seconds, stirring constantly. Add the cut-up asparagus and salt. Stir-fry the mixture quickly over high heat, tossing to coat the asparagus with the oil and seasonings.

Lower the heat to medium. Add the chicken broth, give everything a big stir, and cover the skillet. Cook the asparagus for 5 minutes, or until it is just tender.

Restir the cornstarch mixture and add it to the skillet, stirring constantly. Cook for 1 minute. Sprinkle in the sesame oil and sesame seeds, stir once more, and transfer the asparagus to a serving dish.

You can also serve this at room temperature. Chilled, it gets a little clammy.

Serves 6 to 8.

 ### It Happens To Everyone

As a child in rural Iowa, I preferred margarine to butter, canned green beans to fresh, and TV dinners to Mom's home cookin'. This led to a showdown at age eight or so, when I told my mother that I would vomit if I had to eat Grandpa's fresh peas from the garden. Mom laid down the law: I would not leave the table until I had eaten every last handpicked pea. 7:00, 8:00, 9:00 ticked slowly by as I glared at my mother from the table. It was a school night. At 10:00, I cleared my place in silent triumph, threw the peas to the dog, and went to bed. Mom and I never had another standoff about anything.

—Jill Dickey

Roasted Green Beans

Roasting beans is just as easy as microwaving them, and more interesting. Get your kids to trim the beans for you.

Strips of red bell pepper are also good cooked this way, but you don't need to add the water because the peppers are already so juicy. Asparagus works too.

1 pound fresh green beans, trimmed

1 teaspoon vegetable oil

1 teaspoon water

Salt and pepper to taste

Preheat the oven to 500 degrees. Line a rimmed baking sheet with foil.

Stir the beans, oil, and water together in a bowl until the beans are coated—another task a child would like. (You can shake them all in a plastic bag too.) Spread the beans out on the baking sheet and sprinkle them with salt and pepper. Bake for 8 minutes, or until cooked through. These are good hot or at room temperature.

Serves 4.

Bacon-Baked Green Beans

Want to know why I have so many green bean recipes in this book? Because *my children like green beans.*

If you feel guilty about adding so many extra calories to nice, lean beans, you can just serve this as a main dish. If your children squawk about cooked tomatoes, you can just leave them out. Don't leave out the bacon. You may think I use bacon a lot, but believe me—it's nothing compared to what I *could* do.

4 bacon strips

1 small onion, chopped***

3 cups trimmed whole fresh green (or yellow) beans, cooked halfway

1/3 cup mayonnaise

1/3 cup sour cream

2 ounces cheddar or Parmesan, grated (about 1/2 cup)

Salt and pepper

2 tomatoes, peeled, halved, deglopped, and chopped

Preheat the oven to 325 degrees. Grease a medium baking dish.

Cook the bacon in a medium skillet until crisp. Take it out, drain, and crumble it, but leave a couple tablespoons of the bacon fat in the skillet. Fry the optional onion in the fat until it's browned. Turn off the heat and add the beans to the skillet. Stir them around a couple of times so that they get coated with all those good oniony bacon drippings. Put them into the dish along with the bacon and toss to combine.

Blend the mayonnaise, sour cream, and grated cheese in a small bowl. Stir this mixture thoroughly into the beans. Add the chopped tomatoes. Season to taste.

Bake for 15 to 20 minutes, or until heated through and slightly browned, and serve.

Serves 6 as a side dish, 4 as a main dish.

The Other Green Bean Casserole

In other words, the one that doesn't have crumbled onion rings and mushroom soup on top. I'm sure you have a recipe for the onion-ring one, and besides, this is slightly less processed.

By the way, you can order excellent "canned" onion rings (crumbles, actually) from the King Arthur Flour Baker's Catalog. (See the note on page 22.) They're way better than the grocery-store kind, and delicious on top of, say, meat loaf or toasted-and-buttered pita. And yet they still retain that deliciously evil quality that makes the grocery-store kind so crave-worthy.

1 pound fresh green beans, trimmed

1 tablespoon unsalted butter or vegetable oil

1 medium onion, thinly sliced, or 1 large garlic clove, crushed***

1 8-ounce container sour cream

1/4 cup flour

Salt and pepper to taste

4 ounces extra-sharp cheddar, grated (about 1 cup)

1 cup fresh bread crumbs

Preheat the oven to 350 degrees. Grease a 9-x-11-inch casserole dish.

Blanch the green beans in boiling water or steam them for about 2 minutes; they should still be *very* crunchy. Drain.

Heat the butter or oil in a large skillet and sauté the optional onion or garlic for about 5 minutes, until translucent. Remove from the heat and stir in the beans.

In a small bowl, mix the sour cream with the flour and salt and pepper until smooth. Stir the sour cream mixture into the beans until well combined. Transfer them to the casserole dish; top with the cheese and then the crumbs.

Bake the beans for 25 minutes, until heated through and browned on top. Serve hot.

Serves 4 to 6.

ALWAYS reread any hint books you may own from time to time. (Keeping them in the bathroom is a good idea.) There are lots of great ideas in these books, but no one except Heloise could actually keep all the hints in her head. My current favorite is *Cooking Hints & Tips*, written by Christine France and published by Dorling Kindersley. If I didn't own this book, it would never have occurred to me to keep a freezer logbook (page 8), to thread hot dogs onto long skewers so I can turn them all over at once (page 86), or to "shop wisely" (page 46).

A Few Other Things About Green Beans

"Are these *bean skins*?" my daughter asked incredulously when I first served those frozen "French" green beans. That's what we've called them ever since. Some vestigial childhood association still makes bean skins seem "elegant" to me, and I haven't renounced them the way I have most other frozen vegetables. Remember how fancy they used to seem when people served them with butter and chopped toasted almonds? Well, they're even better with butter and chopped *smoked* almonds. Just buy one of those cans of Smokehouse almonds and chop up as many as you think you'll need. (You don't have to toast them—duh, they're already smoked.) You can eat the rest while you wait for the beans to cook.

Smoked Bean Skins—now, there's an elegant name.

A great thing to do with trimmed whole green beans is to cook them until they're about half-done. Meanwhile, sauté some chopped bacon until it's crisp.

Drain the bacon, but leave a couple tablespoons of fat in the skillet. If you think your family is up to it, fry a chopped onion in the bacon fat until brown; if not, leave out the onion and finish cooking the beans by stir-frying them in the bacon-y skillet with a tablespoon or so of water. Then add salt and pepper to taste and stir in the crumbled bacon. You know what would also be good added to this? *Chopped smoked almonds.*

I sometimes cut fresh green beans into incredibly small slices—say, 1/4 inch. Then I steam them and serve them with butter and salt and call them Pencil Erasers. It amuses *me*, anyway, and reminds me of the days before I had kids, when I would stir-fry these tiny chopped beans with lots of onion and black mustard seed, and the people I served them to would eat them happily, without asking what all those black specks were . . .

ALWAYS let any dishes you wash by hand *air-dry*. Don't dry them with a dish towel—it's a big waste of time. Besides, it's germier, unless you always use a new, clean dish towel.

Various Carrots

Since many children like raw carrots, and rawness is a virtue, why not serve them carrot sticks all the time? Because you just can't, that's all. It's your *job* to make your kids eat cooked carrots once in a while, even if they never do it again when they're grown-ups. One of the following ways—all of which are meant to use 1 pound of carrots—will probably work.

Roasted Carrots

Carrots can be baked just like potatoes. Scrub them well, pare them, cut them however you want, and put them into a baking dish with 2 tablespoons *each* butter and water. You can bake them at 300 degrees for 2 hours, 350 degrees for 1½ hours, or whatever you need the oven set at for as long as seems reasonable. Stir them from time to time. When they're nice and soft and brown, you can coarsely mash them if you want (with more butter and a little milk, and maybe some brown sugar), or serve them whole. This is a good way to use up big, cumbersome carrots—the kind I usually feed to my rabbit, Popcorn.

Glazed Carrots I

Here's the easiest glazing method: Steam or boil the carrots until they're almost done. Then put them into a saucepan with 2 tablespoons *each* brown sugar and unsalted butter. Cook the carrots, stirring, over low heat until the butter and sugar have melted and formed a glaze and the carrots are tender. Test for doneness, season with salt and pepper to taste, and serve.

Glazed Carrots II

No, wait, this is even easier: Put the carrots, 2 tablespoons *each* brown sugar and unsalted butter, ½ teaspoon salt, and ⅓ cup water into a heavy saucepan. Cover and cook them over low heat for 10 to 15 minutes, stirring occasionally, until the water has cooked away, a glaze has formed, and the carrots are tender. (You may need to add a little more water.)

Glazed Carrots III

This is easy too, but you need to start it ahead. Steam or boil the carrots until they're almost done. Melt 2 tablespoons *each* unsalted butter, brown sugar, and undiluted frozen orange juice concentrate in a small saucepan. Add 1 cut-up orange and stir well. Coat the carrots with this mixture and refrigerate them for at least 8 hours and up to 24. Then bake at 350 degrees for 20 to 25 minutes, until tender.

In any of these recipes, you can substitute molasses, honey, dark corn syrup, or maple syrup for the sugar, but the spoon will be a little harder to wash. And you know about giving in and serving raw carrot sticks with peanut butter and raisins, right? As my mother says, it can function as a salad, though perhaps not at state banquets.

ALWAYS decant stuff into airtight containers if you can. This helps protect food products in many ways. Brown sugar, for instance, will stay softer if it's in a jar with a screw-on or snap-on lid. Cornstarch is easier to spoon out of a jar than a cardboard box with a messy paper lining. And any grain product, dried fruit, or other "dry-pourable" food is less likely to be infested by those horrible Indian meal moths if it's stored airtight.

Peanutty Carrots

We serve this carrot puree at Easter. It is one of the only recipes I know in which what is essentially peanut butter works as a savory flavoring. Most children recoil at peanut butter in anything but cookies and sandwiches. For mysterious reasons, mine don't complain about the peanuts in this dish.

5 cups thinly sliced carrots

1 cup salted peanuts

4 tablespoons (1/2 stick) unsalted butter

1/2 cup sour cream

1 tablespoon light brown sugar, packed

1/2 teaspoon ginger

Salt and pepper to taste

Roast the carrots according to my method on page 239, cooking them until they are very tender. Process the peanuts and butter in a food processor until they're—until they're peanut butter! Add the hot carrots and puree until smooth. Add the sour cream, brown sugar, and ginger. Season with salt and pepper and serve immediately.

Serves 6.

Husky Corn

C orn roasted in its husks is vastly different from boiled corn, and I think it's much better. The problem is that doing it on the grill gets in the way of either the griller or the other food that's being grilled. Those in-the-husk ears aren't exactly tiny, you know. Cooking the corn in the oven gives you more control and more space on the grill.

You'll need 8 ears of unshucked fresh corn. Soak the corn in a large bowl or pot of water while you preheat the broiler. When it's hot, put the corn on a large cookie sheet and broil it, turning several times, until the husks are black. Watch the corn very carefully to make sure the husks don't catch on fire.

Take the corn out of the oven, turn off the broiler, and turn *on* the oven to 500 degrees. Shielding your hands with dish towels or oven mitts, husk each ear of corn. Take off as much silk as you can; wiping the corn with a damp paper towel is helpful for this.

Return the corn to the oven and roast it for 5 minutes. Serve immediately, with butter and salt.

Serves 4.

Corn Oysters

a lovely use for fresh corn—and perhaps the only oysters that will ever pass your child's lips. Isn't it funny how giving a food a disgusting name makes children *more* willing to try it?

I didn't give corn oysters their name, though; they came with it. They're really little pancakes. There are no pearls inside them.

Traditionally, these are a side dish. By adding some chopped cooked bacon or ham, you can turn them into a light main course. But don't serve corn on the cob as a side dish with them.

> 2 cups grated-off-the-cob *fresh!* corn
>
> 2 large eggs, beaten
>
> 1/2 cup flour
>
> Salt and pepper to taste
>
> 4 tablespoons (1/2 stick) unsalted butter, plus more as needed

Preheat the oven to 200 degrees so that you can keep the finished corn oysters warm.

Mix the corn, eggs, flour, and salt and pepper in a medium bowl until they're well combined. Shape the mixture into little oyster-sized cakes. Heat the butter in a large skillet until it begins to foam; then carefully set as many oysters into the skillet as will fit. Cook them for 4 minutes per side, or until they're medium-brown. Keep them warm on a cookie sheet in the oven until they're all done, adding more butter to the pan as needed.

Serves 4.

Corn Pudding

I have to admit that I'm not as insanely fond of fresh corn on the cob as most people are. I like it fine, but the thing I like best is getting to put lots of butter and salt on it. If people just served corn on the cob plain, how popular would it be? Probably we wouldn't care so much if raccoons got to it before we could pick it.

So when corn is in season, I serve it maybe twice a summer. Then I also make corn pudding a couple of times, because corn pudding is one of those delicate, summery dishes that *have* to use fresh corn. Otherwise, it loses all its meaning.

2 cups *fresh!* corn kernels (from 3–4 ears)

2 cups milk or half-and-half, heated to a simmer

2 large eggs, beaten

2 tablespoons (¼ stick) unsalted butter, melted

1 teaspoon sugar

Salt and pepper to taste

Preheat the oven to 350 degrees. Grease a 2-quart baking dish.

Mix everything together in a medium bowl and pour into the greased baking dish. Bake the pudding until it's set—35 to 45 minutes. Serve warm.

Serves 4.

Panfried Corn

You must not exit this world without eating a batch of fried corn, one of the best barbecue accompaniments there is. It's 100 percent worth buying salad seasoning for, even if you would never dream of using salad seasoning and never plan to go near the jar again. And it's one of the world's few recipes in which a canned vegetable works best—though the can certainly doesn't save you much time. To be properly chewy, fried corn needs to cook forever. Be warned: you have to drain the corn at least 4 hours in advance to get out every bit of the juice that would keep it from being chewy enough.

After dinner you can have a contest to see who has the most corn stuck in their teeth.

- 1 15-ounce (or thereabouts) can white corn
- 1 15-ounce (or thereabouts) can yellow corn
- 2 tablespoons (¼ stick) unsalted butter, plus more if needed
- 1 tablespoon vegetable oil, plus more if needed
- 1 tablespoon cheese-flavored salad seasoning (available at some supermarkets, as well as from Penzeys; see page 22)
- Salt and pepper

Drain both types of corn for at least 4 hours in a sieve or colander.

Heat the butter and oil in a large skillet. When the butter is melted, add the drained corn. Cook the corn over very low heat, stirring frequently, for at least 2 hours. (You may need to add more butter or oil from time to time.) It should be well browned and chewy. About 15 minutes before you remove it from the heat, stir in the salad seasoning and salt and pepper to taste.

Serves 6.

The Only Onion Rings

I thought it was my duty to pass along a couple of eggplant recipes that children might try. Then I realized, why? I hate eggplant so much myself! So I substituted my favorite onion rings instead.

Deep-frying at home is complicated unless you're used to it. If you're not, I recommend reading the deep-frying directions in *The Joy of Cooking* or a similar book to prepare yourself. When I make onion rings, I serve them as a main course. No *way* am I doing all that work for a side dish.

They're worth it, though.

3 cups milk

1 large egg

4 large Spanish onions, cut into 1/2-inch slices and separated into rings

Approximately 2 quarts vegetable oil

1 1/2 cups flour

1 1/2 cups yellow cornmeal

1 tablespoon pepper

2 teaspoons salt, plus more to taste

A pinch of cayenne***

Beat the milk and egg together in a bowl. Pour into a 9-x-13-inch pan and layer the onion rings evenly in the pan. Some of the rings will break, but that's okay. Let the onions soak for 1 hour, turning them occasionally.

Pour enough oil into a deep fryer or large, heavy saucepan to reach a depth of 3 inches. Preheat the oil to 375 degrees. Be patient with this; the onion rings will be slimy if you fry them at a lower heat.

While the oil heats, put the flour, cornmeal, pepper, salt, and the optional cayenne into a brown-paper grocery bag. Shake the dry ingredients to blend. With a slotted spoon, transfer the onions from the milk into the bag. Shake them gently until they're thoroughly coated with the dry ingredients. (A child might like to do the shaking.)

Preheat the oven to 200 degrees, unless you plan to serve each handful of onion rings as soon as it is fried.

A few at a time, take the onions out of the bag, shake off any excess coating, and drop them carefully into the hot oil. Fry until they're well browned. Drain them on paper towels, salt them to taste, and keep them warm on a baking sheet in the oven. Keep going until all the onions have been fried. Serve immediately.

As I said in an earlier cookbook, "When the oil cools, you can strain and reuse it a couple more times. But do you really want to? I'd get rid of it, myself."

Serves 4 to 6.

Sugar Snap Peas with Orange

We haven't yet gotten tired of eating sugar snap peas raw. My rabbit likes them, too; I always let him have three pods when I'm serving them to the family. But this recipe works well for summertime company, when I don't want to do a lot of hot kitchen work but I don't want it to look as though I've done *nothing*.

1 pound fresh sugar snap peas

1 teaspoon grated orange rind

3 tablespoons fresh orange juice

2 tablespoons (1/4 stick) very cold unsalted butter, cut into small pieces

Salt and pepper

Trim and destring the peas.

Steam the peas for 2 to 3 minutes, or until they just begin to become tender. Transfer them to a saucepan. Over low heat, toss the peas with the orange rind, orange juice, butter, and salt and pepper to taste until the butter melts. Serve immediately.

Serves 4.

Cheesy Mashed Potatoes

The great thing about this recipe is that it can be done ahead—unlike regular mashed potatoes, which are so often a last-minute, last-straw production when you're trying to haul a turkey or a prime rib out of the oven.

4 pounds Idaho or Yukon Gold potatoes

4 tablespoons (1/2 stick) unsalted butter

1 teaspoon salt, or to taste

1–1 1/2 cups milk

1 8-ounce package cream cheese, at room temperature

8 ounces cheddar, grated (about 2 cups), divided

1 red bell pepper, minced***

1 medium onion, minced***

Bake or microwave the potatoes until they're very soft. Set the oven to 325 degrees if you'll be baking the tates right away.

Scoop out the insides into a large bowl. Dump the butter, salt, 1 cup of the milk, the cream cheese, and 1 cup of the cheddar on top of the potatoes. Using an electric mixer, beat until smooth and fluffy; add more milk if you need it, then add the optional vegetables. Transfer the mixture to a greased large baking dish and bake immediately, or refrigerate it until you need it. (You can refrigerate it for up to 24 hours.)

About 2 hours before you need to serve the potatoes—if you chilled them, that is—take the dish out of the fridge and let it sit at room temperature for an hour to take the chill off. Preheat the oven to 325 degrees.

Cover the tates and bake them for 1 hour. Top them with the remaining 1 cup cheddar, bake uncovered for 15 more minutes, and serve.

Serves 8 to 10.

SWEEEEEEEET Potatoes

You'd better not serve these any other time except Thanksgiving. They'll give your kids way too exalted an idea of what a sweet potato should taste like.

3 cups cooked mashed sweet potatoes (6–8 baked sweet potatoes)

1/2 cup heavy cream

1 cup sugar

4 tablespoons (1/2 stick) unsalted butter, at room temperature

1/4 teaspoon salt

Topping

3/4 cup light brown sugar, packed

1/4 cup flour

4 tablespoons (1/2 stick) unsalted butter, at room temperature

A pinch of salt

A pinch of nutmeg

1 cup chopped pecans (optional)

Preheat the oven to 350 degrees. Grease a 2-quart casserole.

Combine the mashed sweets, cream, sugar, butter, and salt and beat until smooth and light. (Well, as light as possible. This isn't a *fizzy* recipe.) Spread the mixture in the casserole dish.

For the topping: Combine all the ingredients in a small bowl. Crumble the mixture with your fingers and sprinkle it over the casserole.

Bake the casserole for 45 minutes, or until heated through and browned on top.

Serves 8 to 10.

Tomatoes

In honor of my sister Cathy and her childhood hatred of tomatoes, I have not included any tomato recipes in this book. Everyone in my family knows why.

Zoocakes

The only challenge here—and I'm not downplaying its difficulty—is: will your kids eat green pancakes? If you don't think so, add some blue food coloring to the batter and call them Bluecakes. Then they might not spot the zucchini. If your children are familiar with latkes, you can just call these Green Latkes and see if *that* works. I serve these like latkes, with sour cream and applesauce. I don't have to make them blue, either; for some reason, my kids have always liked zucchini. I must be a really great mother.

1 pound zucchini, grated and squeezed in paper towels
   to remove excess moisture

$^1/_3$ cup grated Parmesan (about $1^1/_2$ ounces)

1 large egg, beaten

1 small onion, minced***

$^1/_2$ cup flour

Salt and pepper

$^1/_2$ cup vegetable oil

Sour cream and applesauce

Stir together the drained zucchini, Parmesan, egg, and the optional onion in a medium bowl. Gently mix in the flour and season to taste.

Heat the oil in a large skillet until hot. Add spoonfuls of the zucchini batter to the skillet, flattening them down with your spoon. Cook until crisply browned on both sides, about 5 min-

ALWAYS remember my mother-in-law Carol's dictum about dishwashers: "My dishwasher works for me. I do not work for it." Don't spend precious time trying to fit every last dish into your dishwasher with lapidary precision. It's okay to leave some of them in the sink until the next time you run it. Also, don't feel you *have* to run the dishwasher only when it's jammed full of dishes. If you've got, say, a couple of pots in there that you're going to need in the next couple of hours, just run it now! Naturally, ignore me if you live in an area where there's a water shortage.

utes per side; if you get bored just standing there, it's okay to flip these pancakes more than once.

You can keep the finished pancakes warm on a cookie sheet in a 200-degree oven until the batter is all used up, or you can serve them immediately. In either case, serve them with sour cream and applesauce.

Serves 4.

Golden Delicious Salad

G o back and read my notes about salads (page 229) if you're worried that this isn't respectable enough.

2 Golden Delicious apples

1 13-ounce can crushed pineapple in its own juice

2 carrots, grated

1 3-ounce package cream cheese, at room temperature

1 1/2 teaspoons grated lemon rind

2 tablespoons fresh lemon juice

2 teaspoons sugar

1/4 teaspoon nutmeg

Salt to taste

Lettuce leaves (optional)

1/2 cup chopped salted peanuts

Core the apples, but don't bother peeling them. Chop them into 1/2-inch cubes.

Drain the pineapple, but save 2 tablespoons of the juice.

Toss together the apples, pineapple, and grated carrots in a medium bowl. Blend the cream cheese, the reserved pineapple juice, the lemon rind and juice, sugar, and nutmeg in a small bowl. Season with salt. Carefully stir this dressing into the apple mixture.

Serve on lettuce leaves if you want to give your children a more salad-y experience. Sprinkle with the chopped peanuts just before serving.

Serves 4 to 6.

ALWAYS have a bag of walnuts in the shell when there's a toddler in the house. Thirty or forty whole walnuts and a colander are the best bath toy there is. True, the walnuts will sometimes stain the porcelain for a while after they're used, BUT I KNOW YOU HARDLY CARE ABOUT A LITTLE THING LIKE THAT WHEN YOUR CHILD'S HAPPINESS IS INVOLVED.

"Come on, all you idduw fuddows"—that would be "little fellows"—my daughter used to say lovingly to her herd of bathtub walnuts. Whole cranberries are great bath toys, too, though they're of a swallow-able size so you'll need to be watching little Joey very carefully. But then, you *would* be watching him very carefully, wouldn't you?

Morning Glory Salad

I don't know how this salad got its name, because why on earth would you serve it in the morning? And it certainly doesn't contain any morning glories, which is just as well, because their seeds are supposed to be hallucinogenic. But mine not to reason why.

Salad

1 head romaine lettuce, shredded

1 large banana, sliced into "coins"

³/₄ cup raisins

³/₄ cup chopped walnuts

1 large apple, peeled, cored, and chopped

Dressing

Half of a 6-ounce can frozen orange juice concentrate, thawed

¹/₂ cup vegetable oil

2 tablespoons honey

2 tablespoons cider vinegar, distilled white, or balsamic vinegar

1 teaspoon poppy seeds

For the salad: Gently stir together all the ingredients in a large bowl.

For the dressing: Fiercely whisk together the dressing ingredients in a small bowl.

Toss the two together and serve.

Serves 4 to 6.

Strawberry Salad with Poppy Seed Dressing

The children will pick out all their strawberries, of course. But if you cut the romaine very fine, some of it may cling unavoidably to the berries.

The original version of this recipe called for red onions to be added along with the berries. I think this counts as cruelty to children. If you want the onion, chop it separately and add it to your own helping, you meanie.

1 head romaine lettuce, chopped

1 pint fresh strawberries, washed, hulled, and sliced

Dressing

1/2 cup mayonnaise

1/4 cup whole milk or half-and-half

2 tablespoons cider vinegar, raspberry vinegar, or distilled white vinegar

1/4 cup sugar

2 tablespoons poppy seeds

A pinch of salt

1 red onion, chopped***

Put the romaine and strawberries in a salad bowl.

For the dressing: Whisk the dressing ingredients in a small bowl and toss the salad with the dressing. Add the onion at the table for them as wants.

Serves 8.

It Happens To Everyone

I didn't really like any fruits except seedless grapes when I was little—and everyone was boycotting grapes, so there was basically no fruit I liked. One winter, for a few weeks, a rat got into the house and kept eating all the skin off the pears that my mother kept in a bowl on the kitchen table. Mum kept saying, "Nelie, if you want a pear, you should have the whole pear." I kept saying, "But I don't *like* pears."

—Nelie McNeal

Sunny Broccoli Salad

My original copy of this recipe called for mushrooms. Raw mushrooms! In a kid's recipe! Don't make me laugh.

1 bunch broccoli (2 or 3 stems)

1 cup dried currants or raisins (currants are cuter)

1 cup sunflower seeds

10 bacon strips, cooked until crisp, and crumbled

1/4 cup diced red onion***

1/2 cup mayonnaise

1 tablespoon red wine vinegar

3 tablespoons sugar

Chop the broccoli into small pieces. Steam or boil it *for 1 minute only;* then quickly rinse it under cold water and drain very well. Combine the broccoli with the currants or raisins, sunflower seeds, bacon, and the optional onion in a medium bowl.

Mix together the mayonnaise, vinegar, and sugar in a small bowl. Pour over the broccoli mixture and toss. Refrigerate the salad for at least 2 hours before serving.

Serves 6.

Vaguely Asian Cabbage!? Salad!?

y friend Gina brought this dish to a potluck at which an eleven-year-old girl named Alexa said to me, "I just want you to know: this is the first time I've ever liked cabbage." Say no more, Alexa: the recipe goes in the book.

I've made two slight changes to Gina's recipe. I add a tablespoon of sugar to the dressing and I toast the noodles and almonds in the oven, instead of in a skillet, to give me a little more control over the browning.

Salad

1 package "Oriental-Flavor" Top Ramen noodles
  (reserve the "flavor packet")

1/2 cup slivered almonds

1/4 cup sesame seeds

1 tablespoon vegetable oil

1 1-pound package of that wonderful, already-chopped-
  in-the-bag cabbage slaw or 5 cups shredded-by-you
  cabbage

2 large carrots, grated or shredded

Dressing

The "flavor packet" from the noodles

1/4 cup vegetable oil

2 tablespoons rice vinegar (seasoned kind is good but
  not essential)

2 tablespoons soy sauce

1 tablespoon sugar

2 teaspoons sesame oil

Preheat the oven to 300 degrees.

For the salad: Break up the noodles into shreds and put them into an 8-inch square pan with the almonds, sesame seeds, and oil. Give them a couple of stirs and bake them for 10 minutes, or until they're browned.

Toss together the cabbage and carrots in a large salad bowl.

For the dressing: Whisk together all the ingredients in a small bowl.

To assemble: Toss together the vegetables, noodle mixture, and dressing. Gina says, "Some people like to mix these kinds of salads with the dressing early; I prefer a crisper salad and toss just before serving." She also says, "A million bucks would be fine"—as payment for the recipe, that is. Would someone please oblige?

Serves 6.

"Just-Might-Work" Coleslaw

Many children are dead set against coleslaw. But if you can force them to try some of this, and if they're not too stubborn to admit they like something you've forced them to try—well, then! As they get older, you can gradually make the recipe more adult.

Slaw

1 cup coarsely shredded red cabbage

1 cup coarsely shredded green cabbage

1 cup coarsely shredded carrots

1 14-ounce can chopped pineapple in its own juice, drained well

1/3 cup slivered almonds, toasted

Dressing

2/3 cup mayonnaise

2/3 cup sour cream

1 tablespoon fresh lemon juice

1 teaspoon grated onion***

1 teaspoon sugar

Salt to taste

 I Can't Believe I'm Doing This

As preschoolers, my kids always ate steamed red cabbage because I sliced it thin, called it "worms," and let them pretend they were frogs gobbling it up with the appropriate sound effects. Frogs *do* eat worms, in case you're wondering.

For the slaw: Toss together all the ingredients in a medium bowl.

For the dressing: Stir together all the ingredients in a small bowl.

Combine the two and chill the slaw for at least an hour, or until it is "cole."

Serves 4 to 6.

Note: If you really think the cabbage won't rope 'em in, you could use all carrots.

Layered Salad

In an earlier cookbook, I upgraded this recipe for adults. Now I'm downgrading it: I have actually witnessed children eating this version but have never seen them go near my fancier one. True, this recipe is a cliché, but you don't have to tell the kids that. Anyway, foods become clichés for a reason . . .

You'll need a very big salad bowl, one that can hold 4 quarts. Ideally, it should be transparent and straight-sided, to give the layers their full due.

Salad

1 10-ounce bag fresh spinach, well washed and well drained

1 pound thick-sliced bacon, cooked until crisp, and crumbled

6 hard-boiled eggs, sliced

Salt and pepper to taste

1 head romaine lettuce, sliced very thin

1 10-ounce package tiny frozen peas, thawed and drained

Up to 1 bunch scallions, chopped***

Dressing

1 cup Hellman's or Best Foods mayonnaise

1 8-ounce container sour cream

1 tablespoon sugar

A sprinkling of paprika

1 pound Swiss cheese, grated (about 4 cups)

For the salad: In your nice big bowl, layer the salad ingredients in order, starting with the spinach and ending with the optional scallions.

For the dressing: Mix all the ingredients in a small bowl and "ice" the salad with them. *Do not stir in the dressing.*

Sprinkle the grated cheese over the dressing. Cover the bowl with foil and chill it overnight, or for 24 hours. (It takes that long for the dressing to percolate down.)

When you serve this, you should plunge the salad spoon way, way down to the bottom of the bowl so that you'll get all the layers. Some people say to toss the salad, but I think that misses the point.

Serves 20, so don't make this for a family of 4.

Couscous Salad with Add-Ins

Using add-ins in this kind of salad (or rice salad, or potato) helps reduce the risk of "Yuck, I hate it." Even plain, however, this dish may seem alien to kids. If that's the case, they can just pick at the add-ins. Or at least the raisins. It's hardly your responsibility to make your children eat fresh vegetables *all* the time.

2¹/₂ cups chicken broth

2 cups couscous

²/₃ cup mayonnaise

Grated rind of 1 orange

¹/₄ cup fresh orange juice

2 tablespoons tomato paste

1 tablespoon fresh lemon juice, or more to taste

Salt and pepper

Optional Add-Ins

3 large tomatoes, halved, deglopped, and chopped

1 cucumber, peeled, seeded, and chopped

¹/₄ cup fresh mint leaves, chopped

¹/₄ cup fresh basil leaves, chopped

1 bunch scallions, minced

1¹/₂ cups raisins or dried currants, soaked in boiling water for 5 minutes and drained well

1¹/₂ cups slivered almonds or pine nuts, toasted at 300 degrees for 10 minutes

ALWAYS get the strongest refrigerator magnets you can find—not the cutest ones. Go to an office-supply store and get a couple of those magnetized "file pockets" that are meant to be fastened to file cabinets. They work great on a fridge, and they hold whole reams of paper. Whatever you put in there—a school permission slip, say, or a camp medical form—will at least stay safe, even if you forget about it.

Bring the chicken broth to a boil in a small pot and stir in the couscous. Remove from the heat and let the mixture stand, covered, for 5 to 10 minutes, fluffing the couscous occasionally with a fork.

Combine the mayonnaise, orange rind, orange juice, tomato paste, and lemon juice in a small bowl. Add this dressing to the couscous, stirring well. Season to taste with salt and pepper. Chill the couscous for at least 2 hours.

Taste the couscous for seasoning; it may need more lemon juice. At serving time, accompany the couscous with bowls of your chosen add-ins.

Serves 4 adults, with small dabs for the children.

Crunchy Pea Salad

My original copy of this recipe called for celery (which I hate) and red onions (which I love but am making optional here because of, you know, the kid thing). This recipe can stand in for a nice summer main dish as well as work as a salad. And it is further proof that tiny frozen peas are one of the world's best ingredients.

Most salads are improved by a few drops of Maggi seasoning, and this one is no exception. (Maggi is an all-purpose savory liquid found in the condiment section of most supermarkets.)

1/2 cup mayonnaise

2 tablespoons vegetable oil

4 teaspoons vinegar (I use balsamic)

1 teaspoon sugar

1/4 teaspoon Maggi seasoning (optional)

Pepper to taste

1 10-ounce package tiny frozen peas, thawed and
    drained

1 cup salted peanuts

6 bacon strips, cooked until crisp, and crumbled

1/4 cup minced red onion***

Combine the mayonnaise, oil, vinegar, sugar, the optional Maggi, and pepper in a medium bowl; whisk until well combined. Gently stir in everything else. Chill the salad for at least 1 hour before serving.

Serves 4.

"If You Don't Eat That, You Can't Have Any . . ."

Dessert, of course.

Dessert raises a lot of emotional issues. Before I get into them, let me say that when I first started this book I didn't plan to include any desserts at all. They didn't seem to fit the theme. You never have to bargain to get kids to try *dessert,* after all, or make dire predictions about what will happen to their bones if they don't get enough sugar. Desserts are the easy part. What's more, everyone has tons of dessert recipes already. Why even mention them?

A couple of reasons. For one thing, no one who knows me would believe I'd written this book if it didn't have some sweets in it. (Here's what's sitting next to my keyboard now, to reward me for doing all this hard work: a Lindt Mocca bar, a Lindt Orange bar, and eight ounces of Lindt chocolate hearts. I went to a Lindt store today, you see. Then later I went to a drugstore and bought a pound of assorted hard candy to be the "fruit" part of the reward.) Also, a cookbook that doesn't include a dessert chapter is like a meal that ends with salad. You may not have planned to eat dessert, but you'd rather be given the choice.

So my flimsy notion collapsed like the First Little Pig's straw house. But I decided to restrict the desserts in this book to very simple ones—and not too many, either. All of

The Recipes

them are either easy enough for a child to make without much supervision or simple enough for *you* to make on a busy night without driving yourself crazy. I'm confident that you'll be able to track down recipes for drop-dead desserts that take three days to make. They're just not in this book.

Now on to the emotional stuff. Desserts can sometimes make parents wish their children were birds instead of people. Adult birds have to flap around ceaselessly to get food into their babies' mouths, but at least mealtimes are pretty much invariant. The parent stuffs the food into the baby's mouth and that's it. There's not all this *discussion*. The baby bird doesn't complain that she's getting sick of caterpillars. She doesn't ask if it's okay to eat just the grasshopper's head and skip the legs. She doesn't point out that she's eaten nothing but seeds all day and the bluejay babies get berries whenever they want. She just eats, grows, and one day either topples out of the nest onto the sidewalk or flies away.

Whereas we human parents are stuck for years and years with offspring who know how to get to us.

Like many (human) parents, I started out resolving that my first child, Laura, would not taste any sweets at all, ever. Fresh fruit and an occasional smoothie would be the only sugar she knew. She would never attach emotional importance to desserts, because she'd never get the chance; instead she'd respond to the natural deliciousness of, say, wheatgrass juice. For my part, I would never tell her she had to finish her vegetables before she could have dessert, and I'd never try to cheer her up with a cookie when she stubbed her toe. In our family, desserts would never become the bargaining issue they were in all the sloppy, mismanaged households around me.

This notion lasted for about two seconds. As I say, Laura was my first child. As soon as she started having friends over for lunch—friends with older brothers and sisters, friends who knew about cookies—I started serving them. And even if I hadn't started giving them to Laura, at some point she might have noticed that I was eating them myself. Like ants, children are good at tracking down sugar.

Once you've seen how much a small child likes dessert, it's hard to turn back. I can still remember taking Laura to a Friendly's when she was about eighteen months old. David and I ordered sundaes, and we ordered a small dish of vanilla ice cream for Laura. When the waitress brought it, Laura reared up in her high chair and shrieked, "Baby ice cream *too*?" with such incredulous joy that it brought tears to my eyes.

What can you do? Desserts make people happier, and

you want your child to be happy. So you start serving them more often, and the child starts preferring them to proteins and vegetables, and you start using them as bribes to get her to try a shred of spinach—and before you know it, you're exactly where you didn't plan to be.

But once in a while a child takes a bite of something he thought he'd hate—and realizes that it's not that bad. And anyway, weren't many of us raised this way? And haven't we turned out pretty well? I'm sorry, folks, but it's just not that big a deal. As my mother once said, "Save your tears for *real* tragedies."

Besides, you may end up with a child like my son, John, who doesn't particularly like desserts. He's never responded to the "if you don't eat your meat" threat. He just says, "Okay," clears his plate, and leaves the table.

That'll show me.

Buttermints

These simple unbaked candies are perfect for children to make at Christmas. The "dough," or whatever you'd call it, is so malleable that it can be shaped and reshaped and cut with tiny canapé cutters, and then the cutouts can be filled with a contrasting color of dough cut out in the same shape, and on and on.

Peppermint oil works better and has a fresher taste than extract. You can buy it at gourmet stores, by mail order, and in some craft shops and pharmacies. Just be sure not to sprinkle it around your kitchen like holy water, because you'll never get rid of the smell. Of the peppermint oil, I mean.

8 tablespoons (1 stick) unsalted butter, at room
    temperature

1 pound confectioners' sugar (about 4 cups)

2 tablespoons ice water

A pinch of salt

$1/4$ teaspoon peppermint oil or $1/2$ teaspoon peppermint
    extract

Green and red food color

With two knives or a pastry blender, cut the butter into the sugar in a large bowl. Add the water. Knead the mixture by hand until it's smooth and satiny. Add the salt and oil or extract and knead again.

Divide the dough into thirds. Tint one-third pale green and one-third pale pink; leave the last third alone.

Rolling the dough into $1/2$-inch balls and flattening them slightly is the most basic thing to do.

Making the mints fancier depends on your child's age, ambition, and fine motor skills. However fancy or plain the mints are, they should be placed on waxed paper for 2 to 3 hours, until they've set. Then they can be moved to a covered container in a cool place, where they should ripen for 2 days before being eaten.

Makes a little over 1 pound.

ALWAYS remember that any mint-flavored dessert or candy will contaminate any other dessert or candy it's closed up with. I even keep my little jars of peppermint extract and oil sealed up in plastic containers so that the mint won't permeate other foods in that cupboard, like the peanut butter.

Rainy-Day Fudge

C ooking classic fudge, or any candy, on a rainy day is a bad idea because the sugar crystallizes too easily. This recipe is for a rainy day when your house is filled with bored children who aren't old enough to use the stove. The fudge is fine— better than the store-bought mix kind, anyway—but the really great thing is that it's so easy to make. For one batch, the electric mixer is incredibly easy; if several small children are doing the cooking, it's better to use a zipper-lock bag and let them mash it around. I once supervised seventeen children making seventeen batches of this recipe, and at the end of the class there wasn't a trace of fudge anywhere but in the pans where it was supposed to be.

2 cups confectioners' sugar

2 ounces unsweetened chocolate, melted

1 3-ounce package cream cheese, at room temperature

1 tablespoon milk

1 teaspoon vanilla

A pinch of salt

Either thoroughly beat everything together in a bowl, or thoroughly mash everything up in a zipper-lock bag. (Make *sure* that the bag is tightly and completely "zipped.") When the ingredients are smooth and completely mixed, pat the fudge into an 8-inch square pan.

If you're in charge of several children who are each making a batch of fudge, it's perfectly acceptable to have them use the premelted chocolate that comes in packets. In that case, omit the milk, or the fudge will be too soft.

Makes about 1 pound.

Soft-as-a-Cloud Dip

 **I Can't Believe
I'm Doing This**

Serve this once in a while as a summer lunch and dessert in one, with various fruits to dip into it. Your children will call you blessed.

1 8-ounce package cream cheese, at room temperature

1 7-ounce jar Marshmallow Fluff

1 teaspoon grated orange rind

3 tablespoons fresh orange juice

1 teaspoon ginger

Beat everything together in a medium bowl until smooth. Chill for an hour or two before serving.

Makes about 3 cups.

Ambrosia

Okay, okay, so it has mini-marshmallows in it. Also coconut, which my kids and husband hate. *I don't care.* I love this stuff, and this is my book.

Marshmallows used to be considered elegant. In *Betsy's Wedding*, by the incomparable Maud Hart Lovelace, Betsy has terrible trouble learning to cook for her new husband, Joe. Why, that meat pie she makes!

> Joe took a bite. So did Betsy. Where the crust wasn't burned, it was soggy, and the vegetables tasted very queer. Joe took a second bite. "A mighty good idea," he said briskly, "using up that pot roast in a meat pie. It's tasty too."
>
> . . . Betsy began to cry. She pushed back her chair and ran out of the living room and threw herself across the white bed. Joe followed. "What's the matter?" he asked anxiously. "Didn't I say your meat pie was good?"
>
> "That's just the trouble!" Betsy sobbed. "It's so awful—and you were so—so—nice about it!"
>
> At this Joe laughed his ringing laugh and kissed her tears away. "Next time I'll beat you."

That's how you know the book was written a long time ago. But soon Betsy learns to make dinner for company: "Chicken fricasseed in cream, and a marshmallow pudding!" She would have been proud to serve ambrosia. And Joe, unlike some husbands I could mention, would have liked it.

ALWAYS cut a bunch of grapes into small bunches the minute you get it home. The only thing that keeps a bunch of grapes from looking horrible as people help themselves is precutting it into single servings.

1 cup mandarin oranges, drained

1 8-ounce container sour cream

1 cup shredded sweetened coconut

1 cup canned crushed pineapple, drained

1 cup miniature marshmallows

Fold everything together gently but thoroughly in a medium bowl. Chill for at least 2 hours before taking the bowl away somewhere that you can enjoy it in private.

Serves 4, or me.

Cranberry Kissel

I 've never understood why cranberry kissel—a sort of Jell-O—isn't more mainstream. My mother used to make it when I was growing up, and I always loved it. Let's *all* work to make it more popular after the millennium, shall we?

2 tablespoons plus 2 teaspoons cornstarch

1/4 cup cold water

3³/4 cups cranberry juice cocktail

1/4 cup fresh lemon juice

4 teaspoons sugar, plus more to taste

Heavy cream or whipped cream as a topping (optional)

Dissolve the cornstarch in the cold water in a small bowl and let it sit.

Heat the cranberry and lemon juices with the sugar in a medium nonreactive pot and taste to see if the mixture's sweet enough for you. Add more sugar if it's not. (It's supposed to be quite tart, though.) Add the dissolved cornstarch and, stirring constantly, bring the mixture to a boil. Pour it into a serving dish and cover the dish immediately. Let it come to room temperature; chill it thoroughly, and serve it with the cream or whipped cream, if desired.

Serves 6.

30-Second Smoothies

There are dozens of smoothie recipes around. I'm including this one for the excellent reason that it's from one of my best friends, Bill Sorensen. "For hot summer days when your kids have no desire to eat, only want to drink, this is a great way to give them something more substantial," says Bill. "And if you're pissed off to be taking care of cranky, sweaty kids, you can pretend you're really on an island blending up Southsides or frozen daiquiris."

> 1 container Dannon Orange-Banana "kid" yogurt (the kind that comes in little six-packs)
>
> 1 banana
>
> 6 large ice cubes
>
> 1 cup fresh orange juice

Put everything into a blender and blend until the ice is all crushed.

"Makes 2 kid-size drinks; your kids will gleefully guzzle them in under 30 seconds, and it takes just 30 seconds to make a second batch," says Bill. "I've used other Dannon 'kid' flavors, like Raspberry-Lemon, and substituted fresh raspberries for the banana. It was tasty, but kids under the age of four hate drinking raspberry seeds."

Apple Cidersauce

Store-bought applesauce is one of those desserts that don't really count as a dessert to most children. You have it on hand, like instant pudding, and you pull it out when there's nothing else around, and your kids droop in disappointment. You pull out some Girl Scout cookies from the freezer, but it doesn't do much to improve things.

This applesauce is different. You can still serve it with a cookie alongside, but you certainly don't have to.

6 cups apple cider

8 large apples, peeled, cored, and chopped into large cubes

1 teaspoon cinnamon

1/4 teaspoon nutmeg

1/8 teaspoon ginger

A pinch of salt

1 tablespoon unsalted butter

1/4 cup light brown sugar, packed, or to taste

 I Can't Believe I'm Doing This

Parents of picky eaters will find their lives easier once they declare that apples are vegetables. They are then free to call applesauce "soup."

Boil the cider in a large, heavy nonreactive saucepan, stirring frequently, until it's reduced to 3 cups. This may take 45 minutes, so have a book on hand.

Stir in the apple chunks, spices, and salt. Cover the pot and simmer the apples until they're so soft they're starting to fall apart—at least another 45 minutes. By then the mixture should look like applesauce. If there's too much liquid, cook it uncovered, stirring frequently, until the sauce has the texture you want.

Take the applesauce off the heat and stir in the butter. Sweeten with brown sugar to taste. This is delicious hot, at room temperature, or cold.

Makes 1 quart.

Making Jell-O More Grown-up

Isn't it hard to believe that Jell-O has been around for five hundred years? Why, Christopher Columbus and his sailors only missed it by—

Oh, wait a minute. Looking at the press release again, I see that Jell-O is only *100*. That's almost as hard to believe, though. Most of us probably assume that Jell-O—like Play-Doh—came into being somewhere around our own third or fourth birthday. Can a food that's so brightly colored really be so ancient and full of history?

Yup. In 1893, the Knox company invented the first granulated gelatin, and fancy salad-making took off among the American bourgeoisie. Of course these salads were only remotely saladlike by our standards; they contained virtually no vegetables or fruits. One 1890s recipe for "cheese salad" consisted of a gelatinized boiled dressing with whipped cream and grated cheese. Another memorable effort contained gelatinized chicken salad molded into the shape of a meat chop, with an almond as the chop bone. A plaintive letter written to a women's magazine in 1896 begged for "directions to a jelly where pieces of oranges, bananas, white grapes are used and are seen in the jelly." When Jell-O—an even easier, even shinier, presweetened, precolored version of granulated gelatin—came along a year later, it must have seemed like an answer to a prayer.

"What flavors!" an early Jell-O pamphlet exclaimed rapturously. "Crimson strawberries, luscious raspberries, great gold oranges . . ." Today, with boxes of Jell-O tucked into 64 percent of all American homes, we can also marvel over mango, strawberry kiwi, and peach passion fruit Jell-O. We can make Jell-O Popcorn Balls, Jell-O Poke Cake, and Jell-O Pie in a pretzel crust. If we're Canadian—where the third-most-requested Jell-O recipe is for something called "Jell-O Jelly Powder with Milk"—we can amuse ourselves for hours thinking about the way "Jell-O" sounds like *"J'ai l'eau,"* as in *"J'ai l'eau à la bouche"* (my mouth is watering). Or so suggests the Canadian Jell-O home page on the Kraft Foods web site.

But it seems so predictable to be a Jell-O basher. Jell-O and other Middle American foods are probably genetically encoded in our DNA by now. I have no problem with colorful industrial foods. They're part of my heritage, and I cleave to them proudly. Besides, Jell-O is fun to play with—and very easy to fix up so that it seems like a from-scratch gelatin dessert. Not that kids object to being served straight-up Jell-O, but sometimes we parents have to look out for our own needs.

The main obstacles to homemadeness are Jell-O's color and its rubbery texture. (I realize that a preschooler would object to losing these, but we are not in preschool.) The flavor isn't much of an impediment: Jell-O tastes more like Jell-O than like any particular fruit. It doesn't even taste like "fruit flavoring." With my eyes closed, I can hardly distinguish even between the "red" and "nonred" flavors. It's easy to disguise the basic Jell-O taste by replacing the water in the recipe with a more interesting liquid—which means pretty much any liquid.

Adding more liquid than the recipe on the box calls for produces a dessert that's more tender and less bouncy than regular Jell-O. (It's not possible to unmold my Jell-O variations, but they still look pretty in a glass bowl.) Using fresh lemon juice—anywhere from 2 tablespoons to $1/2$ cup—as part of the liquid improves all Jell-O recipes immeasurably. And using lemon Jell-O as your base means that you won't have to stare at a dessert the color of crayons. Yellow Jell-O is bright enough, God knows, but it's still easier to disguise than the other colors.

Here's a master recipe I'm especially fond of, and two permutations. Choose any add-ins you want; just stir them into the mixture when it's half-jelled.

ALWAYS remember that frozen unsweetened raspberries have a better flavor than fresh if you're straining them for a sauce or dessert. The only time this isn't true is if you have access to hundreds and hundreds of delicious, perfect raspberries that you can pick yourself. (And if you're as lucky as *that,* you'd probably rather eat those delicious, perfect berries whole than mash them up.) Frozen raspberries—thawed, forced through a sieve, and sweetened to taste—make pretty much the perfect sauce for any kind of cold, white dessert (custard, vanilla ice cream or frozen yogurt, white chocolate mousse). A little lemon juice brightens up this sauce even more.

Master Recipe for Grown-Up Jell-O

    1 3-ounce package lemon Jell-O
    1¼ cups tea
    ¾ cup cold fresh orange juice
    ¼ cup fresh lemon juice
    1 tablespoon grated fresh ginger***

Put the Jell-O in a bowl, heat the tea to boiling, pour it over the Jell-O, and stir until the Jell-O has dissolved. Stir in the juices, then transfer the mixture to a serving dish and chill until it starts to jell. Stir in the optional ginger and continue to chill the mixture for 3 to 4 hours, or until firm.

Serves 4.

Variations

Grapefruit: Substitute 1¼ cups boiling grapefruit juice for the tea; substitute 1 cup chilled grapefruit juice for the OJ and reduce the lemon juice to 1 tablespoon.

Lemon Cream: Use 1¼ cups water instead of the tea; use ½ cup chilled heavy cream (or lemon yogurt) instead of the orange juice; increase the (chilled) fresh lemon juice to ½ cup. When the mixture is semisolid, stir in 1 tablespoon grated lemon rind, then let it jell completely.

My kids and I also love what my grandma Donna called "Raspberry Bavarian." It's a teeny bit too pink, but that's its only flaw. Dissolve 1 package of cranberry Jell-O in 1 cup boiling water. Stir in 1 12-ounce bag of frozen unsweetened raspberries. You don't need to defrost them; just break them up. When the mixture is partially jelled—and that will happen pretty fast, since the berries are so cold—whip 1 cup heavy cream with 2 tablespoons sugar in a medium bowl and fold in the Jell-O mixture. Chill for another couple of hours and serve to 6 people.

Blue Brains

 **I Can't Believe
I'm Doing This**

So-called not because it makes children smart, but because it looks like a pile of brains on the plate. It does have plenty of protein, though.

> 1 6-ounce package Berry Blue Jell-O
> 1 16-ounce container small-curd cottage cheese
> ³/4 cup frozen blueberries, thawed and drained

Make the Jell-O according to the directions on the box. Chill it until it begins to set. Fold in the cottage cheese and blueberries and chill for another 3 hours. It really does look horrible.

Serves 4. Four kids, that is; I doubt any grown-ups will eat it.

Homemade Creamsicles

Why make them when you can buy them? Partly because it's nice to have some easy cooking projects in the summertime, and partly because it's nice to teach your children that even foods that scream "store-bought" can, in fact, be made from scratch. (Sort of, at least. You might want to warn the kids that these *taste* like store Creamsicles but don't *look* like them.) A good life lesson, in other words. Another good life lesson: patience. These have to chill for 12 hours to be firm enough to eat without melting all over the place.

1 3-ounce package orange-flavored Jell-O

1/4 cup sugar

1 cup boiling water

1 cup cold milk

1 cup orange-flavored yogurt

In a medium bowl, dissolve the Jell-O and sugar in the boiling water, stirring constantly for at least 2 minutes to make sure all those little crystals have melted. Stir in the milk. Refrigerate the mixture for 45 minutes to 1 hour, or until it's partially set.

Use an electric mixer to whip the mixture until fluffy. Beat in the yogurt. Pour the mixture into six plastic "frozen pop" holders or 5-ounce paper cups and freeze them for at least 12 hours, or until quite firm, before handing them out. (If you use the paper cups, insert wooden sticks or those flat wooden spoons into each pop when it's frozen enough to hold the stick upright.)

Makes six 5-ounce pops.

G.I. Joe-Sicles

 **I Can't Believe
I'm Doing This**

If you have any spare G.I. Joes or other small action figures lying around, boys love it when you freeze juice in paper cups with a G.I. Joe stuck upside down in each cup, so that the legs form a handle. We call these "G.I. Joe-Sicles" at my house.

Don't try this with Barbies: a) girls tend not to enjoy destroying their toys in this way, and b) the hair problem.

Another good G.I. Joe activity that's kind of food-related, in that it involves kitchen ingredients and is best done in a sink: Make a paste out of baking soda and water. Pat this all over a G.I. Joe. Catapult him into a bowl of vinegar (or, for a more Dr. No-ish touch, tie a string to him and *dip* him into the vinegar) and watch him hiss and foam. Hours of fun! And baking soda's cheap, and you can use up that old tarragon vinegar you bought for one recipe and never used again.

Should I make it clear that this is an activity for your kids, not you?

Better-than-My Chocolate Sauce

There's always room for one more chocolate sauce in the world. And my friend Ellen says this recipe is even better than the one I use. My daughter agrees.

> 8 ounces unsweetened chocolate (I use Ghirardelli), chopped
>
> 1 13- or 14-ounce can evaporated milk
>
> 8 tablespoons (1 stick) unsalted butter
>
> 1 pound confectioners' sugar (about 4 cups)
>
> 1 teaspoon vanilla
>
> A pinch of salt

Heat the chocolate, evaporated milk, and butter in the top of a large double boiler or in a small heavy pot over very low heat, stirring frequently, until everything is melted and the mixture is smooth. Whisk in the confectioners' sugar, vanilla, and salt. Remove the mixture from the heat and continue to whisk it until no lumps remain. Store the sauce in the refrigerator and reheat gently before using. On bad days, scoop out spoonfuls of it directly into your mouth.

Makes about 3 cups.

ALWAYS double the vanilla extract called for in a recipe. (A dessert recipe, that is.) Perhaps that's a risky recommendation. How do I know you're not using a recipe that calls for 1 cup of vanilla? But you're probably not. Anyway, I always double the vanilla, and it invariably improves whatever I'm making. Also, ALWAYS buy the best vanilla you can afford. I buy a quart of Nielsen-Massey Mexican vanilla extract every year or so, and into it I stick two Nielsen-Massey Bourbon vanilla beans, cut in half the long way. Honest to God, it only costs "pennies more per serving"— and considering how often most of us use vanilla, it's worth using the best available.

Caramel-Apple Fondue

The days of people getting several fondue pots as wedding presents were long past even before I got married twenty-one years ago. In *my* day, what we got millions of were woks. I don't know what the multiple gifts are now. Juicers, maybe, or espresso makers or bread machines.

But you probably have one fondue pot, and elsewhere in this book (page 180), I've suggested that you drag it out of the closet and dust it off. Once it's clean, you can also use it for this recipe. Then back into the closet goes the fondue pot for another decade or so.

Reassure your kids that the coffee won't make the fondue taste like coffee. (As if that would be so bad!) It just enriches the flavor.

  2 pounds caramels

  1 cup heavy cream

  1/4–1/2 teaspoon instant coffee crystals

  A pinch of salt

  1 teaspoon vanilla

  6–8 apples, cored and cut into wedges or chunks

Unwrap all those caramels—a task for your children if ever there was one. Put them into a double boiler over boiling water. In a separate pot, bring the cream to a boil with the instant coffee and salt; as soon as it reaches the boil, pour it over the caramels. Stirring frequently, melt the caramels and blend them thoroughly with the cream. Add the vanilla. Pour the fondue into a fondue pot (or just leave it in the double boiler) and serve with the apples.

Serves 6 to 8, depending on the size of the apple wedges you use; the leftovers can be refrigerated and remelted.

Toffee Shortbread

What's better than regular shortbread? Brown sugar short-bread. What's better than brown sugar shortbread? Shortbread with double the normal amount of sugar, so that it bakes into a caramely, crisp sheet that you cut into wedges and ration out, hiding a disproportionate quantity for yourself.

8 tablespoons (1 stick) unsalted butter

1 1/4 cups cake flour

1/2 cup brown sugar, packed

1/2 teaspoon vanilla

1/4 teaspoon salt

Preheat the oven to 350 degrees.

Melt the butter over low heat. Stirring constantly, heat it until it's a light caramel color. Then take it off the heat and *immediately* stir in the remaining ingredients.

Pat the mixture into an ungreased 8-inch round cake pan, making sure to spread it evenly. Bake for 20 minutes. While it is still hot, cut it into 12 wedges. Cool the pan on a wire rack. Then gently separate the shortbread into its 12 wedges.

Makes 1 dozen pieces.

Fudgies

Fudgies, says my friend Cindy Kane, "are the most wonderful food in the world." She must *really* think so, since she's sent me the recipe three times. It is pretty great, though, and not only that—it's also easy enough for children aged eight and up to make themselves. And, says Cindy, "it makes more than you'd think."

The only change I've made from her recipe is that I've substituted unsweetened chocolate for cocoa.

    4 cups sugar
    4 ounces unsweetened chocolate
    1 cup milk
    1 cup (2 sticks) unsalted butter
    A pinch of salt
    1 cup smooth peanut butter
    1 18-ounce container Quick Quaker Oats
    2 teaspoons vanilla

Bring the sugar, chocolate, milk, butter, and salt to a boil in a large, heavy saucepan, stirring frequently. Let the mixture boil for 2 minutes; take the saucepan off the heat.

Stir in the peanut butter, oats, and vanilla. "Mix swiftly but well," Cindy says. Drop from a teaspoon onto waxed paper. Let the Fudgies set for at least 1/2 hour before anyone touches them.

Makes about 4 dozen fudgies.

I think that M&Ms—stirred in after the peanut butter and oats have cooled the mixture slightly—would be even more kid-friendly. But maybe that's overkill.

Damn Decent Brownies

Why do they always spell it "dam'" in British mysteries, I wonder? "Thanks, old bean. That's dam' decent of you."

As with my oatmeal cookies, the all-time best of the best brownie recipe is in my first cookbook. But must you serve your kids the all-time best of the best recipe *every single time*? Do they do their all-time best of the best jobs cleaning their rooms every single time? Sometimes it's okay to serve B+ brownies—especially when, to many people, these would be an A. They're so far above "mix" brownies (and hardly any more trouble to make) that it's laughable. *Dam'* laughable.

3 ounces unsweetened chocolate (see Note, opposite)

8 tablespoons (1 stick) unsalted butter

2 large eggs

1 cup sugar

$\frac{1}{2}$ teaspoon salt

1 teaspoon vanilla

$\frac{1}{2}$ cup flour

1 cup chocolate chips

Preheat the oven to 350 degrees. Thoroughly butter an 8-inch square pan.

Begin to melt the chocolate and butter in a double boiler over simmering water. When they're half melted, turn off the heat and let them continue to melt over the gradually cooling water, stirring once in a while. Let them sit while you go on to the next step.

Beat the eggs, sugar, and salt in a large bowl with an electric mixer for 8 to 10 minutes, or until very thick and very pale. Beat in the vanilla. Fold in the slightly cooled chocolate

 ALWAYS remember that there are some simple ways to improve cake and brownie mixes:

· Add a teaspoon of vanilla to any kind of sweet mix.

· Add chocolate extract (available at Williams-Sonoma stores) to brownie mix; failing that, add 2 tablespoons of unsweetened cocoa. It should be mandatory for people to add chocolate chips to all brownie mixes. A cupful of chocolate chips is better than any of those little flavor packets or cans of syrup that come with some brownie mixes.

· Substitute orange juice for the water (especially in yellow and white cake mixes). Grated orange and lemon rind work well too.

· Use unsalted butter instead of oil.

· Put the dry mix into a food processor and grind up $\frac{1}{2}$ cup pecans or walnuts with it. Then put it into a bowl and follow the directions.

Alas, there's nothing you can do to improve canned frosting. The chocolate varieties are passable if you have nothing to compare them to, and very useful when you're making a gingerbread house (page 349); the other flavors all taste like poisoned cheese.

mixture, then fold in the flour and, last of all, the chocolate chips. Scrape the batter into the prepared pan.

Bake the brownies for 15 minutes. This is the correct amount of time, assuming your oven is accurate. (There is no doneness test for these brownies.) Cool them to room temperature on a wire rack; then chill them for at least 2 hours. Serve them very cold.

Makes 16 creamy—almost custardlike—brownies.

Note: Until a few years ago, you could find only two basic brands of unsweetened chocolate. Unfortunately, both of these brands taste like chalk. Now that Ghirardelli unsweetened chocolate is more widely available in stores, I strongly urge you to make the switch. If you can't find it, you can order a couple of brands of excellent unsweetened chocolate from the King Arthur catalog (page 22).

Mile-High Strawberry Squares

From my friend Laura Lloyd, mother of my goddaughter Sarah, this recipe combines a shortbread crust with a fluffy, light, pale-pink strawberry topping. I see no reason it wouldn't work with frozen raspberries just as well.

Crust

8 tablespoons (1 stick) unsalted butter, melted

1 cup flour

1/4 cup light brown sugar, packed

A pinch of salt

1/2 cup chopped almonds (optional)

Topping

1 10-ounce package frozen strawberries in syrup, thawed

3 large egg whites

1 cup sugar

1 tablespoon fresh lemon juice, or to taste

A pinch of salt

1 cup heavy cream, whipped to soft peaks

Preheat the oven to 400 degrees. Grease a 9-x-13-inch pan.

For the crust: Stir together the melted butter, flour, brown sugar, and salt in a medium bowl. Stir in the almonds, if using. Pat the mixture into the greased pan and bake for 10 to 12 minutes, or until it's lightly browned. Cool the crust thoroughly. Then take it out of the pan, crumble it all up, and pat it back into the pan.

For the topping: Beat together the thawed strawberries, egg whites, sugar, lemon juice, and salt in a large bowl with an electric mixer for 15 minutes. You need to incorporate a *lot* of air into the mixture to get it "mile-high." After 15 minutes or so of hard beating, it should be very thick, almost like Marshmallow Fluff, and a very, very pale pink. Fold in the whipped cream. Spread the topping over the crust and freeze it for at least 6 hours, or overnight.

Makes one 9-x-13-inch pan, which you may cut into as many squares as you want.

Lime Cheesecake Bars

I'm including this recipe not only because it's very good but because it embodies two crucial Ann Hodgman philosophies. One: ground oats make a substitute for nuts that most children will accept. Two: almost all cheesecake recipes work better as bars. I rarely make regular cheesecake anymore; it's just so *massive*. I'd much rather eat it in a nice flat bar where the ratio of crust to squishiness is better and you don't need a fork.

Crust

1 cup flour

1/2 cup old-fashioned rolled oats

1/3 cup light brown sugar, packed

1/2 teaspoon vanilla

A pinch of salt

6 tablespoons (3/4 stick) unsalted butter, chilled and cut into 6 slices

Topping

1 8-ounce package cream cheese, at room temperature

1/3 cup sugar

1 tablespoon grated lime rind

3 tablespoons fresh lime juice

1 large egg

1 teaspoon vanilla

A pinch of salt

If you have to give a dog a pill, **ALWAYS** hide the pill in cream cheese. It's much harder for a dog to lick cream cheese off a pill than butter. If you let him lick your fingers after giving him the pill, you can be sure he's swallowed it. Dogs aren't as smart as children about hiding food in their cheeks.

Preheat the oven to 350 degrees. Grease a 9-inch square pan well or line it with parchment paper.

For the crust: Process the flour and rolled oats in a food processor into a fine powder. Add the brown sugar, vanilla, and salt and pulse a few times until they're incorporated. Scatter the butter slices over the processed ingredients and pulse until the mixture has the texture of coarse meal. Pat the crust into the prepared pan, reserving 2 tablespoons to use as a garnish.

Bake the crust for 15 minutes. Let it cool on a rack while you prepare the topping. Wipe out the food processor bowl with a paper towel; there's no need to wash it.

For the topping: Process all the topping ingredients until smooth. Pour/scrape the mixture onto the semibaked crust. Sprinkle the reserved crust mixture evenly over the top. Bake for about 25 minutes, or until the topping is beginning to puff and turn golden around the edges. Cool the bars completely in the pan, then refrigerate for at least 4 hours.

Makes 2 dozen bars, which should be served chilled.

Better Rice Krispies Treats

 **I Can't Believe
I'm Doing This**

You're only hurting yourself if you don't make your Rice Krispies Treats with actual Kellogg's "Rice Krispies Treats"–flavored cereal instead of plain old Rice Krispies. And while you're at it, the bars will be a lot better if you also use less cereal than in the standard recipe. The "treat" in Rice Krispies Treats is the marshmallow part, not the crisp part.

Oh, aaaaaaall riiiiiiiight, here's the recipe—for the *kids*, for the *kids*, I'm not giving it to *you*.

1/4 cup (1/2 stick) unsalted butter

5 cups miniature marshmallows

4 cups Kellogg's Rice Krispies Treats cereal

M&Ms (optional)

Grease a 9-x-13-inch pan.

Melt the butter and marshmallows together in a large saucepan over very low heat, stirring frequently. When they're smooth, stir in the cereal. Butter your hands and press the mixture into the prepared pan. Why not go ahead and press a few M&Ms on top while you're at it? Cool completely and cut into bars.

Makes one 9-x-13-inch pan.

Pecan Crispies

Somehow, Pecan Crispies taste like more than the sum of their rather basic ingredients. I first tasted them at a New Year's Eve party the year we moved to the town where we live. That's one memory from the party. The other is that I introduced myself to a cranky old lady who said, "Another writer from New York? That's the last thing this town needs!" And it was a party at a *church!* But I did come away with this recipe, so everything turned out fine.

> 2 "packs" graham crackers, broken into individual sections
> 1 cup pecan halves (you may not need them all)
> 1 cup (2 sticks) unsalted butter
> 1/2 cup sugar
> 1/4 cup light brown sugar, packed
> A pinch of salt

Preheat the oven to 350 degrees. Line a 10-x-17-inch jelly-roll pan with foil and grease the foil. Or you can use baking parchment. But line it with one of these two.

Cover the pan with the graham crackers and put a pecan half on each section.

Combine the butter, sugars, and salt in a heavy saucepan. Stirring constantly, bring them to a rolling boil. Spoon the syrup over the crackers—first onto the nuts, to sort of glue them down, and then onto the remainder of each cracker.

Bake for 10 minutes, or until browned and bubbly. Quickly lift the crackers off the pan with a spatula and place them on waxed paper to cool.

Makes 7 to 8 dozen crispies.

Honest to God, the BEST Peanut Butter Cookies, I Swear

I've gone on and on about my chocolate chip cookies for long enough. From now on, I'm only going to talk about these (and perhaps the oatmeal cookies on page 302). You'll notice that there's no flour in them. That's correct—and it's probably why they're so great.

There's another flourless peanut butter cookie recipe floating around out there—one in which you fold the peanut butter into some meringue and make "kiss"-shaped cookies. That one is *paltry* compared to this.

2 cups creamy peanut butter

2 cups sugar

2 large eggs

2 teaspoons baking soda

A pinch of salt

1 teaspoon vanilla

Preheat the oven to 350 degrees. Grease two cookie sheets or cover them with parchment paper.

Beat the peanut butter and sugar in a medium bowl with an electric mixer until fluffy. Beat in the eggs and then the baking soda, salt, and vanilla.

Roll the dough into 1-inch balls and place them 2 inches apart on the cookie sheets. With the tines of a fork, press crosshatches into the balls to flatten them.

Bake the cookies, one sheet at a time, in the middle of the oven, for 10 minutes, or until they're puffy and golden brown. Let them sit on the cookie sheets for a couple of minutes; then transfer them to a wire rack to cool.

Makes 3 to 4 dozen cookies.

Aggression Cookies

"Safer than tranquilizers," says the headnote over this recipe in my daughter's preschool cookbook. This is one recipe you should really let your children make.

3 cups old-fashioned rolled oats

1½ cups light brown sugar, packed

1½ cups flour

1½ cups (3 sticks) unsalted butter, at room temperature

1½ teaspoons baking powder

¼ teaspoon nutmeg

A pinch of salt

Preheat the oven to 350 degrees.

Make sure you've washed your hands first! Dump all the ingredients into a large bowl. Mash it! Knead it! Pound it! Flatten it! The longer and harder you mix the dough, the better the cookies will taste!

Roll the dough into 1-inch balls—it spreads—and place them 3 inches apart on ungreased cookie sheets. Bake for 10 to 12 minutes, or until the cookies are nicely browned. *You* take them off the cookie sheets. An "aggressive" touch would break them; they're more fragile once baked than you'd expect.

Makes 4 to 5 dozen cookies.

Honest to God, the Second-Best Oatmeal Cookies, I Swear

Because I have to be really honest: the all-time best oatmeal cookies are in my first cookbook. On the other hand, these are an *extremely* close second—and they take only half as long to put together. Fifty percent of the work for 85 percent of the results? I think that's a pretty good ratio.

1 cup (2 sticks) unsalted butter, at room temperature

1 cup sugar

1 cup light brown sugar, packed

2 large eggs

1 teaspoon vanilla

1 1/2 cups flour

1 teaspoon baking soda

1 teaspoon cinnamon

1/2 teaspoon salt

1/4 teaspoon nutmeg

3 cups old-fashioned rolled oats

1 1/2 cups raisins, dried cranberries (better), or dried
    cherries (best)

Preheat the oven to 350 degrees. Grease two cookie sheets or cover them with parchment paper.

Beat the butter and sugars together in a large bowl with an electric mixer. Add the eggs and vanilla and beat well. Add the flour, baking soda, cinnamon, salt, and nutmeg; beat thoroughly. Add the oats and raisins; beat slowly or stir by hand until all is evenly mixed.

With wet hands, roll the dough into 1-inch balls and place them 2 inches apart on the cookie sheets. Bake for 10 to 12 minutes, or until the cookies are golden brown around the edges. Let them set for 1 minute before you transfer them to a wire rack.

Makes about 4 dozen cookies.

 It Happens To Everyone

We were serving chocolate chip cookies to my family and to a four-year-old friend of my older daughter. When we finished, we were puzzled to see an odd pile of leftovers on the friend's plate. This always-picky eater revealed, on questioning, that she liked chocolate chip cookies but did not like the "crust." She had somehow consumed only the interior.

—Nicholas Christenfeld

Butter-and-Sugar Cookies

I t's not possible to praise these enough.

1 cup (2 sticks) unsalted butter, at room temperature

1 cup sugar

1 large egg

1 teaspoon vanilla

2 cups flour

1/4 teaspoon salt

Sugar and water, for glaze

Put a rack in the middle of the oven. Preheat the oven to 350 degrees. Grease two cookie sheets or cover them with parchment paper.

Beat the butter and sugar together in a large bowl with an electric mixer until light and fluffy. Beat in the egg and vanilla, then the flour and salt.

With wet hands, roll the dough into 1-inch balls and space them 3 inches apart on the cookie sheets. Fill one small bowl with sugar, and another with water. Somewhere, track down a flat-bottomed drinking glass or cup.

Dip the cup first into the water, and then into the sugar; then press down each ball of dough until it's about 1/8 inch thick. This isn't as easy as it sounds, but keep plugging along. Re-dip the glass as often as you need to, and don't get discouraged if the sugar in the bowl gets so gloppy that you have to get a new bowlful.

Bake the cookies, one sheet at a time, for 8 to 10 minutes, or until pale gold. Reverse the sheet from back to front halfway through the baking. If the cookies have been baked on parchment, you can let them cool right on the sheets. If you haven't used the parchment, you should remove them to a wire rack right away.

Chewy Chocolate Meringue Cookies

T his recipe comes from my aunt Gail, who understands about desserts. I've made it for thirty years. When you serve the cookies to friends, you might as well have copies of the recipe to pass out; everyone will want it.

4 large egg whites, at room temperature

1/4 teaspoon salt

1 cup sugar (superfine works best)

2 teaspoons vanilla

1 12-ounce package chocolate chips, melted and cooled
   to lukewarm

Preheat the oven to 350 degrees. Line two cookie sheets
parchment paper or greased foil—you'll want to shoot y
if the cookies stick, and they *will* stick if you don't
cookie sheets.

Beat the egg whites with the salt in a medium bow
electric mixer until they hold stiff peaks. Continue
you add the sugar 1 tablespoon at a time. Beat in th

Fold the cooled chocolate into the meringue mi
but well. Drop the batter by the tablespoonful, 2
onto the prepared cookie sheets. Bake the cooki
utes. (There's no test for doneness; you just
them.) Cool them for 3 minutes if you're usin
fully transfer them to a wire rack. If you're
paper, it's okay to let the cookies cool
removing them.

Makes about 3 dozen cookies.

Tiparillos

Do children know what a Tiparillo is? Explaining will give you a few seconds of civilized dinner-table conversation.

This is a good recipe that children will enjoy helping you with, and they'll also like flourishing their "cigarettes" at the dinner table.

If you're worried that this recipe glorifies smoking, call it "Sticks" and tell the kids to pretend they're beavers.

1 cup demerara or other large-crystalled sugar (available in the baking section of most supermarkets)

¹/₄ teaspoon cinnamon

16 sheets filo dough (read the defrosting directions on the box very carefully)

10 tablespoons (1¹/₄ sticks) unsalted butter, melted

Preheat the oven to 350 degrees. Cover a cookie sheet with parchment paper. (Don't skip the paper, or there will be weeping and gnashing of teeth later.) Toss together the demerara sugar and cinnamon in a small bowl.

One at a time, KEEPING THE UNUSED SHEETS *COVERED*, brush each sheet of filo with melted butter and sprinkle evenly with about 2 teaspoons of the sugar mixture. Then *tightly and firmly*, working from a long side, roll up the filo into a long Tiparillo and set it on the cookie sheet. Brush the top of the Tiparillo with more melted butter and sprinkle on a little more sugar from one end to the other. Don't just idly sprinkle sugar in the middle of the roll and forget about the ends. They're the first thing people will be biting into!

Bake the Tiparillos for 15 minutes, or until crisp and brown. Don't lift them off the parchment until they're completely cool.

Makes 16 long, long cookies, which should be eaten the day they're baked.

It Happens To Everyone

I've always tried to cook creatively, and our daughter Krissy was always happy to try what I made. One year I asked her what kind of cake she wanted for her birthday. "I want an ice cream cake," she told me.

So I went to my cookbooks and found a recipe for a mocha ice cream cake. I had never put that much time and care into a cake before, and I was quite proud of this beautiful pièce de resistance. I brought it to the table expecting oohs and aahs. What I got was, "I meant a *Carvel* ice cream cake!"

That was Krissy's last homemade birthday cake.

—Kristina Creighton

Killer Cupcakes

as I always say, cupcakes are the kneesocks of the dessert world. There's nothing exciting about them, except to kids. These lava-centered marvels, however, are another story. You can't frost them, but believe me—frosting would be excessive. A little whipped cream would be fine, though.

  8 tablespoons (1 stick) unsalted butter

  4 ounces semisweet chocolate

  2 large eggs

  2 large egg yolks

  1/4 cup sugar (superfine works best)

  A pinch of salt

  1 teaspoon vanilla

  1 tablespoon flour

  Whipped cream for topping (optional, but not really)

Preheat the oven to 450 degrees. Lavishly butter and flour four custard cups or ramekins.

Melt the butter and chocolate in a double boiler over simmering water. When it's about half melted, turn off the heat and let it continue melting. Meanwhile, beat the eggs, egg yolks, sugar, and salt in a large bowl with an electric mixer until they're thick and light. Beat in the vanilla.

Stir the chocolate and butter together thoroughly. Gently fold them into the egg mixture, then quickly fold in the flour. Spoon the batter into the custard cups. Put the custard cups onto a cookie sheet and bake them for 12 minutes. (They won't look done, but they are.)

Wearing oven mitts, upend each custard cup onto a serving plate and count slowly to 10. Then carefully lift up the cup and let the cake slide out. Serve the cupcakes with whipped cream, if desired.

Serves 4.

Mud Puddle Cake

I doubt it's legal to write a cookbook for children without including this recipe, which is amazingly good considering its humble messiness and the fact that it has cocoa in it instead of chocolate—usually a sign of weakness in a dessert. You really do make it in the pan, it really works, and kids really can make it themselves with hardly any help from you except for cleaning up the half-gallon of vegetable oil they accidentally pour into the stovetop.

1 1/2 cups flour

1 cup sugar

1/4 cup cocoa (I use Dutch-process)

1 teaspoon baking soda

1/2 teaspoon salt

6 tablespoons vegetable oil

1 tablespoon cider vinegar or distilled white vinegar (I
  suppose you could also use raspberry vinegar if you
  want to get fancy)

1 teaspoon vanilla

1 cup cold water

Preheat the oven to 350 degrees. Grease and flour an 8-inch square baking pan, tapping out the excess flour.

Sift the flour, sugar, cocoa, baking soda, and salt directly into the pan. Stir these ingredients with a fork to blend them. Use the back of a spoon to make three evenly spaced wells in the dry ingredient mixture. Pour the vegetable oil into the first hole, the vinegar into the second, and the vanilla into the third. Pour the water carefully and as evenly as possible over the whole thing. Use your fork to mix everything together vigorously and thoroughly. Get the fork into all the corners.

There are no egg whites or anything to deflate in this batter, so you can stir long and hard if you need to.

Bake the cake for 35 to 40 minutes, or until it just begins to shrink from the sides of the pan. Cool thoroughly in the pan. When cool, frost as desired, or simply sprinkle powdered sugar on top.

Makes one 8-inch square cake.

 ### It Happens To Everyone

When I was five, my family went on vacation to a cabin on a lake. One day, my mom bought some fresh boysenberries and started making a pie. My sister told me Mom was making a poison-berry pie. It didn't matter how many times my parents told me otherwise, or that I could see them eating and enjoying the pie—once I'd made up my mind that I wasn't having any, there was no way I could back down.
—Rob Zacharias

Fudge Pie

This recipe comes from our family friend Anne Lombard, and a child aged eight or so can easily make it. My parents chose the Lombards to be guardians for me and my siblings if anything, you know, *happened*. I knew we'd be safe with the Lombards because once when my sister and I went to visit them for a few days, Anne got us Kentucky Fried Chicken for lunch.

When my mom faxed me this recipe, she noted that the original called for ¹/₂ cup pecans, "which I never add and never will." AGREED!

  8 tablespoons (1 stick) unsalted butter

  2 ounces unsweetened chocolate

  2 large eggs

  1 cup sugar

  ¹/₄ cup flour

  A pinch of salt

  1 teaspoon vanilla

Preheat the oven to 325 degrees. Grease a 9-inch pie pan.

Melt the butter and chocolate in a double boiler over simmering water, stirring occasionally. When they're half melted, take them off the heat and let them melt the rest of the way unheated. (Melted chocolate and butter should be lukewarm or cooler when other ingredients are added to them.)

Add the eggs one at a time, beating well after each one is added. Add the sugar and beat well; then fold in the flour, salt, and vanilla.

Pour/scrape the mixture into the pie pan and bake for 15 to 18 minutes, or until a toothpick stuck into the center comes out damp and brown but not sticky and butter-covered. Serve with what Mum calls "something white"—whipped cream, ice cream, or just a big dollop of lard if that's your preference.

Serves 6.

Pear-Cranberry Crumble

I sometimes add dried apricots to this, but not often. That's because once, when I braggingly asked my daughter, "Didn't you like the pear crumble better with those dried apricots?" she looked at me in amazement. "Mom," she said, "they ruined it."

No, they didn't.

2 teaspoons sugar

1 teaspoon cinnamon

1/4 teaspoon nutmeg

3 1/2 cups peeled, cored, and sliced pears

1 cup dried cranberries

1/2 cup chopped dried apricots (optional)

1 tablespoon fresh lemon juice

1 cup dark brown sugar, packed

3/4 cup flour

8 tablespoons (1 stick) unsalted butter, at room temperature

A pinch of salt

Preheat the oven to 375 degrees. Butter a 9-x-5-inch loaf pan.

Combine the sugar, cinnamon, and nutmeg in a small cup. In a large bowl, toss together the fruits with the lemon juice and the cinnamon mixture.

In a small bowl, blend the brown sugar, flour, butter, and salt together—first with a pastry blender or two knives, and then with your hands. Put the fruit mixture into the loaf pan and pack the brown-sugar topping down over it.

Bake for 1 hour, until the fruit is tender and the topping is nicely browned. Serve hot or cold, with vanilla ice cream or whipped cream.

Serves 4 to 6. Leftovers are great for breakfast.

Two Excellent Things to Do with Chocolate Pudding Mix

 **I Can't Believe
I'm Doing This**

For *good* chocolate pudding, turn to page 316. For *useful* chocolate pudding, stay right here. Both of these "techniques" use the same "recipe."

    1 3-ounce box instant chocolate pudding mix

    3 cups cold milk

In a medium bowl, mix the, uh, mix and the milk with an egg beater, whisk, or electric, uh, mixer until smooth.

For homemade "pudding pops," freeze the mixture in 12 plastic "frozen pop" makers or 5-ounce paper cups. If you use the paper cups, insert a wooden stick or flat wooden spoon into each pop as soon as it's frozen firm enough to hold the stick upright. Freeze the pops for at least 12 hours, to make sure they're really firm.

Try to keep your kids outside while they eat these; they're good, but the dripping is formidable.

Makes 1 dozen pops.

For homemade pudding-paint, cover every surface in your house with plastic wrap. Cover the children with smocks—or better yet, strip them down to their underpants or diapers. Give them big sheets of paper and let them finger-paint with the pudding mixture. If you've used chocolate pudding mix, you won't want to add food coloring; if you used vanilla instead, you might. If the kids are young enough, they won't care.

This project will require a superhuman amount of tolerance on your part, but your kids will never forget it. You might even invite a few extra kids into the house for this project, so as to bolster your neighborhood rep as a super-parent.

Three Real Puddings (not the boxed, chalky kind)

For heaven's sake, let's bring real puddings back to family dinners. They're not easy to make; the amount of effort they require equals that of, say, a from-scratch cake; but boy, are they worth it.

Unless you're my husband, who hates puddings and mousses and soft stuff like that. (Although, for some reason, he loves the Corn Pudding on page 244.) But you aren't my husband, are you? Because if you are, I hate to think who's typing away in the next office.

We'll start with the hardest one first.

REAL Butterscotch Pudding

6 large egg yolks

2 cups (yes!) heavy (yes!) cream

1 cup milk

1/4 cup dark brown sugar, packed

1/2 teaspoon salt

3/4 cup sugar (superfine works best)

1/4 cup water

1 teaspoon vanilla

Preheat the oven to 300 degrees. Have 6 custard cups or ramekins ready.

Put the yolks in a large bowl and beat them until they're well combined. Set aside.

Whisk together the cream, milk, brown sugar, and salt in a medium saucepan over medium heat. As soon as the mixture reaches a boil, remove it from the heat.

Now, in another saucepan, stir together the sugar and water. Over *low* heat, stirring *constantly*, cook until the sugar has dissolved; this may take up to 10 minutes, so be prepared. When the sugar's all dissolved, turn the heat up high and cook the syrup, still stirring constantly, until it's golden brown. (About the color of an imported beer, is how I like to think of it. Not a Guinness—just a nice medium amber ale.)

As soon as the syrup (which is now called a "caramel") is the right color, take it off the heat and stir in the hot cream-milk mixture. There will be a terrible hissing and bubbling, and the caramel may well clump up. Don't worry; it's going to be okay. Keep stirring until all the liquid has been added. If the caramel stays clumpy and hard, put the saucepan over low heat and stir for a few more minutes until everything's smooth again.

Pour a little dollop—say, ¼ cup—of the hot milk-caramel mixture into the eggs. Whisk well. Then, whisking constantly, add the rest of the liquid to the eggs. Stir in the vanilla.

Are you getting tired? It's almost over. Pour the mixture through a fine strainer into the custard cups or ramekins. (You *do* have to strain it, or little gross bits of egg will end up in the pudding.) Put the custard cups into a large roasting pan, and put the pan into the oven. Pour enough boiling water into the big pan—around, NOT INTO, the cups—to come halfway up the sides of the cups. Drape a sheet of aluminum foil over the pan.

Bake the puddings for 50 minutes, or until they are almost set. Carefully remove them from their hot bath and put them right into the refrigerator. Chill for at least 6 hours, or overnight.

Serves 6.

REAL Chocolate Pudding

1 3-ounce bar Lindt or Tobler bittersweet chocolate

1 cup heavy cream

2/3 cup plus 2 tablespoons milk, divided

2 teaspoons cornstarch

3 large egg yolks

1/3 cup sugar

A pinch of salt

1 tablespoon unsalted butter

1 teaspoon vanilla

Whipped cream for topping (optional, but why not go the distance?)

Chop the chocolate as fine as your patience permits.

Scald the cream and 2/3 cup of the milk in a medium, heavy saucepan over low heat. (Tiny bubbles will appear at the edge of the liquid, but the mixture shouldn't boil.) This may take up to 5 minutes.

While the cream and milk heat, stir together the cornstarch and the remaining 2 tablespoons milk in a small bowl. Beat the egg yolks, sugar, and salt in a medium bowl with an electric mixer or eggbeater until the mixture is light.

Now switch to a whisk. Whisking constantly, slowly add half the hot cream mixture to the egg yolks. Still whisking constantly, add the egg-cream mixture to the rest of the cream in the saucepan. Whisk in the cornstarch mixture. Bring to a full boil, whisking constantly. STILL whisking, boil it for 1 minute, or until it heavily coats a wooden spoon. Take the saucepan off the heat (and turn off the stove too).

Add the chopped chocolate, butter, and vanilla to the saucepan. Stir until the chocolate is melted and the mixture is

**I Can't Believe
I'm Doing This**

Homemade Silly Putty

You've always wondered how to make your own Silly Putty, I'm sure. What you need is Elmer's or other white glue and Sta-Flo liquid starch. In a bowl that you don't care if you ever use again, using measuring cups that you don't care if you ever *see* again, mix 1 cup of glue and ½ cup Sta-Flo with your hands until you have a thick, smooth, rubbery glop. I think this is really too messy for preschoolers to do themselves, but I'll leave that up to you.

Let the mixture dry, uncovered, for an hour or two, until it's not sticky anymore. (You can spend that time getting glue out of the prongs of your engagement ring.) It will keep its Silly Putty–ish qualities for a week or so if you store it airtight.

By the way, this Silly Putty isn't edible.

smooth. Strain it through a sieve (you have to do this, or the pudding will have gross curd-y bits) into a bowl. Refrigerate for at least 4 hours, or overnight. Serve with whipped cream, if desired.

Serves 6.

REAL Vanilla Pudding

Do everything I said to do in the Chocolate Pudding recipe, with the following changes: Omit the chocolate. Use 4 teaspoons cornstarch instead of 2, and 2 tablespoons (¼ stick) unsalted butter instead of 1.

This, too, serves 6.

"Oh, My God, It's Christmas Again!" —and Other Holiday Woes

The Recipes

My central holiday philosophy is: once a year is too often.

I love holidays. I do. And yet they always induce the same feeling I have when a bat gets loose in my house, or a visiting child throws up on the floor. *Where are the grownups who are supposed to be running this show? Why do I have to take care of things all by myself?*

Every time I turn around, it seems, I'm having to make some kind of holiday decision. Whether I'll really go for it and polish the silver for the first time in fifteen years. Whether there's going to be time for me to take a shower before The Big Dinner so that I can change out of the sweats I've been wearing for the last two days while I cooked. Whether we *have* to eat in the dining room, and if we do, where's the cover for the pool table? (We used our old dining room table so rarely that we finally decided it made more sense to replace it with a pool table. Now the room gets used more, but eating in it requires some adjustments. Our dining room chairs need extra-high cushions, for instance, and the table's massive sides deflect you from your plate.)

Most of all, I have to decide how to balance the amount of work I'll be doing with the amount of fun I'll be having.

No matter how much fun the holidays are, they're

work. Part of this is simply that they involve so many changes in routine; part is that—not to get too obvious here—the increasing commercial focus on holidays tends to make everyone's expectations rise beyond what they can handle. But the hardest holiday work is emotional. Generally, whoever does the holiday cooking in a family also worries the most about *pulling it all off*. This is especially true when there are children lurking in the background. Can you involve the younger members of the family without irritating the older ones? Can you provide food that is simultaneously traditional, easy, festive, and so delicious that you don't have to trick anyone into eating it? Can you make things perfect for everyone else without shedding tears of rage and exhaustion at the end of the day, as you stare at a sink clogged with turkey grease?

For many of us, of course, Christmas is the worst offender. And it's not enough to say—as so many husbands and other "concerned" adults do say—"Yes, but we'd all enjoy the day more if *you* were more relaxed." This is only true up to a point. You'd be plenty relaxed if you spent Christmas Day lying on the sofa eating candy and reading mysteries. But it wouldn't be much of a Christmas for anyone else.

And what about the nonmajor holidays, ones you don't

really care about all that much but feel you should honor in some way? The Fourth of July, for instance? When I was a child, this was a semi-important day in our family, one on which we always had a traditional New England meal: poached salmon, green peas, and blueberry pie. When I grew up, I dutifully endeavored to produce the same meal, although poached fish has never much interested me. Then the kids came along, and they *really* found the salmon uninspiring. So I switched to another Fourth of July classic, fried chicken. Only: why is fried chicken a Fourth of July classic? Did the Founding Fathers really intend us to stand over a hot, spitting skillet on a summer afternoon? Even if they did—and I wouldn't put it past a couple of them—do we have to pay attention?

. . . At this point, I suppose it would make sense for me to say that there's no solution to holidays. But that's only partly true. The solution lies in making yourself believe that holidays have to be fun for you as well as for other people.

That's not as easy as it sounds—if it even sounds easy. It means that *every single time* you begin to dust off *every single holiday tradition,* you need to ask yourself, "Do I want to be doing this, or am I doing it because I think I should?" And any time you only think you should, you probably shouldn't.

I have a genetic predisposition for frantically cleaning up the house whenever a holiday is coming—even if no one is coming to spend it with us. Okay, not for Arbor Day; but for a lot of the others, my built-in assumption is that I can't enjoy the day until the house is perfect. This means that I tend to do more and more rushing around the closer the holiday approaches: how can the fun start until everything is picked up? At one point I got so I couldn't even relax until all the pets' cages were cleaned—and I just don't think a clean cage made that much difference to the parakeets' enjoyment of the festivities.

This attitude might make some sense if I enjoyed cleaning up, as Anne of Green Gables always seemed to. In *Anne of Windy Poplars,* she says, in her dreamy way, "It's fun to make dirty things clean and shining again." Never mind that the woman she says it to (Nora Nelson, who reminds Anne of a "black moth") snaps back, "Oh, you ought to be in a museum." For most of my adult life—*until I was forty-one*—I reminded myself of Anne's little quote at every holiday. Only very recently have I realized that Anne of Green Gables is not a real person, and—well, okay. To me, she is a real person, but that still doesn't mean I have to be like her. If I liked making dirty things clean and shining again, I wouldn't need to do it so often, would I?

 **It Happens
To Everyone**

When our son Charlie Will was nineteen months old, we took him to London for two weeks. When my wife, Alex's, grandfather died midvacation, she had to leave early to fly all the way from London to Los Angeles with Charlie. She got one seat on a jam-packed flight full of holiday vacationers and left London in such a rush that she forgot to bring a change of clothes for Charlie. Early in the fourteen-hour flight, Charlie ate the in-flight meal, and you can guess what happened. It went all over him, all over Alex, onto the seat, onto the armrests, and onto the floor. Alex had no choice but to take her sweater and all of Charlie's clothes off.

She put her damp T-shirt on Charlie and sat in the middle of her row, wearing only her pants and exercise bra. A flight attendant finally offered her a T-shirt. The other passengers were so enraged by the smell that the flight attendants made Alex stand in the aisle while they rubbed coffee grounds into the wet seat, carpet, and armrests. She and little, sick Charlie had to sit amid coffee grounds for the next ten hours.

—Bill Sorenson

So essentially I was spending the bulk of the major holidays cleaning up the house and putting laundry away—two jobs I shun at any other time of year. I put it to you, people of the jury, that doing something you hate is a terrible way to get ready for a holiday. Even if it troubles your conscience to leave the task undone.

If you're like me, and you find yourself starting to tense up and race around automatically on the holidays, I cannot recommend the book *Unplug the Christmas Machine* highly enough. This book (by Jo Robinson and Jean Coppock Staeheli; published by Morrow) is in about its eleven-millionth printing, partly because of me. I never have fewer than three copies on hand, in case I need to pass one out. One year, I bought nine. Even if you don't celebrate Christmas, you should own it; it's a great blueprint for, as the authors say, "putting love and joy back into the season." Any season. Any holiday. Any *day*. At some point, if you read the book enough, you may even find yourself learning to unplug your *whole life*.

HOW-ever! Let's get back to the food.

For years I thought every holiday had to have perfect food to match the date. I do love cooking, so this wasn't quite as much of an emotional reach for me as cleaning up. But inevitably I found that the more perfect I tried to make the food, the less time I had to spend the holiday with my children. When I found myself wanting to scream, "I'm doing this for *you*!" as I baked the nine-millionth batch of Christmas cookies that my kids didn't want, I realized that even my holiday cooking was out of hand.

So I'm not giving you lots and lots of cooking ideas in this chapter—just a few that have withstood the test of time, my hysterical personality, and my children's desire not to have the holidays pass entirely unmarked. (As my friend Lisa Lasagna says, "Keep things simple, but not too simple.") I'm also suggesting a few traditions—again, just a few, and they're *easy*—that we've had fun with.

I'm very sorry that these suggestions aren't more multicultural. My family's holidays are pretty white-bread. Luckily, things like the Fourth of July and April Fool's Day can be dreaded by *all*.

Birthday Parties

I'm only making suggestions for the preschool set here. Past that, your children will instruct you as to where the party should be held and how many game tokens each guest should get.

Let me say right off that a piñata is a bad idea at a birthday party. First of all, my son was standing directly under the piñata at his third birthday party, and all the candy came crashing down onto his head. Also, children tend to trample each other to death in their mad rush to grab as much as they can. (This is especially true for children who don't get enough candy in their day-to-day lives.) And somehow it always ends up that when all the trampling is done, one poor little slug has half an opened pack of off-brand Necco wafers when everyone else has several pounds of Milk Duds and Twix bars.

The only way to have a piñata that's fair to everyone is to fill it with individually wrapped bags, one for each child. And no matter how sternly you explain to the kids that they must take only the bag with their name on it, they're still going to get frantic, and some of the bags will get broken, and—as grandmothers always seem to say—it will end in tears. So I'm afraid you have to do without a piñata. What else is there?

Thank God this isn't a party handbook, so I don't have to answer that question. But the main challenge at any birthday party is filling up the time until the parents come to take their children away. For this reason, it always makes sense to include a meal in the party. What do parents do at those two-hour afternoon extravaganzas in their backyards? A meal can kill *a whole half-hour*!

And you can make it take even longer than that if you give each child her own pita and have them make their own pizzas. All you need besides the pitas is pizza sauce (the kind that comes in a squeeze jar will be neater) and various toppings. Have the oven preheated to 400 degrees before the party starts—otherwise, you might forget all about it—and line sev-

**It Happens
To Everyone**

On my birthday, I always asked to have liver and beets, because that was what my brother Chuck hated the most.

—Joanna Hodgman

eral cookie sheets with foil or parchment paper. As each guest finishes making her pita pizza, put it on the cookie sheet and *write her initials next to it.* (You can write on foil with a pencil or a Sharpie marker.) This is a key step, since all those little cheese and pepperoni faces will look different—even to their creators—after they've been baked.

If you want to make the meal take even longer and be even messier and even more fun, you can also give each guest his own unfrosted cupcake and a pile of frosting to spread on it. (The birthday child gets an unfrosted cupcake with candles in it.) On the table, put millions of little bowls filled with sprinkles and gumdrops and M&Ms and other cupcake decorations. Be as lavish as you can here, because this is one party activity that really thrills kids. Have lots of wet paper towels ready toward the end, for cleaning off the guests' hands and faces before they go on to their next activity. And make sure the table isn't standing on your favorite rug.

Keep the dog out of the way too. If you've invited really small children, it might even make sense to board the dog somewhere else for the day—for both the dog's sake and your guests'.

 **It Happens
To Everyone**

I hated *all* food when I was little. On my birthday, when I was allowed to pick whatever meal I wanted, I always asked to have an empty plate while the rest of my family ate.

—Patty Marx

New Year's Eve

. . . is traditionally known as "The Worst Eve of the Year" and "The Hardest Night to Get Babysitters For." I assume you've learned by now that New Year's Eve parties are always terrible, and that it's useless to make New Year's resolutions. Resolve that you'll never make them again.

Instead, write predictions for the coming year with your children. Everyone gets a piece of paper and a pencil and writes down a few things they expect to happen. Real examples from our family—all of which, oddly enough, came true:

"We will own at least two more pets."

"I will get my handicap down to 8."

"On *ER*, Carol and Doug will get into a fight, then make up. Carol will be pregnant."

Everyone reads them aloud. Then I put them into a box and save them until the next New Year's Eve, when we read them again and write some more.

New Year's Day is a better time to have eggnog than Christmas—it's just as festive, and it gives you one less thing to do in December. The following recipe was sent to me by a reader named George Love. His children are frighteningly good eaters, so I couldn't use his food recipes in this book—but even children will love his eggnog.

George Love's Eggnog

"**T**ruth to tell," George wrote when he sent me this recipe, "this is the recipe that I expect to knock your socks off. It's entirely my own creation and I've never seen anything like it in a cookbook. Try it once and you'll toss out whatever recipe you've been using until now."

Not quite, because the recipe I'd been using was in a book, and I didn't feel like throwing away the book or even tearing out the eggnog page. But everything else he said is true.

In this recipe you cook the eggs, so there's no risk of salmonella. Not that there ever is, as far as I'm concerned. I buy my eggs from a wonderful, wonderful farm called The Country Hen, and they're very safe (and the chickens lead nicer lives than many). The only person I ever knew who got salmonella was a little boy who caught it from kissing his turtle many years ago. I'm willing to live on the edge and eat raw eggs once in a while—in chocolate chip cookie batter, for instance. But I'm not going to *complain* if a recipe is safe.

You'll need a candy or meat thermometer. And not only for this eggnog, but for many other occasions. Go buy both if you don't have them. That's the only New Year's resolution worth keeping.

4 large eggs

3/4 cup sugar (superfine works especially well), divided

1 1/2 teaspoons nutmeg, divided

1/4 teaspoon salt

5 cups milk, divided

1 teaspoon vanilla

2 tablespoons bourbon or dark rum (optional, and only for adults, obviously)

1 cup heavy cream, divided

Beat the eggs well. Blend in all the sugar except 2 tablespoons. Add 1 teaspoon of the nutmeg, the salt, and 1 cup of the milk. Also, measure out another cup of milk to have ready.

Cook the egg mixture in a double boiler, stirring constantly, until it has reached 140 degrees. (Steam will just be beginning to rise from its surface.) Remove from the heat and stir constantly for 1 minute. Then stir in the second cup of milk.

Strain the egg-milk mixture through a sieve into a 2-quart pitcher with a lid. Add the vanilla, bourbon or rum (if using), 1/2 cup of the cream, and the remaining 3 cups milk. Refrigerate overnight.

When you're ready to serve the eggnog, whip the remaining 1/2 cup cream with the reserved 2 tablespoons sugar until thick and frothy but not stiff; stir into the eggnog. Sprinkle each serving with a dash of the remaining 1/2 teaspoon nutmeg.

Makes about 1³/₄ quarts.

For Extra-Rich Eggnog: Increase the eggs to 6 and cook them with 1¹/₂ cups milk. Replace 1 cup of the remaining milk with heavy cream.

Valentine's Day

. . . also happens to be my husband's birthday, which would make a nice reason to use a heart-shaped pan for his birthday cake except that his favorite dessert is hot fudge sundaes. You'd be surprised how many birthday/Valentine's Day cards they sell, by the way.

For breakfast on Valentine's Day, we always have Cranberry Scones. I cut them with a heart-shaped cookie cutter, but you don't have to. They're pink, which is already Valentine-y enough. They're also delicious, and they can be made ahead and frozen without suffering.

Speaking of Valentine's Day: one of the easiest and nicest ways to decorate your house (and cheapest, *and* easiest to store) is to use old Valentines from previous years. I always save a couple of the cards the kids get at school as well. It's fun to see the fashions kids' Valentines follow throughout the years —from Curious George to *Space Jam* to, I don't know, dark millennial themes—and also to watch their handwriting mature.

Cranberry Scones

2 cups sweetened dried cranberries (I use Ocean Spray Craisins), divided

2$\frac{1}{4}$ cups flour

3 tablespoons sugar

1 teaspoon baking powder

$\frac{1}{2}$ teaspoon baking soda

$\frac{1}{4}$ teaspoon salt

8 tablespoons (1 stick) cold unsalted butter, cut into 8 slices

$\frac{2}{3}$ cup heavy cream

$\frac{1}{2}$ teaspoon vanilla

Sugar for rolling the scones

Preheat the oven to 350 degrees. Grease a cookie sheet or (better) cover it with parchment paper.

Grind 1 cup of the dried cranberries in a food processor with the flour. For a long time, the cranberries will sullenly whip around and around without changing their shape at all, but ultimately they'll give in and allow themselves to be pulverized. Add the sugar, baking powder, baking soda, and salt and process for 1 minute.

Scatter the slices of butter over the top of the flour mixture. Use on/off pulses until the butter has been assimilated and the mixture resembles bread crumbs. Now put the contents of the food processor in a large bowl. With a fork, stir in first the cream and vanilla and then the remaining 1 cup cranberries. Knead the dough a few times, until it's smooth.

On a work surface that has been liberally coated with sugar, gently press half the dough to a thickness of $\frac{3}{4}$ inch. Cut out 2-inch scones with either a cookie cutter dipped in flour or a sharp knife. Flip them over (so the sugar is on top) and place them on the cookie sheet an inch or so apart. Repeat with the rest of the dough. It's okay to gather up scraps and press them together so you can cut out more scones; the trace of sugar that will get mixed in won't matter.

Bake the scones for 20 minutes. The bottoms should be pale brown but the tops shouldn't be. It's a little hard to tell if they're done just by looking; I always bake a couple of the left-over dough scraps so I can break one open to check for done-ness. Serve hot, or allow the scones to cool on a rack; if you're not going to use them within 8 hours, freeze them.

Makes about 16 scones.

St. Patrick's Day

If you ask me, the card-and-decorations business should come up with more tasteful St. Paddy's Day products. The bulk of the decorations you can buy for this holiday are really hideous. Isn't there some way to render a leprechaun so that he doesn't look like a lecherous old man with skinny legs?

But anyway. Green is the order of the day here. Don't forget to have the kids wear something green to school—it always matters more than you'd think. And use green food coloring wherever you can.

Oddly, kids don't always warm to this tradition. My friend Charmaine wrote me, "One year I decided to surprise the kids with green eggs and ham. When it was all ready and plated up, I called them in. They took one look and no one touched a bite. Virtually the same thing happened when I made green mashed potatoes for St. Patrick's Day. My daughter Camille's kids *ask* for food coloring in their oatmeal. What does she do right that I did wrong?"

Nevertheless, scrambled eggs, mashed potatoes, and oatmeal are three of the foods that take food coloring best. So do milk and chicken noodle soup. And not too many children object to green icing on cupcakes.

April Fool's Day

You'd think my family would take St. Patrick's Day more seriously than April Fool's. After all, the former honors an actual *saint*, while the latter is just about tricking people. But if you'd think that, it would show that you don't know us at all.

It's easier to think of April Fool's Day tricks when your kids are very little. Then you can just get away with things like, "Look! There's a goat in the yard!" At that stage, though, your payback is having to pretend you believe the kids when they shriek, "Mom, I'm bleeding!" and you go running in and see that they've VERY OBVIOUSLY drawn on themselves with Magic Marker, and you have to let out this big fake gasp.

As the children mature, they expect more of you. Here are several April Fool's Day pranks that have worked for me.

Covering my nose with a huge bandage just before the kids came home from school and saying I fell off the treadmill at my health club. All afternoon, they kept saying, "Mom, you look so horrible! Does it hurt?" Finally, when one of them mentioned it at supper, I crossly said, "Do you want to *see* how much it hurts?" and peeled off the bandage.

Renting crutches would probably work too.

Spiking my hair with lots of gel. Again, this was just before the kids came home from school and I picked them up at the bus stop. (You don't think I'd go around like that, do you?) When they said, "What did you do with your hair?" I snapped, "Just get in the car." I continued to pretend to refuse to talk about it and finally said that my hairdresser had given me something completely different from what I was expecting, "but it doesn't really look that bad, does it?" "Is it permanent?" my son asked timidly, to which I said, "No, it will grow out after a few months." It almost made them think my real hair looks nice.

Leaving a letter on the table that was allegedly from their school and that claimed the dress code was about to be made much, much stricter. My husband wrote this, and it was a work of genius. Among other things, it claimed that girls as well as boys would wear neckties and that "all students will be required to wear the same style of shoe." At the end, the letter asked parents please to keep the news confidential until a press release could be sent out.

We gave a copy of this letter to a friend, who used it on her daughter. When the daughter read it, she burst into tears and pounded the kitchen table with her fist, screaming "Why? Why?" It's hard to see them get so upset, but they cheer up right away when you tell them it's just a joke.

Making fake ice cream. I learned this trick from a food stylist, who makes fake ice cream for photo shoots. If you mix equal parts light corn syrup, Crisco, and powdered sugar (and a little food coloring, if you want), you get something that can be scooped exactly like ice cream. The only problem is that you have to pre-plate it before you give it to your kids. Otherwise they'll wonder why you're scooping it out of a bowl instead of the usual ice cream container.

You can also frost and decorate a balloon filled with water or an overturned cake pan. And you can put mustard in Oreos and re-sandwich them, but even I think that's a little too mean. April Fool's Day is aggressive enough already.

If you do pull a food prank, be sure you have a real dessert on hand. You're asking too much of your children if you require them to be good sports about a joke dessert that's replaced with *no* dessert.

Easter

It's hard to believe that people used to think of eating eggs as a big part of Easter. When I was little, I brought dyed hard-boiled eggs in my lunch bag for days after Easter. Now I wouldn't eat a hard-boiled egg if—forget it, I can't even think of an "if" that would make me eat one.

But I do hard-boil most of the eggs we dye at Easter. Blowing them is too much work, and blown eggs tend to float in the dye. I know some people who don't even bother hard-boiling their eggs; this is especially true if you make *pysanky*, those intricate Ukrainian eggs, because the dyes don't work as well when the eggs have been boiled. Unfortunately, the eggs work a little too well if you drop them on the floor.

Even with cooked eggs, Ukrainian pysanky dyes are still a billion times better than anything Paas or any of the other supermarket guys make. And they don't come with all those stupid gimmicky duck and lily stickers, either. You can buy Ukrainian dyes at craft stores. They come in an unbelievable range of colors—even black and maroon and forest green— and they're unbelievably bright and glowing in an Easter basket. I *beg* you to try them. But first you should coat your work surface with lots of big plastic garbage bags and then with lots of newspaper, unless you like bright, glowing, permanent blotches of maroon and forest green on your kitchen counters.

You can also wrap eggs in several layers of onion skins and then tie them up tightly in cheesecloth, sealing the knot with a twist tie. Boil them for longer than usual—at least half an hour —and you'll end up with beautifully marbled eggs. They're too subtle for children, being a range of earth colors and yellows, but *you'll* like them. And you should get to have *some* of the fun.

I haven't had much luck with all those tips for keeping eggs from cracking or leaking when they boil. It helps, some, to prick one end with a needle or one of those egg-piercing devices; it also helps to start them in cold salted water, bring them to a boil very gently, and immediately turn off the heat and let them cool. Probably the most useful plan is to boil lots more eggs than you think you'll need so that you won't go crazy when some of them ooze out those gross warty bubbles of egg white.

This Easter, I'm going to experiment with baking a few of the eggs at 200 degrees. And I bet that won't work either.

My kids like neither of the traditional Easter main courses, ham and lamb. I'd get depressed cooking a chicken or turkey at Easter, so I just go ahead with ham for myself and my husband and put more effort into Easter desserts, like the one on page 338.

ALWAYS keep a small holiday notebook in your kitchen so that you can jot down various observations as they occur to you. Things like, "Kuchen leaks unless you squeeze the dough *tight* around the filling" and "The Santa mugs are in the bathroom cupboard under the guest towels."

Strawberry–Lemon Bavarian Tart

Orange Shortbread Crust

1½ cups flour

3 tablespoons sugar

A pinch of salt

1–2 teaspoons grated orange rind

¾ cup (1½ sticks) unsalted butter, chilled and cut into
    12 slices

3–4 tablespoons fresh orange juice

Lemon Bavarian Filling

1 envelope plus 1 teaspoon (3½ teaspoons) gelatin

½ cup cold water

½ cup fresh lemon juice

2 cups heavy cream

⅔ cup sugar

A pinch of salt

1 teaspoon grated lemon rind

1 pint fresh strawberries, rinsed, hulled, and sliced

Sliced strawberries for garnish

For the crust: Process the flour, sugar, and salt together in a food processor for a few seconds. Add the orange rind and process until it's all mixed in. Drop the slices of butter over the flour mixture and use on/off pulses until the mixture resembles coarse meal. Sprinkle 3 tablespoons of the orange juice over the top of the dough and use on/off pulses until the dough begins to come together. You may need up to 1 more tablespoon of orange juice. Gather the dough carefully into a ball.

Grease the bottom and sides of a 9-inch springform pan.

Divide the dough into 8 chunks and scatter them evenly over the bottom of the pan. Use your fingers to pat the dough into a crust that covers the bottom and extends up the sides of the pan about 1/2 inch. Chill for 1 hour.

Preheat the oven to 350 degrees.

Prick the dough in several places with a fork. Bake for 20 minutes, or until it's golden brown. Cool completely before you add the filling.

For the filling: Sprinkle the gelatin over the water in a small, nonreactive saucepan and let it stand for 10 minutes, or until softened. Add the lemon juice and, over *very low heat,* stirring constantly, mix the juice and gelatin just until the gelatin has melted. An even safer way to do this so the gelatin doesn't lump would be to place the saucepan in a larger pan of boiling water while you stir.

Whip the cream with the sugar and salt in a large bowl until stiff. Fold in the lemon juice mixture and the lemon rind gently but thoroughly, then fold in the sliced strawberries. Pour the mixture into the cooled crust.

Chill for at least 6 hours, or overnight. Garnish with more sliced strawberries just before serving.

Serves 6 to 8.

Halloween

More than any other holiday, Halloween lends itself to good kid food. And the first thing you should have on hand is a jar of black paste or gel food coloring. You can get black food coloring from craft stores, baking supply shops, and by mail-order from the King Arthur Flour Baker's Catalog (page 22). Adding it to ordinary foods like Jell-O (you put it in with the boiling water), peanut butter and/or jelly, soup, and chocolate pudding is a great—and incredibly easy—way to Halloween up your children's meals. You can also use it to make bat-shaped sugar cookies that are actually black. Now, that's the way to win "Classroom Parent of the Year" award.

Strangely enough, it's not that easy to find bat-shaped cookie cutters. Brooms, yes, even though broom-shaped cookies break the second you look at them. Witches, yes. Pumpkins, yes. *Dinosaur* cookie cutters are everywhere, but a living, breathing creature, the only flying mammal in the world, a great mosquito-eater—oh, *no!* The manufacturers can't be *bothered!* So I took a pterodactyl-shaped cutter and bent it to look more like a bat. (You make the beak shorter, so it looks more like an ear, and pinch a corresponding ear on the other side of the head.) The following sugar cookie recipe works very well.

Halloween Sugar Cookies

1 cup (2 sticks) unsalted butter, at room temperature

2 cups sugar

2 large eggs

1 teaspoon vanilla

1 tablespoon milk

3½ cups flour

2 teaspoons baking powder

½ teaspoon salt

2 teaspoons black food coloring (to start with; you may need more)

Confectioners' sugar for rolling out the cookies

Cream the butter and sugar together in a large bowl with an electric mixer until light. Add the eggs and vanilla. Beat until fluffy, and add the milk.

In a separate bowl, stir together the flour, baking powder, and salt. Beat the flour mixture into the butter mixture until well mixed. Then add the black food coloring. If it doesn't look black enough to you, keep adding more until you've achieved the right saturation. Wrap the dough in plastic wrap and chill it for at least 1 hour.

Preheat the oven to 375 degrees. Grease two cookie sheets or line them with parchment paper.

Break off a hunk of black dough from the refrigerator. Dust your rolling surface, your rolling pin, and all sides of the dough with confectioners' sugar. Roll the dough out ⅛ inch thick and cut into Halloween shapes with cookie cutters. It doesn't spread much, so you can put a lot of cookies onto each baking sheet.

Bake for 10 to 12 minutes. Obviously there's no way to tell when these are done by looking; you'll have to break one open to see. Cool the cookies on racks.

Makes about 16 dozen cookies.

On a delicate note: Black food coloring is actually a very, very dark green. If you have a child in diapers who eats some of these cookies, don't be worried the next day if the diaper looks, well, different.

Thanksgiving

This one's the toughest for me, for some reason. I just can't get that worked up about a holiday whose main purpose is eating. I realize that giving thanks is supposed to be the point, but I personally would feel more thankful if all I had to prepare was three grains of parched corn—the legendary meal that's supposed to be all the Pilgrims ate on their first Thanksgiving. (So said Laura Ingalls Wilder, anyway.) It's my husband's favorite holiday, so I try to be a good sport about it. (I always fail, though, so we tend to eat Thanksgiving dinner at a restaurant.)

A common problem with most people's Thanksgiving menus is that they're simply too big and contain too many foods with similar, pureed textures. It's disgusting to think of people so stuffed after Thanksgiving dinner that they have to lie on the floor before they can start on dessert, yet this is the norm in many families. Remember that you don't have to have every single one of your favorite Thanksgiving foods at Thanksgiving dinner. You won't be able to appreciate each side dish if there are thirty of them—too much food, too much work. Why not serve them all through the fall so that you get your Thanksgiving fix in smaller, steadier, less-sickening doses?

Another common problem with Thanksgiving is that the menu tends to duplicate Christmas dinner, or vice versa. Why on earth should you serve turkey at the end of November and then again at the end of December? Both meals will be more interesting to cook and eat if you make sure that none of the food overlaps.

Knowing that you won't have to cook a turkey again for a whole 'nother year also gives you the patience to perfect it. As long as I'm doing a turkey at all, I want it to be the best. That means brining it (see page 94 if you want to read about the greatness of brining), which in turn means I can't do a huge turkey. (You can brine a 20-pound bird only if you have a bowl big enough to hold the turkey and its brining liquid *and* a refrigerator big enough to hold the bowl overnight—or a reliably cold day and no prowling neighborhood dogs, so you can put the turkey on the porch.) I don't mind, though. Using a 12-pounder leaves at least a few tiny spaces in the oven where I might be able to fit a couple of rolls or something. A turkey breast would work even better (and be much better value for the money), but I suppose we can't get away with that.

Here's a somewhat streamlined version of the technique. Go to *The Joy of Cooking* to figure out the size of turkey you need. Go to your bowl collection and your fridge to see how much storage space you have. Then get started, keeping in mind the fact that this turkey needs to chill overnight before you cook it.

It will be the prettiest turkey you've ever served—a dark, glistening mahogany. Roz Chast, the artist who did this book's illustrations, says, "When I served this at Thanksgiving, my mother gave it her highest compliment: 'It looks *bought.*'"

Magnificent Ultra-Turkey

The cooking times below are for an *unstuffed* turkey, which is so much better and safer that you should really consider making the switch and baking your stuffing separately.

Brining Solution

1 *pound* salt

1 very large bowl or nonreactive pot

1 turkey, fresh or defrosted

Basting Solution

8 tablespoons (1 stick) unsalted butter

1/2 cup dark corn syrup

For the brining solution: Rinse the turkey thoroughly in cold water, inside and out. Put it into a bowl or pot big enough to hold it easily. Pour the salt all over the turkey. Rub some into the skin, rub some inside the body cavity (which you've taken the giblets out of, by the way), rub some into the neck cavity—just rub and rub and rub until the whole turkey is well coated. Pour enough cold water over the turkey to cover it entirely. Cover the bowl or pot, too, and chill the turkey for 12 to 24 hours.

When you're ready to roast the bird, remove it from the brine, rinse it obsessively with cold running water, and pat it dry, also obsessively, with lots and lots of paper towels.

Preheat the oven to 325 degrees. Grease your roasting rack heavily, so you won't have horrible problems later on. Or else—much better—line it with several thicknesses of parchment paper. Put a pie pan filled with water on the oven's lower rack. Refill as needed while the turkey cooks.

For the basting solution: Melt the butter in a small saucepan and whisk in the dark corn syrup until smooth. With a pastry brush, paint the entire outside of the turkey with the glaze. Flip the turkey's wings backwards to pin down the neck skin. Tie its legs together with twine or unflavored dental floss. Plunk the turkey down on the rack and somehow get it into the oven.

Roast the turkey for 15 minutes a pound if it weighs less than 16 pounds. If it weighs more than that, cook it for 12 minutes a pound. For the first hour, keep it covered with foil. After that, remove the foil and baste the turkey every 15 minutes or so. About halfway through the roasting, you'll be able to start basting with pan juices as well.

The turkey is done when a meat thermometer inserted into the leg pit and breast reads 165 degrees. Leave the turkey covered on top of the stove for 15 minutes before carving it.

Another good addition to the Thanksgiving table is:

Cran-Blueberry Relish

"How can anyone get tired of regular cranberry sauce?" you're asking. And I agree, it's impossible. But what if, like me, you love novelty for its own sake? What if you feel like showing off? What if you've been asked to someone else's house for Thanksgiving, and you don't want people to think you just opened a can? (Although in some circles, those little "can lines" on the cranberry sauce are considered something to be thankful for.)

This is excellent, and beautiful, and the stains it leaves on your best Thanksgiving tablecloth will be excellently beautiful too. Maybe you can dish it out in the kitchen.

1 12-ounce bag fresh cranberries, rinsed and picked over

1½ cups frozen unsweetened blueberries

⅓–½ cup sugar (start with the smaller amount)

1 teaspoon grated orange rind, plus more if needed

Juice of 1 orange, plus more if needed

¼ teaspoon cardamom, plus more if needed

A pinch of nutmeg, plus more if needed

A pinch of salt

Combine all the ingredients in a large, heavy saucepan over medium heat. As soon as they reach a boil, taste to see if you need to add more sugar, orange rind, juice, or spices. Cook the sauce for 30 to 40 minutes, or until it has visibly thickened. It can be served hot, warm, or cold, so fit it into your Thanksgiving plans in whatever way works best for you.

Makes about 1 quart.

Christmas

Once again: go right out and buy a copy of *Unplug the Christmas Machine,* by Jo Robinson and Jean Coppock Staeheli. How many times do I have to tell you?

I wouldn't dream of adding more traditions and more recipes to your Christmas. I know you have enough already. But I think it's worth reminding you that Christmas is 12 days long, not one. It does not end on the night of December 25— or at least it shouldn't.

This doesn't mean you need to plan a full-scale holiday for each one of the 12 days: It means you should *spread things out. Never, never, never try to cram everything into the 25th of December.*

You might consider, for example, not serving Christmas dinner until the 27th or 28th of December. We discovered this trick one Christmas Eve long ago, when my daughter was sick. To cheer her up, I said we'd just do the presents on Christmas morning and have Christmas dinner a few days later than usual. What an improvement! It meant that we could spend most of Christmas Day together, playing with presents and just hanging out, rather than what had always happened before: I'd rush through opening my presents and then dash into the kitchen to start cooking for several hours, resisting the kids' pleas to play with them. At the end of the day, when we were all tired and let down, I'd serve a meal no one even wanted because everyone would have been eating candy all day.

Waiting a few days for Christmas dinner gives us something else to look forward to, rather than slamming that end-of-Christmas door in our faces. It also lets some fresh air into the schedule. On the night of the 25th itself, my rule is: no cooking, only reheating. I buy lots of frozen appetizers and finger foods and smoked salmon and stuff, and serve them on beautiful paper plates. Then we all loll around cozily instead of having to get dressed up.

Another good way to space things out is to save certain traditions for the days after the 25th. We never do a gingerbread

ALWAYS buy a couple of presents for yourself— things you really want— wrap them nicely, put them away with the other presents you're giving your family, and don't open them until Christmas morning. Don't you know better than anyone else what you want? And wouldn't you like the chance to open a couple more things as your children rip open box after box while you watch politely? Grown-ups can't rely on other people to baby them at Christmas; they have to do it for themselves. Yes, buying presents for yourself may seem a little pathetic at first. But it can be oddly cheering, as you're racing around buying things for other people, to think, "Well, at least I *know* I'm getting those earrings I wanted."

house before then; there's just too much going on. We wait a few days, and then make the house. And we never actually make it out of gingerbread.

Gingerbread houses are a pain to assemble unless you enjoy that kind of finicky work. If you do, you might want to consider assembling the house before you bring your kids into the project. Otherwise they'll go crazy waiting for you to finish, and you won't want them breathing down your neck anyway. If you just want something that the kids will have fun decorating, make a house out of cardboard covered with frosting. No one ever eats the gingerbread anyway, do they? What most kids like is the decorations. And there's no way a cardboard house can shatter if a child pushes a Lifesaver onto the roof too hard.

Speaking of Lifesavers, you can make really incredible stained-glass windows for a gingerbread house by baking hard candies at 300 degrees on a greased sheet of foil. They melt and flatten beautifully; you just want to make sure they're larger than the windows themselves, so you'll have a little edge to "glue" inside the windows with frosting.

Making marzipan fruits and vegetables is another good post-December 25 tradition. I buy several rolls of Odense marzipan every year; it's available in the baking section of most supermarkets. Since I do so much baking, we have lots of exotic paste food colorings in the house, but regular food coloring works well too. Whole cloves make nice stems for marzipan fruits; rolling a marzipan orange on a grater makes a nice orange-skin texture. Not that kids always want to make fruits and vegetables, even though they're traditional. My son and a friend once spent a happy afternoon making little men out of marzipan, then stabbing them with toothpicks and dripping red food coloring onto their heads. It wasn't exactly Christmas-y, but they had a good time.

Nevertheless, Christmas does involve at least *some* recognition of the fact that you're supposed to give people something

on December 25. It's awfully nice when kids can give homemade presents to their grandparents, teachers, and other rele-
vant adults. It's not so nice when the making of the gifts
becomes a dreadful chore that you have to force the kids
through as if you were forcing an ox to walk backward up a
ramp into a truck. One Christmas I had Laura and John make
stationery that involved lots of cutouts and a sort of grave-
rubbing technique where you ran the side of a pencil around
the cutouts and made a border or something—it's a little vague
in my mind, there were so many details. At the rate the kids
worked, one piece of stationery per grandparent would have
represented hours of labor. But you can't give one piece of stationery as a present.

Nope, homemade food's the best, definitely. At any time of
year, not just Christmas. It's fun to make; you can make a lot of
it at once, enabling you to "gift" several recipients at the end of
your labors; and people generally like getting it more than they
do, say, slips of tissue paper threaded into a ball, where you
pull off one slip of tissue each day to clean your razor. (That's a
present I gave my father when I was a little girl.) What you
want is food that's unbreakable, packs easily—in a gift tin, for
instance—and keeps well. Buttermints (page 272) and Rainy-
Day Fudge (page 274) are two good examples. So are Apricot
Sugarplums.

Apricot Sugarplums

The original "sugarplums" were crystallized fruit, so this isn't too far off. You need a food processor or a food grinder (as if anyone still has one of *those* anymore), but other than that, the recipe is ridiculously easy. Do make sure to get plump, soft dried apricots, though—not the shriveled brown kind that look like dead ears. *Really* dry dried apricots will never, never grind up properly.

1 11-ounce package dried apricots

2 cups shredded sweetened coconut

1 cup chopped almonds (optional), toasted at
    300 degrees for 10 minutes

About 1 cup sweetened condensed milk

About 2 cups confectioners' sugar, for dusting the
    sugarplums

Grind the apricots and coconut together in a food processor, working in batches if necessary. When they're all ground up, put them into a medium bowl and use your (clean) hands to work in the chopped almonds, if using, and 1/2 cup of the condensed milk. Continue to add the condensed milk until the mixture is well blended and can be molded into balls.

Shape "sugarplums" that are about 1 inch in diameter. Roll them in confectioners' sugar and set them to dry on waxed paper for a few hours. Stored airtight, they'll keep for 2 weeks.

Makes about 4 dozen sugarplums.

One last thing. Holiday meals are one time you should dispense with nutritional concerns entirely, in favor of food the whole family will celebrate. If the only thing you and your family enjoy about Christmas dinner is the special Yule log cake you all decorate together, then just serve that. It's not healthier to plow your way through a whole meal to get to the good parts, so on holidays you should just allow yourself the good parts. Take vitamins if you're worried. You can get back to normal in January—once George Love's eggnog is all gone, that is.

Why None of This Matters

I f you're reading this book, you're probably a fairly comfortable resident of the richest country in the history of our planet. Your concerns about feeding your children are therefore rather trivial compared with those of most of the world's parents, past and present. You wonder how to provide your kids with food they like—not how to provide them with food.

Keep that in mind the next time you worry that your four-year-old doesn't get enough vegetables.

There's an excellent chance that if kids get enough calories, vitamins, and minerals—no matter what the source—they're going to be healthy. When did your son or daughter last pass out from hunger? When did you last see one of your children—any child in your neighborhood—any child at your child's school—suffering from a serious nutritional disorder? Rickets? Scurvy? Kwashiorkor?

Give up the notion that having a child who's a picky eater is a problem. It's not a problem. It's a luxury. True, I wrote this book to make your life easier. But you and I already have easy, easy lives compared to most people, and we should keep that in mind every time we offer our children something to eat.

I'm not saying you should pull out the old "starving Assyrians" line every time your kids refuse to finish their supper. Parents are right to feel a pang when their children snub perfectly good food that could save other children's lives. But the pang should be one of sadness, not guilt. It's terrible that so much of the world is starving. But it's not (directly) your fault—and it's not one bit your children's fault. *Not liking a certain food is not immoral.* What's immoral is that this world could, right now, grow enough food to feed everyone on the planet. Your energy is misdirected if you heap sorrow on your children's shoulders because they don't like broccoli. Teach them to help the poor instead.

Global issues aside, having a child who's a picky eater is not and never will be *your* problem. If it's a problem at all, it's the child's to deal with, when he or she decides she's ready. Your job is putting the food down on the table. The child's job is eating it. And "job" is too serious a word for the process, anyway. Your kids probably won't reach adulthood never having eaten a bite of salad. Or maybe they will! Do you really care?

If you do, I don't want to know you. Our children are only young for a little while. If we can give them enough to eat, we're lucky and so are they. Let's enjoy mealtimes and not waste anyone's time trying to fix a situation that, for most of us, is already pretty great.

And then let's push in our chairs and go on to more important things.

Index

About the Author

Ann Hodgman started cooking early, and at the age of fourteen was named *Seventeen* magazine's Teen Gourmet of the Year. She is the author of two previous cookbooks, *Beat This!* and *Beat That!*, has written over 40 children's books, and is coauthor of the *1003 Great Things* series. She lives in Washington, Connecticut, with her husband, their two children, and many, many pets.